NAPOLEON

. . . .

NAPOLEON

Geoffrey Ellis

LONGMAN
London and New York

Addison Wesley Longman Limited
Edinburgh Gate,
Harlow, Essex CM20 2JE,
United Kingdom
and Associated Companies throughout the world.

*Published in the United States of America
by Addison Wesley Longman Inc., New York*

First published 1997

ISBN 0 582 02548 6 CSD
ISBN 0 582 02547 8 PPR

British Library Cataloguing-in-Publication Data

A catalogue record for this book is available from the British Library

Library of Congress Cataloging-in-Publication Data

Ellis, Geoffrey James.
Napoleon / Geoffrey Ellis.
p.   cm.
Includes bibliographical references and index.
Summary: A biography of the military genius, who in 1804 crowned
himself Emperor of the French and established a vast European
empire.
ISBN 0–582–02548–6 (cloth). — ISBN 0–582–02547–8 (pbk.)
1. Napoleon I, Emperor of the French, 1769–1821—Juvenile
literature.   2. France—Kings and rulers—Biography—Juvenile
literature.   3. France—History, Military—1789–1815—Juvenile
literature.   4. France—Politics and government—1789–1815—Juvenile
literature.   [1. Napoleon I, Emperor of the French, 1769–1821.
2. Kings, queens, rulers, etc.]   I. Title.
DC203.E4   1996
944.05′092—dc20
[B]   96–26814
CIP
AC

Set by 35 in 10½/12pt Baskerville
Produced by Longman Singapore Publishers (Pte) Ltd.
Printed in Singapore

CONTENTS

. . . . .

LIST OF MAPS

1. Europe, January 1799
2. Europe, September 1806
3. Europe, May 1812
4. Departments of the French Empire at its height in 1812
5. Europe after the Congress of Vienna

PREFACE

When an author sets out to publish two textbooks on the same broad subject in the space of less than six years, the second can risk giving the impression of *déjà vu*. I have been conscious of this risk throughout my composition of the present *Napoleon* and have tried throughout to keep the inevitable echoes of my shorter *The Napoleonic Empire* (Macmillan Studies in European History, 1991) down to a minimum. In this respect, the greater length allowed by the 'Profiles in Power' series has been a very considerable help to me. As a result, three of the six main chapters of this volume cover very largely different ground, and in the others I have also been able to develop several common topics in more detail than had been possible in my earlier booklet.

In particular, I have tried on this occasion to say rather more about Napoleon himself and about the way his 'image' was projected to contemporaries and later generations alike. In looking more closely at the man, I became increasingly aware of the great debt I owed to the encouragement and invaluable bibliographical advice of Professor Harold T. Parker, with whom I have quite often corresponded since our first meeting at the 1984 Consortium on Revolutionary Europe in Durham, NC. Over these more recent years, he has generously shared his vast knowledge of Napoleonic history with me, and I should like to thank him in full measure for allowing me to draw so freely on his scholarly erudition and wisdom. He, more than any other, first drew my attention to the influence Napoleon's developing personality had on his evolving ambition, and to the importance of his Corsican background in other ways as well. I could not even have presumed to go down such a road, which before had been so unfamiliar to me, without the skilful guidance of Professor Parker's many learned writings.

As the final sections of this book were being prepared for the publishers, I was among a great many in different parts of the world to be saddened by the death of Professor Richard Cobb on 15 January 1996. I cannot easily express in words all I owed to him, as my former tutor, research supervisor, and close friend for more than thirty years. His brilliance as a scholar and natural generosity as a friend were a constant inspiration to so many of us who knew him. I am not sure that he altogether approved of *yet* another book on Napoleon; but I like to think that he was reassured by the thought that this enterprise at least was in the hands of one of his old pupils! Whatever its reception by others may be, the present volume is a personal tribute to his memory. The study of French history, as I know it, can never be quite the same again.

G.J.E.
Oxford, March 1996

À MADAME LAPINE

Chapter 1

INTRODUCTION

This book is not a biography of Napoleon nor an attempt to trace his military and political career in narrative terms. The sub-divisions of its six main chapters sometimes follow a broadly chronological sequence, but its overall approach is essentially topical. While it draws on my own research into the archival and printed primary sources for Napoleonic history, it is also primarily a synthesis of earlier secondary accounts, both old and more recent, of which many may not be familiar to general English readers. It is an attempt to offer them a series of over-views which deal in turn with Napoleon's rise to fame as a soldier of the French Revolution, with his aims and achievements as first consul and emperor during the years 1799–1815, and with the many different reactions to his rule among not only his contemporaries but observers of later generations as well. My binding theme is the nature of Napoleonic *power*: how it was pursued and won; how it was first elaborated in the extended frontiers of France and then expanded well beyond them; how its initial impact through military conquest was followed up by political subjugation and economic exploitation; how it was resisted; how it was finally lost; and how perceptions of it lived on in both the heroic and black legends of Napoleon well into the twentieth century.

In an earlier and shorter published work, I was less concerned with Napoleon, the man, than with the implementation and effects of his policies, and with the underlying structures of his regime.[1] Such an approach reflected the more recent trends in Napoleonic historiography, away from personalities and towards the wider context in which Napoleon and his subjects lived and worked. The first unmistakable conclusion to emerge was that

1

there had been as much continuity as change across the apparent watershed of Napoleon's *coup d'état* on 18 Brumaire. In view of it, the innovatory and radical nature of his reforms, which had so often been assumed by earlier writers, seemed rather less self-evident. The more one looked at the real aims and effects of his rule in France itself, the more they bore the aspect of a grand consolidation, adaptation, and extension of his Revolutionary inheritance, especially in the earlier years. As first consul (1799–1804), he owed much to the officers and men, to the tactics and weaponry, and to the territorial conquests of the reconstituted line armies of the mid- to later 1790s, in which he had of course played a spectacular part himself. He accepted the Revolutionary sales of the property confiscated from the Church and the émigrés, and indeed formally reaffirmed them in his Civil Code of 1804. In recruiting the administrative and legal personnel of his civil state, he drew heavily on the professional élites of the Revolutionary regimes before him. Similarly, the more one investigated his impact on the conquered territories beyond French frontiers, the clearer still it became that he could not always be considered a uniquely radical innovator.

Some readers will no doubt regard this as a modish 'revisionist' approach, aimed primarily at demystifying the 'myth of the saviour' and his heroic legend. So be it. The present volume at least, as seems appropriate to a series concerned with the central theme of 'Power' in particular episodes associated with major historical figures, has more place for Napoleon the man – for the formation of his character in the years before he gained power, for his own perception of power, for the influence this had on his exercise of power, in short for the whole nature of his personal ambition. Indeed, the chapters which follow might be seen as inter-related manifestations of an essentially *personalized* system of power. As such, they reassess the value of the older 'classic' accounts which have established themselves in the rich seam of Napoleonic historiography over the years. These include a huge and colourful variety of views on Napoleon's character, aims, and achievements, both adulatory and otherwise, evident in writings from the earliest days.

English readers will probably be most familiar with that historiographical debate through Pieter Geyl's long-serving study *Napoleon: For and Against*, first published in 1949, which was deliberately confined to French writers.[2] Yet, even in those terms,

the debate on the major recurring themes in Napoleonic historiography has moved on a good deal since Geyl's time, and the
whole subject now seems ready for review. That is one of my
objects here, and it is supplemented by another: to provide
a critical survey of the earliest (often contemporary) German,
Italian, and British writings on Napoleon in my penultimate
chapter. Geyl never set himself this latter task, and, as far as I
know, such a synthesis of the wider and more immediate European reactions to Napoleonic rule has never before been available to English readers in a general text.

In the course of this volume, then, we shall be confronting
the older and more flamboyant images of Napoleon which
dominated the historiographical debate up to the Second World
War with the findings of more recent research. This will imply
a reappraisal of earlier writings in which he often appeared as
a sort of 'superman' or 'super-demon', who seemed somehow
larger than life, and who (for his admirers at any rate) could
not be judged by the standards of ordinary mortals. It will
also imply a reconsideration of the great thematic accounts
which sought to subsume his ambition and achievements in a
'grand idea' – such as Adolphe Thiers's notion of a 'universal
empire', Albert Sorel's insistence on the 'natural frontiers' of
France as the determining priority of Napoleonic imperialism,
Frédéric Masson's detailed exposition of an evolving Corsican
'clan spirit', Émile Bourgeois's more exotic construction of an
'oriental mirage', the 'Roman imperial ideal' elaborated by
Edgar Quinet and Édouard Driault, and the various versions of
the 'Carolingian motif' associated with Leopold von Ranke,
Charles Schmidt, Marcel Dunan, and Hellmuth Rössler, among
others.

A more recent historiographical trend, influenced no doubt
by political developments within the enlarged European Union
today, also needs to be confronted. There are signs that some
writers are now reconstruing Napoleon's great ambition of
nearly two hundred years ago as an early anticipation of 'European integration'. If much of this seems tendentious and specious, Stuart Woolf's more scholarly variant of the analogy certainly merits more serious consideration. Basing his detailed
account on the presupposition of a French administrative
'model' of 'modernity' and 'uniformity', one which could be
exported to all the annexed lands and satellite states of the
Napoleonic Empire, he examines the cases for and against the

efficacy of its implementation there.[3] His general conclusion suggests a crucial social distinction, for, as he puts it, 'the pressure for the integration of elites that was an intrinsic part of the Napoleonic philosophy of administration widened the social gap between the propertied and property-less. This was the final and most profound heritage of the Napoleonic experience.'[4] The issues raised by this argument are an important part of the present study, too.

Otherwise, however, the whole notion that Napoleon was an early architect of the modern 'European idea', topical though it may be, seems at variance with the hard evidence of his declared priority of 'France first' (*la France avant tout*), as he once bluntly put it in a letter of August 1810. The one-sidedness of his military exactions, of his Continental Blockade against Britain, of his 'reserved markets' in Italy, and of his expanding 'spoils system' in the subject states of the 'Grand Empire' all suggest that the argument is simplistic and fundamentally flawed. On the other hand, we need not doubt that Napoleon's Imperial idea and imperial conquests* reached out far across the 'natural frontiers' of France to incorporate Spain and Portugal (however tenuously in fact) beyond the Pyrenees, the whole of the Italian mainland beyond the Alps, a significant slice of the Adriatic hinterland further east, most of Germany beyond the Rhine, and the larger part of Poland.

While all this clearly *did* amount to a wider *European* vision, the crucial question remains: how well were its constituent parts actually 'integrated'? To find an answer, we need to go back a stage in time and consider at what point Napoleon's Imperial vision had emerged as a clearly formulated policy even within the extended frontiers of France itself. 'I am of the race that founds empires', he once remarked to Emmanuel de Las Cases, his companion in exile on St Helena.[5] In retrospect, that may well have seemed to both a poignant reaffirmation of his destiny, in which we are assured he passionately believed from an early age, ambitious Corsican that he was. But just *how early* did this Imperial design really begin to influence his actions? Was

---

* Throughout this work, 'Imperial' (with a capital I) refers to the official delimitations of the French Empire or to Napoleon's own policies or ambitions as emperor within that formal context; 'imperial' (with a small i) refers to the process of empire-building (e.g. through conquest) in a more general sense. 'Grand Empire' refers to all the states which lay beyond the official frontiers of the French Empire but which, at one time or another, came under Napoleonic rule in some form.

it all part of a preconceived plan evident even before Brumaire, or did it form in a more gradual and pragmatic way, as opportunities for wider conquest and greater glory opened up to him?

Those are questions which this study attempts to answer through empirical analysis. The picture of the emperor which ultimately emerges is neither as glorious as his arch-admirers, nor as demoniacal as his arch-enemies, have tried for so long to propagate. The Napoleon of this account cannot be subsumed in a single grand image but is a more changeable and contradictory character, of mercurial moods and only too fallible judgement, constantly adjusting to the immediate situation before him, and trying to exploit it to his own advantage. His capacity for brilliant improvisation on the field of battle is legendary; his adaptations to changing circumstances in the French civil state are perhaps less well known. Moreover, it is really only during the last thirty years or so that important research on Germany, Italy, and Poland has revealed the extent to which Napoleon, the great 'radical' reformer, in practice made his compromise with the old feudal order there, so as to extract his military and fiscal levies and to fuel his 'spoils system' more effectively. Among other effects, this undermined the application of his Civil Code (*Code Napoléon*) in those countries, and his role as a lawgiver there was vitiated.

In his exercise of power, whether at home or further afield, Napoleon was above all a *realist*. As a civil ruler, for instance, he grasped early on that he would need the services of professional loyalists and the support of a social élite. He set out to secure both, by offering them the sort of careers and promotional prospects that would bind them more closely to him, and later by lavishly bestowing honours and material rewards on many of them. In this way, he aimed to establish a system in which the professional and propertied classes would more firmly associate their interests with his regime. While he presumed upon his own popular appeal, not least in the early plebiscites, he was largely indifferent to the popular masses. After the Revolutionary upheaval, he sensed that the French people as a whole wanted stable government and an orderly society, and that peasants and artisans alike would acquiesce in his rule, even if they had no direct part in it. Recognizing the traditional Catholicism of the vast majority of his subjects, he calculated that they would rally behind his Concordat with Pope Pius VII in 1801 and welcome the latter's formal acceptance of his coup. In his later rupture with the pope, however, he *unre*-alistically failed to honour the distinction between temporal power and spiritual authority, and the break with Rome ultimately weakened his position.

Given all this, how might Napoleon's ambition then be redefined? We must resist the temptation of thinking that there is *one* vital insight, be it a particular directive, or letter, or speech, or conversation, or recorded utterance, which provides a conclusive answer. It would be more helpful to identify the constants in Napoleon's character and actions, and see how far these take us. A Corsican by birth, his concept of empire was rooted in a strong sense of clannish honour, which naturally encompassed the dynastic furtherance of his family along with his own imperial ascent. A professional soldier by training and in mentality, he thought that civil society could also be ordered hierarchically on martial lines. A man of extraordinary will-power, supremely confident in his own abilities, utterly convinced that he was always right, intolerant of opposition, and driven by a strong sense of his personal destiny, he was by nature egotistical, authoritarian, and ambitious.

And yet, if Napoleon was thus unquestionably inspired by a vision of his own power and glory, he had to pursue it in a real world of unobliging obstacles and setbacks, more especially at sea. Since his power was effectively land-locked, its practical extensions can be properly understood only in *continental* terms. Moreover, since his continental conquests themselves did not come all at once, but in stages, especially during the critical campaigns of 1805–7, his 'Grand Empire' was forged by the same logic of military circumstances, step by step, in ways which had not always been foreseen. Its dynastic embellishments, that is his family placements on the satellite thrones, followed in their turn, and could be seen as acts of improvised opportunism rather than preconceived planning. Indeed, all its other social accretions, most notably the titles and land-gifts with which he endowed his Imperial nobility, were no less dependent on the prior spoils of conquest. What made Napoleonic imperialism possible was its gradualism, and its course was determined by the chronology of war.

Such empirical evidence suggests that Napoleon's ambition was not driven by any over-arching 'master-plan' or 'grand design', present from the start and systematically worked out, but that it grew by an *evolving* process of pragmatic opportunism,

which eventually over-reached itself. Military strength underpinned the whole edifice of his rule in France, in the annexed
territories which lay within the formal frontiers of the French
Empire, and in the subject and allied states beyond them. His
dynastic claims, even when they seemed to have been recognized by marriage with the ancient house of Habsburg and
enhanced by the birth of an heir, never gave him the legitimacy he so dearly sought to secure the future. The edifice fell
when Napoleon was no longer able to sustain its essential military base, and with its collapse his dynastic pretensions quickly
evaporated as well. In this sense, the end of his 'Grand Empire'
and even of the French Empire itself was already implicit in
the military preconditions of their formation. None of his own
annexations survived his fall in 1815. We are thus left with the
great paradox of his rule. As a military conqueror of legendary
fame, he ultimately surrendered a very much smaller territorial
state than he had inherited; but, as a civil ruler, his legacy to
France was monumental and altogether more enduring. In the
final analysis, this was where his great work of 'integration'
truly lay.

. . . .

NOTES AND REFERENCES

1. Geoffrey Ellis, *The Napoleonic Empire*, Macmillan Studies in European History, Basingstoke and London, 1991.
2. The edition used in this work is Pieter Geyl, *Napoleon: For and
   Against*, Harmondsworth, 1986 impression (Peregrine Books).
3. Stuart Woolf, *Napoleon's Integration of Europe*, London, 1991.
4. Ibid., p. 245.
5. Quoted in Harold T. Parker, 'Napoleon's Changing Self-Image to
   1812: A Sketch', *The Consortium on Revolutionary Europe: Proceedings
   1983*, Athens, Ga, 1985, pp. 457, 463 n. 26

Chapter 2

PRELUDE TO POWER:
THE FORMATIVE YEARS, 1769–99

The traditional biographical approach to Napoleon's life and military career before Brumaire has been ploughed so many times in earlier accounts that nothing very new now seems likely to come from it. And so, while this chapter retains a basic chronological thread, its arrangement is deliberately more topical than narrative. Since Napoleon was thirty years of age when he seized power in November 1799, we may assume that by then his fundamental character had already formed and that his military career had advanced spectacularly enough to make his *coup d'état* conceivable in the first place. Moreover, since the coup also marked the beginning of a political and military regime which was to become increasingly a manifestation of personalized power, it seems appropriate to seek its origins in the formation of Napoleon's own personality.

Two questions are chiefly at issue here. How far had Napoleon's essential character been moulded by the various influences of his Corsican upbringing and subsequent education on the French mainland? And how far had the opportunities opened up to aspiring young officers by the reforms and wars of the Revolution contributed to the same process and assisted his own military career? Taken together, the answers to these questions will also help to clarify the genesis of his earlier ambition, from would-be liberator of Corsica to actual ruler of France. Expressed in terms of power, that same evolution marked the transition from boyhood dream to adult reality.

. . . .

NAPOLEON'S YOUTH AND EDUCATION

Corsica had a long history of invasion but rather patchy col-
onization by outsiders, as Dorothy Carrington has shown in
her brilliant portrait of its land, people, and customs. Its strategic position, safe harbours, and plentiful supply of timber
for shipbuilding had exposed it to ruthless exploitation by a
succession of seafaring states at different times, so that 'the
inhabitants had come to believe that their inescapable destiny
was privation and war'.[1] Greeks, Carthaginians, Romans, Van-
dals, Ostrogoths, Lombards, Byzantines, Saracens, the bishops
(later archbishops) of Pisa, the kings of Aragon, and Genoese
– nearly all had left some mark on the island during their various periods of ascendancy there. The French too had raided it
several times before their more determined arrival at the end
of 1768 to put down the revolt led by the patriot Pasquale Paoli
and assert their rights of annexation acquired earlier that year
through a commercial deal with the Republic of Genoa.

The fierce pride of the Corsican people, reared in a rugged
environment of lofty granite peaks, unhelpful soil, and the
almost ubiquitous *maquis*, that sprawling aromatic scrub which
evoked such powerful memories for Napoleon years later during his exile on St Helena, had been sharpened over centuries
of conflict. Witnesses, then and since, testify to the resilience
of the islanders, to the tenacity of their local customs against
the odds of relentless internecine intrigues and the seemingly
endless intrusion of alien forces and ways. Loyalty was born in
the family, first and foremost, and the instincts of clan were predominant. Charity began, and ended, at home. Commenting
on the phenomenon in general terms, Frédéric Masson speaks
of 'a society for which the idea of the family was superior to
any other social or governmental concept, a society imbued with
the same idea to such an extent that this became the source of
all its laws, the basis of all its undertakings, and the justification
of all its adventures'.[2]

Corsica had never known feudalism, at least in the form in
which it had taken root on the European mainland. Nor, by
the eighteenth century, had industrial capitalism made any

significant impact there. Great extremes of wealth and poverty, of lord and vassal, or of entrepreneur and proletarian, were virtually unknown. If the living standards of the inhabitants were generally low, their social and economic antagonisms had not been sharpened by any clearly defined class structure. Bitter rivalry among families had bred a rugged democracy among the agrarian folk of the mountainous interior and the merchants, shopkeepers, fishermen, lawyers, and administrators of the coastal ports. Brutal vendettas and banditry 'of honour' were endemic, features of a society in which Church and State alike had been unable to eradicate deep-rooted pagan customs going back to megalithic times. It is estimated that vendettas alone accounted for between 900 and 1,000 murders a year in pre-Revolutionary Corsica, whose total population was then around 120,000.[3] They also followed an ancient code of conduct known to and shared by most of the islanders. Within this code, the honour of the family was the overriding purpose of private and social relationships, indeed of life itself. The patriarchal structure of the Corsican family was strict and formidable. The father had command of all its relations with the outside world, not least in determining the most advantageous marriage alliances for his children, whose own feelings were rarely allowed to obstruct his perception of the family's interests and prestige. The mother's sovereignty lay in the domestic management of the home, but in all other respects she and the other females of the family were under the sway of the men, even to the point of being seen as extensions of their property.[4]

This was the society into which Napoleon (originally Napoleone Buonaparte) was born in Ajaccio, a port of less than 4,000 inhabitants on the western coast of the island, on 15 August 1769. Before the birth of his elder brother Joseph in 1768, his father Carlo and mother Letizia (*née* Ramolino), who had married in 1764, had already lost two children in infancy. During the Corsican war of independence against the French, Carlo had supported and indeed actively collaborated with Paoli, 'the Father of the Nation'. But the latter's defeat at Ponte Novo (8 May 1769) and flight to England, where he was to remain in exile for twenty years, presented Napoleon's parents with a choice. There was, on the one hand, the apparently pointless hazard of continuing the rebellion by whatever means could still be mustered; on the other, they could accept the fact of defeat and collaborate with the French conqueror. The latter soon materialized in the person of Count de Marbeuf, French military governor of the island from May 1770 to his death in September 1786.

To Carlo and Litizia, the wisest course of action seemed clear enough. The safety and advancement of the family came first. They rallied to the French in expectation of rewards and honours, which indeed were not long in coming. Both claimed Italian noble blood going back for centuries, a proudly cherished ancestry for which there is in fact very little hard legal evidence, as Dorothy Carrington has concluded in her masterly study of the Bonaparte family up to the year 1786.[5] Nevertheless Carlo, a prudent and ambitious man, was also adept at intrigue and persuaded the French to recognize his title of count in September 1771, some seventeen months after they had created an order of nobility in Corsica. Acceptance of French rule furthermore enabled him to pursue the legal career for which he had qualified, and his election as a deputy of the nobility of Ajaccio to the Corsican Estates duly followed with Marbeuf's approval in September 1771. The defeated Paolists, as subsequent events were to prove, never forgave the Bonapartes for thus looking after their own interests at the expense of the old patriotic cause.

Collaboration brought stability of family life as well as professional advancement, and the young Napoleon was raised in a safe if strict environment, shielded from the legal disputes over property and Letizia's dowry in which Carlo was often embroiled. Studies of the first nine years of his life suggest that he was a self-confident but somewhat unruly child. The self-assurance came from a happy and trusting relationship with his wet-nurse, Camilla Ilari, the quarrelsomeness from an early perception that his mother had a preference for Joseph, and that to attract her attention and admiration he had to compete with his elder brother and show himself superior in deeds. These early contests were often violent, on Napoleon's part at least, although Joseph's natural inclination was to shrink from the physical challenge. Small wonder then that Napoleon soon earned the nickname of '*Ribulione*' – the troublemaker.[6] The traits of aggressiveness, egotism, jealousy of his mother's attentions to Joseph and Carlo, and childish pleasure in winning her admiration of his own achievements formed early in his personality. Sharpened by constant frustrations and some long-remembered physical punishment, they were to prove enduring.

The complexity of his childhood relationships within the family increased with the birth of younger sisters and brothers: Maria Anna (1771, who died four months later), Lucien (1775), Elisa (1777), and Louis (1778) – but none of these came near to matching the early rivalry with Joseph.[7]

One effect of rallying to the French was that the elder Bonaparte children were given a rare opportunity to further their education on the mainland at royal expense. The decisive factor was again the patronage of Marbeuf, whose devotion to Letizia had already become notorious in Ajaccio and the source of much salacious tittle-tattle among the enemies of the family, some of whom even spread the rumour (certainly untrue) that he was Napoleon's natural father.[8] Joseph's prize was a scholarship place at the College of Autun in Burgundy, which he took up in January 1779. In the following March Napoleon similarly received a scholarship to Brienne in Champagne, one of the twelve royal preparatory schools for the sons of poorer nobles founded in 1776 by Saint-Germain, the minister of war. Both were the beneficiaries of the token awards Louis XVI's loyal Corsican nobility were thus offered, among a total of 650 for the whole of France. Similar favours would enable Elisa to win a scholarship to Saint-Cyr in 1782, then the most exclusive school for girls in France, and Lucien to follow Napoleon at Brienne in 1784. Earlier still in 1779, Joseph Fesch, Letizia's half-brother by her mother's late second marriage, had already been elected to a scholarship at the seminary in Aix-en-Provence.

These were to prove momentous steps in the life and fortunes of the whole Bonaparte clan. For Napoleon, one episode of rivalry and attention-seeking within a secure family home had ended; another, of loneliness and alienation from the sons of French nobles who were his academic fellows but also his social superiors, had begun. At the age of nine, uprooted from the only world he had ever known, there were no familiar props to support him. The regime of the school, run by the Franciscan teaching order of the Minims, was spartan. For five and a half years he was not allowed to leave it, let alone return to Corsica, and even visits from his family in 1782 and 1784 were strictly regulated. His courses of study and physical training were carefully supervised, which may indeed have been the very discipline he needed to see him through this painful time of adjustment. His aloofness in the face of gibes from his peers, his proud defence of a Corsican identity, even his strange dialect, all stamped him as an outsider, and a somewhat prickly one at that. Among his schoolmates, only Charles Le Lieur and Fauvelet de Bourrienne (who much later served him first as personal secretary and then as minister plenipotentiary to Hamburg) became close friends during those years.

What effect, then, did Napoleon's schooling at Brienne have on the formation of his character? Clearly, his self-reliance and physical courage were tested to the limit and in the event abundantly proved. Yet something of the impetuous flaunting of his skills, the ebullient spontaneity of his childhood in Ajaccio, had taken cover in the process. He drew into himself more, becoming a loner almost in spite of himself. He read avidly and dreamed of the brilliant service he would one day give in liberating his native land from French rule, convinced of his natural ability to succeed by his deeds. If he remained weak in Latin, dismissing it as a subject without practical value, he was good in history and geography, and excellent in mathematics. From his reading of ancient history, Plutarch's work on Caesar most notably, he formed a powerful impression of the valour and martial glory of classical heroes, exemplary models for what he later presumed to be his own still greater appointment with Destiny. His mastery of mathematics eventually brought him out top of his class.

Napoleon's social and sexual education were much more limited, however, partly by force of circumstance, but mostly through natural inclination. This particular part of his early life has always had its devotees, whether through the older titillating genre of '*petite histoire*', or through more recent and more serious analytical attempts at psycho-historical interpretation. It would, then, be as well to recognize the inherent difficulties of the subject itself. The available evidence, for a start, is limited and often notoriously unreliable. Napoleon himself was always reticent on the matter, and even the insights provided by his private and most intimate letters, whose authenticity is enhanced by the fact that they were never intended for publication, are patchy rather than conclusive. Some of his earlier associates like Bourrienne and Méneval left detailed memoirs, but these were written long after the events they recounted. In particular, the ten volumes published in Bourrienne's name in 1829 were in large part an unauthentic concoction of the writings of others. The unfinished memoirs left by Joseph and Lucien Bonaparte are unhelpful in the present connection.

There is also the problem of anachronism, given that sexual customs and the public perception of acceptable standards of personal morality have changed a good deal since Napoleon's time. For modern readers exposed to the 'explicit' and often sensational revelations of the private 'sex lives' of prominent public figures, it may be difficult to understand the shared restraints and outward decorum of major historical characters two hundred years ago. Indeed, most readers nowadays would probably find earlier Corsican custom on the matter about as unfamiliar as any other in Europe. Its ethic of family honour, its traditional acceptance of what some today regard as outmoded 'gender roles', its stigmas which still attached to adultery, fornication, and illegitimacy, the absence of co-educational schools in the modern sense, of accessible contraceptive methods now taken for granted in most western societies, and of saturated sexual titillation through the mass media – all mark a great distance in moral values between Napoleon's world and our own.

With those caveats in mind, we must try to imagine the *ambiance* in which the young Napoleon, more than two hundred years ago, might have had his early sexual education. We need to understand the moral code and cultural conditioning of his upbringing in a remote Corsican home, and his unfamiliarity in those early years with the laxer customs of the French mainland. The example of his parents, whose own marital fidelity was often questioned by contemporaries, with some real justification in the case of the pleasure-loving Carlo, upheld a strict outward decency, and of course they had even stricter expectations of him. Much later, when his process of assuming a clearer French identity had run a longer course, Napoleon could look down with disdain on the more barbaric excesses of popular Corsican custom. In any case, as petty gentry set apart by social status and some formal education from their ruder compatriots, the Bonapartes had never lived by such brutal tribal rules. But, while Corsica was their *patria*, they well knew and respected its moral rule that sexual propriety was an integral function of family honour. In short, in approaching this private and elusive subject, we need to understand Napoleon's mentality in the context of his own time and situation.

The first thing to be said is that it was virtually impossible for the schoolfellows of Brienne to have social, let alone sexual, liaisons with girls while they were under its regime. The exclusively male ethos of the place was, and was intended to be, an essential part of its educational purpose in forming character. On the other hand, there was nothing at all unusual in this. In any case, Napoleon then seems to have had no great interest in or fantasies about girls, and that too may be thought unremarkable in an ambitious boy with other more immediate priorities in view. While the indulgence of pubescent curiosity with his schoolmates would no doubt have been possible, since the homosexual 'nymphs' of Brienne were notorious, there is no evidence that he ever sought such experiences. Yet who can be sure that there were no carnal stirrings in the growing boy, or whether they were released in the solitary moments of an almost monastic confinement, or tempered by the iron will of self-control?

In any event, until he was a grown man in his twenties, Napoleon certainly *appeared* to be indifferent to sexual relationships. Again, who can say whether this was due more to his sexual indifference, or innocence, or self-consciousness, or moral priggishness at the time? He seems to have had a passing initiation with a young prostitute in Paris when he was eighteen, but otherwise his teenage years were unusually chaste. Some writers, drawing on the more recent personality theories of psychologists, have identified the cause in the deep sense of reverence he felt for his mother, that is in an 'oedipal drive' which was to last well into his adult years.[9] Perhaps so; yet it seems to me just as plausible that Napoleon, the arch-egotist, may have decided early on that sexual intimacies meant physical exposure to others, which might compromise his hard-won effort in emotional self-control, and that this was not the way for an ambitious soldier who would be master of all situations to disarm himself. One *canard* at least can be dismissed with confidence: religious taboos were *not* the motivation. Napoleon indeed received his first communion at Brienne sometime in 1781 or 1782, and was to be confirmed by the archbishop of Paris while at his next school on 15 May 1785, but such affiliation to the faith in which he had been born was in all probability an outward formality, a public token to satisfy family decorum. As his education broadened, he came more and more to espouse the fashionable deism of the Enlightenment. If he ever needed to sublimate the temptations of the flesh, religion was not the inspiration.

Instead, Napoleon's time at Brienne was filled by a passionate devotion to study, by the driving will to demonstrate his superiority over all others in the end-of-year tests (the so-called '*exercices publics*'), as well as in the physical challenges outside the classroom, and by the proleptic dream of his heroic Corsican destiny. In the end it was his intellectual achievements, and his success in mathematics above all, that gained him a scholarship place at the Royal Military School in Paris, which he took up in October 1784. If one regards Brienne as in a sense of a sort of 'prep school', his new affiliation marked the beginning of his training as a professional soldier, although it too was abstract and dominated by mathematics. While his acceptance there was also somewhat warmer, it appears, he continued to resent the snobbishness and arrogant posturings of fellow cadets from the high nobility. As he formed new friendships, his social life assumed more ease. After rather less than a year, instead of the usual two or three, he passed as a sub-lieutenant of artillery, that is as a lieutenant of the second and lowest degree, at the age of sixteen. In a national list of 300, he was placed forty-second. His letters of that time, signed '*Buonaparte, officier*', exaggerated the true status of his modest grade, but they testify to his pride in the attainment. One of his early ambitions had at last been concretized in rank. Postings followed during the next three or four years to the La Fère Regiment in Valence (November 1785–September 1786), where he was commissioned as a lieutenant, and to the artillery school at Auxonne (June 1788–September 1789).

The artillery, moreover, was a specialized and something of an élite section within the royal army. Napoleon's acceptance into it was itself a mark of distinction and of recognized promise. The artillery regiments made up less than 10,000 of the total complement of some 237,000 officers and soldiers in the 1780s, the regular infantry accounting for 113,000, the cavalry for 32,000, the royal household troops for something over 7,000, and the militia or provincial reserve for the remaining 75,000.[10] Napoleon's military training exposed him to the important innovatory teachings of men like Gribeauval and the Du Teil brothers in artillery formations and guncraft, and to those of Bourcet and Guibert in the infantry tactics of mobile warfare. Indeed, while at Auxonne he received personal instruction from the commandant, General Jean de Beaumont, the chevalier du Teil, catching his eye and earning his commendations. New intellectual interests also opened as he turned to political thought and literature, becoming an enthusiastic reader of Rousseau and Voltaire, of Corneille and Racine.

Reading the record of Napoleon's career in the years 1785–89, one is struck not only by its precocity but also by its mobility. At Brienne, he had had to accept a form of educational incarceration. After graduating from the Royal Military School, his transfers between postings were interspersed with prolonged periods of leave, which to some extent went with promoted rank. For the first time since his departure from Ajaccio in 1779, he was able to return to his family. His first Corsican leave lasted from September 1786 to June 1788, interrupted only by a three-month trip to Paris towards the end of 1787. Among his ambitions at this time was a grandiose plan to write a monumental history of Corsica, for which he was already assembling documentary material. Without the help and support of Paoli (still in exile) and his followers on the island, the project was unlikely to advance. Napoleon was therefore anxious to keep on good terms with these old patriots, who included many of his most seasoned potential sources, and even to collaborate with them in the underground movement for independence.

Meanwhile, major changes had overtaken the family. Napoleon's sisters Pauline and Caroline had been born, in 1780 and 1782 respectively, as had his youngest brother Jerome in 1784. But Carlo had died at the age of thirty-nine in 1785, while on a trip to France, and ominously of stomach cancer, leaving Letizia a widow at thirty-six. During their twenty years of marriage they had had twelve children, eight of whom survived into the adult years. Napoleon, then still at the Royal Military School, appears to have felt little genuine remorse at the death of his father; in later years he even conceded that it might well have been advantageous to his own career. Following Corsican custom, Joseph was now head of the family, a role he evidently took very seriously. Leave brought Napoleon back into the family fold, gave him the chance to meet his new younger siblings, and also to challenge Joseph's authority as head of the house. All the evidence suggests that he formed a particular liking for Louis, a babe in arms when he had left Ajaccio for Brienne, whom he later took with him on trips to the mainland and coached in his studies with almost paternal devotion. As the Revolution approached, the Bonapartes were often on the move, but the solidarity of the clan was as close as ever before. In the case of Napoleon, now an officer on the army payroll, the luxury of a regular salary had to be shared with his family. The obligation was accepted and duly discharged.

. . . .

SOLDIER OF THE REVOLUTION

When the States General met in Versailles in May 1789, very few could have foreseen the ructions that would follow in the royal army within three or four years. By 10 August 1792, when the monarchy was overthrown, the military high command had been thrown into disarray by a long succession of emigrations. It is true that this trend was significantly much less pronounced among the officers of the *petite noblesse* serving in the artillery than among those of the *haute noblesse* who up to then had dominated the infantry. But, over all sections of the royal army, the best estimates suggest that perhaps as many as 6,000 commissioned officers, more than 60 per cent of the authorized complement, had emigrated by the end of 1791, and that the proportion then rose to around 75 per cent of the pre-Revolutionary officer corps by the early months of 1793.[11] They had thus only too plainly dissociated themselves from the Revolution, and in many cases they had joined its active enemies as émigré commanders. Such a massive exodus would surely have crippled the Revolutionary regime once war was declared on Austria and Prussia in April 1792, and then extended to Britain, Holland, and Spain in February–March 1793, had there not been a ready supply of talent to step into the breach.

The fact, not without its irony, is that there *was* that source of talent ready to hand. What saved the Revolution from military collapse in the critical campaigns of 1792–94 was the emergence and rapid promotion of a core of talented young soldiers, NCOs and lesser commissioned officers, regulars and volunteers alike, mostly of bourgeois origin but including a significant number of former nobles of varying status. The vast majority of them had had at least some experience of service in the old royal army, however brief, and this crucial line of continuity must be stressed. Those years marked the start of a process aimed at professionalizing the officer corps and was to have a major influence on the military careers of thousands within it during the Revolutionary wars. Such opportunities would no doubt have been unthinkable in the venal system of officer promotions current under the old regime, when financial

18

means and social connections had often been the main determining factors.

Now, it would of course be altogether misleading to imply
that the whole process was easily and tidily managed. The
demands of war created their own uncertainties, anxieties, and
upheavals. Successive changes of government in Paris, not least
in the high personnel of the ministry of war, had repercussions
on the military command. Since the test of ideological loyalty was
never constant, there were several military purges, as officers
in favour with one political regime fell foul of another which
had replaced it. The patronage of particular ministers or superior military officers still counted for much. In other words,
the simple luck of being in the right place at the right time,
or enjoying the favours of those who had the power of promotion at a given moment, could suddenly enhance or blight the
careers of aspiring young officers.

What those changes implied for the wider reorganization of
the French army, and for its progression to a new code of military conduct and honour, is more fully discussed in chapter 4
(below, pp. 87–101). The emphasis here is on Napoleon's own
experience of that process, since no one personifies the extraordinary transition, the massive yet often turbulent remobiliza-
tion of human resources, better than himself. The most striking
feature of his military career in the early years of the Revolution, up to 1793 at least, is how messy and uncertain it all was.
There was a wild, even anarchic, quality about his activities at
that time. On more than one occasion, disobedience towards
the Revolutionary authorities could have left him stranded in
virtual exile, but somehow fortune always seemed to favour
him. After his second Corsican leave (September 1789–February
1791), he did brief service as a first lieutenant at Auxonne and
then with the Grenoble Regiment at Valence, but in October
1791 he was allowed to transfer from the regular army and
joined the volunteer Corsican National Guard at the rank of
lieutenant-colonel. This brought him into more immediate
contact with Paoli, who had returned from exile in July 1790
to become Louis XVI's royal governor of Corsica, and who was
also then head of its National Guard. A quarrel with the military authorities in Paris soon afterwards confronted Napoleon
with the real prospect of professional disgrace. He had prolonged his second Corsican leave by three and a half months
without permission, and the rebellion of the volunteer battalion

of Ajaccio under his command in 1792 was a serious embarrassment to him. It took a hasty trip to Paris to sort out the mess, win the exoneration he sought, and secure his reinstatement in the French army at the promoted rank of captain.

At the same time Napoleon's rupture with Paoli, now in open revolt against the new Republic in France, left him exposed to the threats of more immediate enemies. The project for his great 'History' seemed doomed. Lucien Bonaparte had for a time been Paoli's secretary, but his impetuous denunciation of the latter's royalist 'despotism' before the Jacobin club in Toulon in April 1793 embittered relations between the parties still further. Taking sides, the National Convention in Paris responded by outlawing Paoli as an Anglophile traitor and ordering his arrest. Where then, given his growing isolation from the Corsican rebellion, was Napoleon's cause? For not the first or last time he found it in himself, above all, and by extension in his family. Less than a year earlier, on 24 June 1792, Lucien had observed perceptively in a letter to Joseph that he had always distinguished in Napoleon 'an ambition not altogether egoist, but one that surpasses his love of the public good'.[12]

The events which now bore down on the Bonapartes and forced the family to leave their home to the depredations of the Paolists and take refuge in Toulon in June 1793 are familiar enough. What matters here is the psychological impact that whole affair had on Napoleon's own sense of identity. As a French collaborator or '*francisé*', bereft of a patriotic cause and following in Corsica, his perilous position left him only one option. He had to assume a more obviously *French* identity, not only outwardly by education and professional training, but also by inner conviction. The Corsican dream, nourished since the early years at Brienne, but now sullied by the clannish feuds and implacable enmities of his native land, had evaporated. This was in fact the culmination of a process lasting several years. As Dorothy Carrington puts it, 'the Corsican traits in his [Napoleon's] character which his years at school served only to reinforce, were progressively shed between 1789 and 1793, under the impact of the French Revolution. . . . Napoleon simply grew out of certain Corsican values as of constricting clothes.'[13] And so, if removal to the south of France at first obliged the family to live in straitened circumstances, its formative influence on Napoleon was much more enduring and significant.

20

It enlarged his whole vision of how the *French* cause might serve his personal ambition. In ideological terms, this also implied his firmer and more public identification with Revolutionary principles. And these in turn, after the formal abolition of the monarchy in September 1792, had become explicitly republican.

Outwardly, then, Napoleon had embraced the French Revolutionary Republic, but inwardly he was clearly more responsive to the opportunities it offered for the advancement of his military career than to the purity of its principles. During most of 1793, while the Bonapartes were preoccupied with their unsettled domestic affairs, the political crisis in Paris deepened. There were serious military reverses on the northern front, culminating in the defeat at Neerwinden in March and the defection of Dumouriez to the Austrians in early April. After the new military levy of February, a major civil war had erupted in the Vendée, and then spread to other areas of the west country on the instigation of royalist seigneurs and refractory priests. It was exacerbated by the so-called 'federalist' uprisings in many other departments, a provincial reaction against the authority of the new Jacobin government in Paris, following the expulsion of the Girondin leaders from the National Convention on 2 June. During the spring and summer of that year major cities like Marseilles, Lyons, and Bordeaux also joined the revolt against Paris, while the vital naval port of Toulon surrendered to the British fleet towards the end of August. Almost everywhere, at home and abroad, the very survival of the Revolution seemed under threat. The instruments of the Jacobin Terror were already in place, but the first necessity was for a *military* recovery.

This was where Napoleon's luck played its hand. He was in the right place at the right time. Stationed in the south, his artillery skills had come to the attention of the younger Robespierre, Augustin, a commissioner to the Army of Italy who was then based in Nice. As it happened, the Corsican deputy A.-C. Saliceti was then the Convention's representative on mission to the army in Toulon. With such fortuitous connections, Napoleon was given the chance to participate in the siege of Toulon and to conduct the artillery offensive which eventually led to the recapture of the port in December 1793. His action earned him immediate promotion to the rank of brigadier-general at the age of twenty-four. At the same time he was appointed commander-in-chief of artillery of the Army of Italy and of its coastal defences. Such opportunities from his association with the Jacobins were not to last much longer, however. Lucien Bonaparte, a wilful young man who was beyond anyone's power to control, not least Napoleon's, had already made something of a name for himself as a Jacobin firebrand, as we have seen. But *he* was also a relative minnow; Napoleon's recognized military prowess marked him out as a far more dangerous suspect in the eyes of the Thermidorian regime which unseated the Jacobins in the coup of 9–10 Thermidor Year II (27–8 July 1794). He had enemies among the new authorities in Paris, the aged and mediocre Aubry among them, and even suffered the indignity of a brief imprisonment in the Château d'Antibes.

After his release and a footloose period in Paris, his loyalty was put to a new test. The royalist rebellion in the Vendée had continued sporadically in spite of its major military setbacks during the last months of 1793. So it was that in May 1795 Napoleon received orders to join the Army of the West with the rank of general of artillery. He refused to take up his post, much less out of any ideological discomfort than for the personal reason that he considered such undignified action within France rather than heroic service against more dangerous foreign enemies beneath his professional reputation. Retribution followed. His name was struck off the officer list for disobedience, and his whole career again seemed in jeopardy. Financial worries also returned to deepen his despair, and it is said that at this time he even contemplated suicide as a way out. He certainly considered abandoning the French army altogether and offering his services to the sultan of Turkey.[14]

Yet favourable opportunity once more came Napoleon's way. The *arrêté* of the committee of public safety formally announcing the removal of his name from the officer list was dated 15 September 1795. The event which changed everything occurred just three weeks later. The legality of the new republican constitution finally adopted in September was challenged by a royalist uprising in Paris on 13 Vendémiaire Year IV (5 October 1795). Whether officially in service or not, Napoleon now had an unexpected chance to demonstrate his loyalty to the retiring National Convention in what has passed down to history as the celebrated 'whiff of grapeshot'. After the incident, itself a minor affair in military terms, his career scarcely looked back. On the very day of the uprising he was formally reinstated in his rank of brigadier-general and now also appointed as second in command of the Army of the Interior. On 16 October following he was promoted to the rank of divisional general in the artillery section, and on 26 October to the post of *général en chef*, of that same Army.

. . . .

'A DAZZLING FAME'

The Directory, the new regime which succeeded the Convention in November 1795, inherited a military position which had been improving appreciably since the French victory over the Austrians at Fleurus in June 1794. So far from having to defend the home frontiers by desperate means, by Terror and the extraordinary military exactions it implied, on which the Jacobins had staked their survival but also overplayed their hand, the late Thermidorian Convention and early Directory were able to take the war to the enemy. Belgium and Luxemburg were overrun and annexed in September 1795. The German left bank of the Rhine was brought under effective military occupation during that same year, and although its new departments were not formally annexed to France until January 1802, their resources were already being systematically exploited. The Revolutionary wars of conquest and territorial aggrandizement of the French Republic were under way.

Early in 1796 their direction switched to the south-east, where Piedmont and Italy beckoned, and this was where the next phase of Napoleon's military career was brilliantly realized. In March 1796, at the age of twenty-six, he was promoted to the rank of general and also appointed supreme commander of the French Army of Italy. The spectacular victories over the Austrians and Piedmontese which followed during his first Italian campaign are too well known to need detailed recounting here. It is a textbook platitude that the years 1796–97 were a crucial period in the evolution of Napoleon's character and professional career, that is in his private and public life alike. They were a time of new challenges and experiences, when personal ambition, real military genius, and the infatuation of first love all combined to produce a warrior increasingly conscious of his heroic mission. In other ways too those years tell us much about the historical circumstances in which such career-soldiers could rise to prominence. We need to identify all elements of the case, three at least, since their interaction influenced its development in several ways.

There was, first, the intervention of patronage at crucial moments, and here the role of Paul Barras in the advancement of Napoleon's career was certainly very fortunate. Barras, formerly a member of the National Convention, a regicide and then representative on mission to the south of France in the autumn of 1793, with a bloody reputation for dealing with captured counter-revolutionaries, had first met Napoleon during the siege of Toulon. Indeed, he had played his part in the latter's military promotion after victory there. Fearing for his life as the Jacobin Terror intensified, Barras had been active in the coup which eliminated Robespierre and his colleagues. During the Thermidorian interlude which followed, he had become commander of the Army of the Interior and of the police, and had also served terms on the committee of public safety and on that of general security. The start of his affair with Josephine de Beauharnais (*née* Rose Tascher de la Pagerie), who had already been the mistress of General Hoche, also dated from this period. At the time of the Vendémiaire uprising, when he was charged with the defence of the Tuileries, he had been the key figure in giving Napoleon another chance to make his mark. The episode had also enhanced his own political career, for in the elections which shortly followed Barras became one of the first five directors, and was certainly the most popular among them. He, and only he, was to hold that high executive office throughout the years of the Directory (1795–99). His patronage was decisive in securing Napoleon's promotion to the rank of general and his appointment as supreme commander of the Army of Italy.

The rapport between the two men, still trusting and mutually advantageous, was again demonstrated when a more serious royalist threat to the Directory, following electoral gains that year, was foiled by the coup of 18 Fructidor Year V (4 September 1797). On Barras's request for help, Napoleon sent General Augereau, his own deputy on the Italian campaign, to put down the attempted insurrection in Paris. Not all the implications of this affair were immediately apparent. In the short term, Fructidor strengthened the position of Barras and enabled him to get rid of his main political enemies, notably the directors Barthélemy and Carnot, as well as of the compromised military commander Pichegru. It also greatly enhanced Napoleon's reputation as a military custodian of the French Republic. In the medium term, the coup could be seen as one of a series of interventions by the line army in Parisian politics, as a precedent for and major step on the road to Brumaire, or in other words as part of a conditioning process from which the civil authorities would then emerge as servants rather than masters of the military high command. In the longer run, as events were to prove, it was the last serious royalist challenge to the new political order in France until 1814. In that sense, Fructidor had provided the opportunity for Napoleon, no doubt unwittingly at the time, to play his part in removing one major obstacle to the political ambition which was to unfold in the coup of November 1799.

Could the Barras of Fructidor possibly have foreseen his shattering fall from grace only a little more than two years later? Plainly not; and yet the seeds of enmity between him and Napoleon were already being cast in the years of their apparent trust and collaboration. The second element of the formative years 1796–97 lay in the vicissitudes of Napoleon's emotional development. We do not know when exactly he became aware that Josephine had been Barras's now apparently discarded lover, but it *is* clear that Napoleon first met her through the social favours of his patron. She already had the reputation of being a bosom friend to several scions of *salon* society. This indeed was the context in which Napoleon first met her, and the extent of his infatuation was altogether unprecedented. It would be too much to call this a whirlwind romance, since Josephine's affections towards him appear to have been shallow. He inspired no great love or passion in her; she probably did not even like him. What, then, can have been her motives for their marriage by civil ceremony on 9 March 1796, just a week after the announcement of his Italian command? From her point of view, he was obviously a rising star, already a popular military hero, with favour in high places, a superior officer who seemed likely to go far. She was thirty-two years of age and a widow, with passing affairs rather than an honourable alliance to expect from her other consorts of the *salons*. His passion for her was beyond doubt, and she had not had a better proposal. Most important of all perhaps, she had the interests of her children, Eugène and Hortense, to consider. In short, her reasons for marrying Napoleon were material and prudential. They were based on calculations of the head rather than quickenings of the heart.

Harold Parker has suggested that Napoleon's infatuation with Josephine may have been a projection of his oedipal fixation, indeed that he had married his own deceptive image of Letizia. The celebrated beauty of the mother, with her radiant black hair, chestnut eyes, and fine limbs, barely spoilt by her frequent pregnancies, was reflected in the wife, whose fading good looks were enhanced by an elegant aristocratic charm. Parker asks whether this same mother-image may itself have been a powerful inspiration of Napoleon's brilliant actions during the first Italian campaign.[15] It is an intriguing lead: the public cause of France was also his private cause, where military glory and the celebration of love could coincide in his own person. Just as he had once wished to impress his mother and win her admiration by his deeds, so he now sensed that the way to Josephine's heart lay in demonstrating his still more conspicuous success. That at least was achieved in victory after victory south of the Alps, but the battle for her love turned out rather differently. He wrote her frequent and ardent letters from the front, only to receive occasional and miserable scraps of acknowledgement in reply. Her liaisons with other men were already becoming notorious.

In fairness to Josephine, it should be said that Napoleon had walked into this impasse with his eyes wide open, and wholly against the wishes of his family. In their view, Joseph had shown how it should be done in marrying Julie Clary, daughter of a rich silk merchant of Marseilles, in 1794. This had brought not only honour but also the prospect of greater ease to the penurious family. For a time thereafter it had seemed that Napoleon might pull off a remarkable double-act by marrying Julie's sister, Desirée, and by so doing shrewdly tie up the family fortunes in a sort of *alliance à quatre*. Joseph had been very much in favour of it, and Napoleon's own feelings had appeared fervent enough to encourage talk of an engagement. But Desirée, only fourteen at the time, had been unresponsive to his attempts at a correspondence after his transfer to Paris. Although their relations remained cordial, there had in all probability been no very serious commitment between them. She was to marry General Bernadotte (the future marshal) in 1798, and so much later to become queen of Sweden. One can only speculate about what sort of figure she might have cut as empress of France.

But none of those future eventualities, nor any indulgence of what might have been, was even remotely conceivable when the bombshell of Josephine burst on the unsuspecting Bonaparte clan in March 1796. Their immediate reaction was almost wholly unfavourable: for here was a woman whose reputation left a lot to be desired, of noble origin but doubtful intentions, a widow with encumbrances, and six years older than Napoleon. Furthermore, he had chosen to marry her behind the back of his family, without even the courtesy of a prior introduction to them. Even Lucien's marriage in 1794 to Christine Boyer, an innkeeper's daughter, to which the family had also objected, scarcely compared with this new affront. Letizia reckoned soon enough what Josephine's motives must have been and always disliked her. In fact, of all Napoleon's close relations, only Pauline had the generosity of spirit to show any warmth towards her. As for Josephine, the marriage had brought the security she sought, public prominence and official acclaim for herself and her children, but no deep emotional fulfilment in the conjugal bond.

The third element in the development of Napoleon's character during the years 1796–97 might be called an enlargement of his professional vision, and in the long run it was to have the greatest influence on his relationships with others. Hitherto, he had acted, or rather been forced to act, within bounds determined for the most part by those around him. Whether one thinks of the family constraints of his Corsican childhood, of the institutional rules and discipline of his training in Brienne and Paris, of his earlier service in the French army under superior officers, or of the political authorities who assumed the right to usher him in and out of even his most spectacular military interventions – whatever the scene, he had never been a wholly free agent. His social and professional relationships had been confined to Corsicans, a small and relatively isolated world, and to associates on the French mainland, certainly a wider but still rather restricted constituency.

Napoleon's appointment as supreme commander of the Army of Italy put him in charge of some 50,000 men, not in itself a large military complement, and one distinctly inferior in number to the Austrians and their Piedmontese allies. It included officers of the sort who up till then had been his peers or superiors

27

by rank. Now, *he* gave the orders, and it was for others to obey. Furthermore, the Italian venture exposed him for the first time to foreign troops on foreign soil in a major and prolonged campaign. His previous encounters with the Austrians in 1794 had been comparatively minor affairs in northern Italy, more skirmishes than serious engagements, although he had learnt valuable lessons about the enemy and about the terrain. Besides the fact that he had no experience of dealing directly with Italians, the campaign of 1796–97 provided his first chance to preside over and dictate peace terms to defeated enemies. All the evidence suggests that Napoleon rose to such challenges by mastery of his military craft, capitalizing on the mobility of his troops and his celebrated artillery, by brilliant improvisation, and by quickly asserting his authority over all subordinates. Augereau and Masséna, who at first thought they might have the better of this Corsican upstart, were immediately cut down to size and made to regret their temerity. A steely reserve, a laconic command, or a withering look were enough to silence them. By his superior grasp of detail, his imperious manner, and his intolerance of opposition in the face of firm orders, Napoleon had given an early demonstration of his power to inspire fear in those around him. From his rank and file he had already earned the ironic nickname '*le petit caporal*', which was to become famous.

The Army of Italy was not particularly well equipped, being intended as a southern diversion while the main French offensive was concentrated in southern Germany, where incidentally the results were much less successful. Speed of manoeuvre and sudden attacks on more isolated enemy positions were the key to its effective deployment, and this was where Napoleon excelled. The succession of battles alone suggests the strategic pattern of the campaign: Montenotte, Millesimo, Dego, Ceva, Mondovi, Lodi, Borghetto, Lonato, Castiglione, Roveredo, Bassano, Arcola, and Rivoli, all of which prepared the way for the long siege of Mantua, which finally surrendered in February 1797. Piedmontese resistance crumbled at a fairly early stage of those operations. The pope was obliged to accept peace terms at Tolentino on 19 February 1797. Then the Austrians, after the loss of Mantua, and with Vienna now threatened, pressed for an armistice. The preliminaries were agreed at Leoben on 18 April, the definitive terms of peace at Campo Formio on 17 October 1797. Out of the territorial spoils Napoleon had also forged the new, enlarged Cisalpine Republic in June that year, a model of its kind, and bearing his own stamp. During this process, as a way of compensating the Austrians for such territorial losses, he gave them the lands of the old Venetian Republic, which he had already summarily dissolved. These high-handed acts scandalized many contemporaries.

Before the first Italian campaign, Napoleon had been an unknown military quantity outside France; after it, his international fame spread rapidly and widely. His popularity at home had never been greater, boosted no doubt by his transfer to France of sundry spoils of war – cash indemnities and works of art most notably. Secure in his position, he had been able to impose terms of peace at Tolentino, Leoben, and Campo Formio on his own authority. Having conducted the war, he was now in effect also conducting diplomacy, on his own initiative. In theory, he was answerable to the political authorities in Paris; in practice, he was his own master in Italy, and in retrospect one can see that Brumaire was a step nearer. As he put it to Count Miot de Melito on his way back from Italy, 'I have tasted supremacy, and I can no longer renounce it.'[16] The whole experience had taught him how to manipulate people to his own ends. Even his French identity had crystallized into purer form. While marching south to Nice in March 1796 to assume his Italian command, he had changed his surname from 'Buonaparte' to 'Bonaparte'.

. . . .

FROM EGYPT TO BRUMAIRE

It was, then, with enlarged professional experience, toughened character, and a considerably enhanced reputation that Napoleon set off on his Egyptian expedition of 1798–99, at the head of 38,000 men who formed this so-called 'Army of the Orient'. It was altogether an extraordinary venture, whose purpose and events are more difficult to relate to the development of his character and career. Some older accounts interpret it as an early sign that his ambition was set on a wider, extra-European emporium.[17] If so, it is interesting to note that his vision was to the east, whereas his nephew Napoleon III in the 1860s was to seek imperial glory in the west, in the ill-fated Mexican fiasco. The dream can seem its own reality, but even then, the Egyptian campaign is a flimsy base on which to pin Napoleon's pretensions to an eastern or even global empire. Without a dominant navy, any such dream was an unattainable chimera.

What, then, did Egypt mean to Napoleon, and what effect did that experience have on his development? For a start, it involved him for the first time in operations that were as much naval as land-based, and so in sustained confrontations with the British. The terrain was more remote, the climate more hazardous, the methods more untried, than any he had known before. Up to a point his naïve economic reasoning was also at issue, believing as he did that British wealth was fictitious, 'a colossus with feet of clay', and that the loss of its spinal cord to India would reduce it to dust and ashes. In this sense, perhaps, one might see the early gestation of an idea that was to take more practical form in his later Continental Blockade, much nearer home.

The naval and military lessons of 1798–99 were real enough. It was comparatively easy to overcome the Mamluk armies in particular battles and colonize the natives by proclamation, but much more difficult to convert them into loyal French subjects. Turkey's early declaration of hostilities and incursions into the region were an unwelcome diversion. The British Mediterranean fleet and land forces could not be isolated and swept aside in the same way. French resources were badly stretched, and the naval defeats which hampered communications between the expeditionary force and the *métropole* became increasingly serious. At a crucial moment, in August 1799, Napoleon himself left Egypt, an act which Kléber (who then assumed command until his assassination by Muslim fanatics in June 1800) regarded as a betrayal, and which prompted him to seek terms with the British for a French evacuation. In the event it was the British who dictated those terms well over a year later, after the French had surrendered at Cairo and at Alexandria during the summer of 1801. The ultimate military failure of the Egyptian campaign is not in doubt.

It is clear, however, that the whole adventure also had more positive results. The cultural and scientific benefit many members of the expedition gained from direct exposure to an alien land, whose illustrious past was only too visible around them, was to bear fruit later in the Institute. It is often said that the 'Institute of Egypt', founded by Napoleon in Cairo in 1798, created the science of Egyptology. The remoteness of Egypt alone bred a powerful sense of *camaraderie* among Napoleon and his closest associates, who included many distinguished *savants* like Berthollet and Monge, for whom the experience was to remain unforgettable. Several of them were to be staunch Brumaireans, his future comrades in arms on many occasions, and recipients of his Imperial honours when the time came. One need only look at the subsequent careers of some of the participants to understand the ties of service and loyalty which were forged in those years. For Kléber, of course, it had all ended in tragic disaffection. For Desaix too, a general of recognized brilliance, the end came in action at Marengo in June 1800. For Reynier, an outspoken critic of the expedition after being ordered back to France in 1801, the future would be patchy, as he fell in and out of Napoleon's favour. For the faithful Menou, who remained a favourite in spite of his military incompetence, administrative and political honours lay ahead. And for many others, most notably the civilian *camarades* of Egypt, there would be distinction at the Institute, along with Imperial titles and other rewards. If the Egyptian campaign had done nothing else, it had added men of some scholarly distinction to the Brumairean party, even if several of them were later to oppose the illiberal policies of its war-lord.

Yet Egypt also had another – no less formative – significance for Napoleon's private life. It was during his absence from France that he learnt from his family of Josephine's repeated infidelities. His earlier suspicions, instinctively felt, were now all too plainly confirmed by those who wished him no harm. After expecting so much, he was the more deceived, notwithstanding the strong probability that his Egyptian adventures included a passing affair with Pauline Fourès, who had recently married a sub-lieutenant of cavalry whom she joined on the expedition (disguised as a man) for what then apparently turned out to be a honeymoon ride with a difference.[18] The disillusioning reports of Josephine bit deep into his character, numbing a whole part of it. Soon enough, however, that void in his emotional humour would be filled by the satisfaction of his ambition in the governable world, by glory and fame. Public charisma would take the place of private love, and the sensation of rising power would be its own aphrodisiac. Napoleon was to have relations with other women, certainly, but Josephine was the only one with whom he ever attempted to find lasting emotional and sexual fulfilment. 'This', in Harold Parker's words, 'is the story of an ego which failed to achieve satisfying

31

intimate human relationships and which learned to cope with and to master other members of the human race instead.'[19]

On his return to France in October 1799, Napoleon found the Directory in terminal discord, lacking clear leadership, fearful of a Jacobin resurgence, the director Sieyès scheming for a change of regime and a new constitution drawn in his – Sieyès' – own image, and the gains of the Italian campaign all but squandered. A coup would need a strong military man, and Napoleon's fortuitous return to and appointment as commander of Paris quickly settled that question. By another lucky chance, his brother Lucien was then president of the council of five hundred, the lower house of the legislature, to which he had been elected the previous year. The plot began when Sieyès and Ducos resigned as directors, soon afterwards persuading the reluctant Barras to do the same, which had the intended effect of incapacitating the chief executive. A majority of the council of ancients, the upper house, supported this move, and on 18 Brumaire (9 November) it voted to move the government to Saint-Cloud. This, it was hoped, would pre-empt any violent intervention by the people of Paris.

Next day, when the council of five hundred proved unwilling at first to go along with the plan, Napoleon faced their raucous hostility in person. During the uproar – the precise details remain unclear – he appears either to have fainted or to have been knocked to the ground unconscious. It was then that Lucien saved the situation. His dramatic declarations on behalf of his brother's good faith and respect for the Republic persuaded both councils to disperse. An undertaking was given that each council would choose twenty-five of its own members to form a commission which would then draw up a new constitution. The immediate upshot was that Napoleon, Sieyès, and Ducos were named as provisional consuls. In the event, the citizens of Paris received the news of the coup without a furore, and the die was cast. Napoleon was the great beneficiary, but Lucien the true hero, of Brumaire.

. . . .

THE FORTUNES OF THE CLAN

This chapter began with the young Napoleon striving for attention and acclaim among his family in a remote Corsican home. It now ends with him in full manhood, his fundamental character

32

formed, and his professional career poised on the threshold of real political as well as military power at the heart of France. If he was more than a little indebted to one of his brothers for the success of his coup, it must be said that Lucien's decisive intervention had been possible only because of his official position in the council of five hundred. That in turn had come about very largely in recognition of Napoleon's rising fame under the Directory and his determination to use it in the interests of all his family. Frédéric Masson made this the binding theme of his multi-volume study of Napoleon's relations with his family, the most ambitious ever attempted, nearly a century ago. Since the instincts of clan had evidently worked to good advantage in the Brumaire coup, it would be appropriate to complete the picture by looking briefly at how the other Bonapartes had fared during the years leading up to that watershed.

Following Corsican custom, the men were expected to take the initiative in public life and play the dominant role in advancing their own and the family's fortunes. We may deal with them first. Lucien, before his election to the council of five hundred, had already benefited from Napoleon's intervention in securing lesser military postings. Joseph, after his marriage to Julie Clary, was for a time heavily involved in their financial affairs, which he improved considerably by judicious investments, while fathering two daughters. Under the Directory he had a more prominent role in public life, following Napoleon to Italy in 1796 and then being sent on a mission to Corsica. In 1797, after brief service in the council of five hundred, and with Napoleon's help, he realized his ambition of becoming French ambassador to Parma and Rome. There, he gained valuable diplomatic experience, which was to be useful later in the negotiations for the Concordat with Pius VII and in those for the treaties of Lunéville and Amiens.

Louis, of all the brothers, had depended most on Napoleon's tutelage. Having chosen a military career, and in the artillery at that, his early progress was unexceptional. His first appointment at the age of fifteen to a subaltern post in a garrison under Napoleon's command, following the latter's spectacular promotions in January 1794, owed everything to blood patronage. He accompanied Napoleon as an aide on the first Italian campaign and was present at the battles of Caldiero, Arcola, and Rivoli, then too at the siege of Mantua. By the end

of the campaign he had advanced to the rank of captain in the
cavalry. He also joined Napoleon on the Egyptian expedition,
but was sent home after the French victory at Alexandria in
July 1798, and in June of the following year again transferred
to the cavalry. His major military promotions were to come in
the years of more lavish patronage after Brumaire.

Jerome, the youngest of the family, and fifteen years Napoleon's junior, had had his schooling at the Oratorian college
of Juilly (near Meaux) and was destined for the navy, which he
eventually entered as an officer in favourable circumstances in
1800. Who at that stage, even allowing for his rumbustious
character, could have predicted the stormy affair of his first
marriage to the American, Elizabeth Patterson, his second
marriage to Catherine of Württemberg a year or two later, and
his subsequent appointment as king of Westphalia?

As for Napoleon's sisters, Elisa's education as a royal scholar
at Saint-Cyr had been cut short by the Revolution, and after
1793 she had shared the troubled migrations of the females of
the clan. In 1797 she married Felix Bacciochi, a Corsican com-
patriot, with whom she was to share high honours under the
Empire. Pauline, whose widely acclaimed beauty is perhaps
best remembered through her later and somewhat scandalous
nude modelling for Antonio Canova's work of sculpture *Venus
Reclining* (1807), made up for her lack of ambition by the
spontaneity of her wit and generosity. Her first marriage, to
General Leclerc in 1797, when she was just sixteen and already
showing signs of her easy virtue, was arranged very much at
Napoleon's behest. To that extent 'tamed' at the time of
Brumaire, and now less embarrassing to the new first consul,
her vivacious spirit had not yet been dampened by the tragic
loss of her husband and of their only child, a son, during the
next few years. How different she was from Caroline, the youngest sister, also good-looking, but an ambitious, scheming, and
fundamentally uncharitable character. Her marriage to Joachim
Murat was to take place only a few months after Brumaire,
while he held the rank of general. She too was part of Napoleon's scheme of things, destined for high honours, though
undeservedly so, as her later betrayal of him would so palpably
show.

Finally, Letizia, mother of them all. Eight years a widow at
the time of her family's evacuation to France in 1793, she had
accepted the loss of their family home in Ajaccio stoically. After

re-establishing a base for her younger children, first near Toulon, then near Marseilles, and finally in Paris, she maintained a regime of frugality and thrift, until they too left home to seek their fortunes. The civil war in Corsica had forced Paoli to turn the island over to the British and again seek exile in London during the course of 1795. The British occupation became untenable after Napoleon's conquest of northern Italy, however, and in 1797 French troops again returned to Corsica. Letizia was now able to reoccupy the old family home in Ajaccio. Dependable, and devoted to her religion, she shunned the limelight which fell increasingly on her offspring, by all accounts doubtful of its future. Her famous remark 'if only it lasts' (*et si ça dure*) dated from the Empire, when she was graced with the title of '*Madame Mère de l'Empereur*', yet might as well have been made many times in earlier years. Alone among her family, she might thus have anticipated Max Weber's much later dictum that 'by its very nature, the existence of charismatic authority is specifically unstable'.[20] But at the inauguration of the Consulate, the end was inconceivable; the parvenu house of Bonaparte was just beginning its fateful date with Destiny.

· · · · · · · · · ·

NOTES AND REFERENCES

1. Dorothy Carrington, *Granite Island: A Portrait of Corsica*, Harmondsworth, 1984 impression, p. 8.
2. Frédéric Masson, *Napoléon et sa famille (1769–1821)*, 13 vols, Paris, 1897–1919, vol. 1, p. 3.
3. Carrington, *Granite Island*, p. 87; Harold T. Parker, 'Napoleon and the Values of the French Army: The Early Phases', *Proceedings of the Annual Meeting of the Western Society for French History*, vol. 18, 1991, p. 234.
4. Carrington, *Granite Island*, pp. 75–6, 84.
5. Dorothy Carrington, *Napoleon and his Parents: On the Threshold of History*, London, 1988, pp. 16–17, 73–7.
6. Carrington, *Granite Island*, p. 12.
7. Harold T. Parker, 'The Formation of Napoleon's Personality: An Exploratory Essay', *French Historical Studies*, vol. 7, Spring 1971, pp. 9–10.
8. Carrington, *Napoleon and his Parents*, pp. 66–7.
9. Parker, 'Formation of Napoleon's Personality', pp. 13, 24–5.
10. Jean-Paul Bertaud, *The Army of the French Revolution: From*

Citizen-Soldiers to Instrument of Power, Eng. edn, Princeton, 1988, pp. 15–16.

11. Samuel F. Scott, *The Response of the Royal Army to the French Revolution: The Role and Development of the Line Army 1787–1793*, Oxford, 1978, pp. 106, 214.

12. Quoted in Parker, 'Values of the French Army', p. 238.

13. Carrington, *Napoleon and his Parents*, p. 89.

14. Masson, *Napoléon et sa famille*, vol. 1, pp. 113–23.

15. Parker, 'Formation of Napoleon's Personality', p. 18.

16. Quoted in ibid., p. 22.

17. E.g. C.F. Lokke, 'French Dreams of Colonial Empire under Directory and Consulate', *Journal of Modern History*, vol. 2, 1930, pp. 237–50.

18. This episode is recounted (from its original source in Jean Thiry, *Bonaparte en Égypte*, Paris, 1973) in Martyn Lyons, *Napoleon Bonaparte and the Legacy of the French Revolution*, Basingstoke and London, 1994, p. 26.

19. Parker, 'Formation of Napoleon's Personality', p. 26.

20. Quoted in *From Max Weber: Essays in Sociology*, trans., ed., and introduced by H.H. Gerth and C. Wright Mills, London, 1982 impression, p. 248.

Chapter 3

THE ELABORATION OF POWER:
NAPOLEONIC GOVERNMENT

On 15 December 1799, when Napoleon presented the Constitution of the Year VIII to the French people two days after its
first formal publication, he declared that it 'is founded on the
true principles of representative government, on the sacred
rights of property, equality, and liberty', and then added: 'Citizens, the Revolution is established on the principles which began
it. It is finished.'[1] So, too, in his letter of 30 December following to d'Andigné, the Chouan leader, Napoleon repeated his
celebrated pronouncement that 'the Revolution is over'. He
also asserted his aim of restoring strong government to France,
one 'solely concerned to re-establish order, justice, and true
freedom – a government which will soon be surrounded by the
trust and respect of all Europe'.[2] Such bold asseverations might
serve as exemplary abstracts against which to judge his actual
policies, as the nature of his regime was elaborated in more
detailed form.

This chapter deals in turn with five aspects of the subject:
the evolving structure of Napoleon's civil government from
the republican legacy of the Revolution to his own Imperial
departure; his treatment of opposition groups, especially in the
earlier years; his Concordat with Pope Pius VII, which at first
seemed a major act of reconciliation with the Catholic Church,
but which bore the seeds of future discord from the moment
of its promulgation; his attempt to restore order and stability
to public finances; and his major reform of the judicial system,
not least through ambitious plans to codify the laws of France.
How far his achievements in all those areas matched his original advertisement of 'order, justice, and true freedom' can
then be assessed more clearly.

. . . .

REPUBLICAN LEGACY AND IMPERIAL VISION

The celebrations which marked the Bicentenary of the French Revolution in 1989 were in many ways a deceptive pageant. One impression left by that less than reflective year was of a selective exercise in republican idealism. For what the French were celebrating, at least in their more popular manifestations, indeed seemed very much like a rarefied version of their *republican* tradition. It will be interesting to see what they make of that other bicentenary – Brumaire – in 1999: whether the Napoleonic interlude is then seen as part of a glorious but buried past, or as a vital legacy for the present.

The question, when set in the immediate context of November 1799, has a direct bearing on what Napoleon inherited from the Revolution, and on what he then did with that inheritance. By the time of Brumaire, the ideological currents emanating from political events since 1789 had certainly not run in the same direction. We need to remind ourselves that, during its first three years at any rate, the Revolution had evolved within a reformed *monarchical* framework. Its first constitution, that of September 1791, was of course a monarchical one, whose practical deficiencies were brutally exposed by war after April 1792. The Revolutionary leaders during most of those three years were not self-avowed republicans, but as it were the 'parliamentarians' of a constitutional monarchy. Their social and professional origins lay either among the privileged orders, or else more generally in the educated élites, of the old regime. It is arguable too that the most enduring institutional reforms of the Revolution were achieved during that same early phase, most notably under the Constituent Assembly of 1789–91. Much the fullest source for the public mood in France on the eve of the Revolution is the lists of grievances (*cahiers de doléances*) drawn up in all the electoral constituencies during the months preceding the States General of 1789. Significantly, these reveal practically no republican sentiment at all among the French people.[3]

The non-implementation of the Jacobin constitution of 1793 is well known. The distortions of republican idealism during the Terror are even more familiar in our textbooks. The Constitution of the Year III, also republican in form, was of a different sort. Liberal it may have been in theory, but in practice it excluded the vast mass of the people from any direct role in the electoral and political process. By any standards, it was far from being a democratic constitution. One might see it as a charter for the incumbent professionals of public life, administrators and lawyers more particularly, and also as a property-owners' charter, resting on a conservative social base. If its institutional ramifications were changed after Brumaire Year VIII, the base itself remained largely intact. Napoleon accepted it, along with its professional and propertied élites, and in one sense the years of the Consulate could be seen as a sustained attempt to broaden and consolidate that base within a new framework of government. He had little hesitation, and perhaps even little choice, in redeploying the same professional élites in his own service, while denying them any real substance of power.

These developments across the Brumairean divide all reinforce one central argument here. The Revolution had indeed given France a radical tradition, which might well be called 'republican' and up to a point perhaps even 'democratic'. But equally, by the end of its course, it had also left France with a reconstituted *conservative* tradition, with some deeper roots going back to the old regime, and whose future would be enduring. In viewing Napoleon's place in that conservative tradition, we need to make more of the Revolution's earlier contribution to it than the Bicentenary celebrations ever did. By the end of the Directory, republicanism in France was still a fairly recent departure, and in many obvious ways it had been a bitterly divisive one as well. In civil terms at least, it had failed to heal the wounds of the Revolution and counter-revolution. Loyalty to it was prudent rather than committed among the great mass of the rural people, many of whom had been alienated by its political excesses and by its hostility or indifference to the old religion. Whatever one thinks of the Revolutionary generals, the politicians had signally failed to realize 'the One and Indivisible Republic'. Republican idealism, defined in the civil sense of a common and active citizenship, striving for the moral improvement of the individual and for the State to be used as a therapeutic instrument for the betterment of society as a whole, was the least part of Napoleon's inheritance. Indeed, most of such idealism had already evaporated after Thermidor Year II.

Nevertheless, the constitutional legacy of the Revolution *was* republican, in formal institutional terms at least. Granted this, one might ask how liberal and how democratic it had actually been in the political process before Brumaire. Who can say how France might have evolved if the Jacobin constitution of 24 June 1793 had been implemented? The vision which its champion, Hérault de Séchelles, presented to the National Convention on the preceding 10 June was indeed both radical and democratic; but, in the event, it was a dead letter almost from the start, and it was formally suspended 'until the peace' on the following 10 October. It had a future in the republican mythology of the French Left, without doubt, especially in and after 1848, but its bearing on the present subject is minimal.[4]

The republicanism which Napoleon inherited in November 1799 was of a rather different sort, and its forms stemmed directly from the Constitution of the Year III, finally completed in September 1795. Quite apart from the notorious decree of 22 August that year, by which the new legislative body was obliged to draw two-thirds of its members from the ranks of the retiring National Convention, the constitutional provisions were designed to perpetuate the rule of the property-owning and professional republican élites in other ways. The element of direct popular elections envisaged in 1793, whether to the central legislature or to municipal office and local magistracies, had disappeared. So had the principles of annual elections and of selective public referendums on proposed laws. The notion of the State as an instrument of social improvement had been discarded too. The principles of legal equality and the rule of law were indeed upheld, but now within existing proprietary relationships, or what the constitution itself defined as the 'Duties' of Man and of the Citizen towards 'the whole social order'. Among other things, this meant that the sales of nationalized Church property, which by the end of the Convention had practically run their course, as well as sales of the lands confiscated from the émigrés, which by then were already far advanced, would enjoy full legal sanction. In 1793, the law itself had been defined as 'the free and solemn expression of the general will; it is the same for all, whether it protects or punishes'. In 1795, it was defined as 'the general will, expressed by the majority of either the citizens or their representatives'. The concept of 'representative' had replaced that of 'deputy', and binding popular mandates were outlawed.

Under the Constitution of the Year III, the electoral will of the people was thus significantly curtailed. At the same time the political powers of the governing élites were reformulated, and great care was taken to prevent them falling into the hands of one strong man or clique. France received a bicameral legislature for the first time, and the principle of the separation of the powers was re-established. The new legislative body of 750 members was to be elected indirectly in two stages through a limited franchise based on residential and tax qualifications. 'Active citizens', those who had the vote, were defined as men born and domiciled in France, and who had reached the age of twenty-one, along with naturalized foreigners who met certain specified conditions. Their role was to meet in cantonal assemblies and there choose some 30,000 secondary electors, who themselves had to be at least twenty-five years of age and much higher taxpayers than the primary voters. These 30,000 were to meet in their departmental assemblies to elect the 250 members of the council of ancients, or elders. The latter in turn had to be at least forty years of age and either married or widowed, which would of course disqualify priests. The secondary electors were then also to choose the members of the council of five hundred, for which the minimum age was thirty years. It was the constitutional role of the five hundred to propose laws, that of the ancients to vote on them, and one-third of each body was to be renewed annually.[5]

In addition, there was to be an executive directory of five men, all of whom had to be at least forty years old, chosen by the council of ancients from a list of fifty members drawn from the legislative body as a whole and submitted by the council of five hundred. One director, chosen by lot, was to retire after each of the first five years, his successor being chosen according to similar procedures. The directors were to meet separately from the legislative body, and to preside in turn for a period of three months. Among their considerable executive functions, they had power to appoint army generals and the seven ministers, whose own duties were largely administrative. As a test of their ideological loyalty, the directors were required each year to take an oath of hatred towards royalty and anarchy.[6]

This latter provision, which may at first seem little more than a formal public token, in fact had an important political purpose. One official aim, after the suppression of the artisan riots in Paris in Germinal and Prairial Year III (1 April and 20–3

41

May 1795), was to lay the ghost of direct democracy once and for all. It was largely achieved, for those were to be the last serious disturbances among radical sans-culottes in the capital for many years. At the same time, the political authorities were determined to stem a resurgence of royalism. The uprising of 13 Vendémiaire Year IV (5 October 1795) had been crushed without difficulty only a few weeks before the inauguration of the Directory. A much more serious plot by royalists some two years later, after the Directory had summarily annulled their electoral gains, was pre-empted by the coup of 18 Fructidor Year V (4 September 1797). The full significance of those events for Napoleon's own career, and for the role of the line army as a force of intervention in Parisian politics, has already been noted in the preceding chapter.

Violent and unconstitutional precedents had thus been set for the Directory's celebrated balancing act to stave off challenges from the Right (royalists and non-juror priests) and Left (neo-Jacobins) alike. In 1798, a new spate of repressive measures against the refractory clergy also followed. But equally, when a large number of Jacobins succeeded in the elections of the Year VI, the Directory again acted above its own laws by annulling those returns and jobbing in its own preferred candidates in the coup of 22 Floréal (11 May 1798). The legislative councils gained their revenge over the executive body just over a year later in the so-called 'coup' (really a purge) of 29–30 Prairial Year VII (17–18 June 1799), when they forced the resignation of three directors hostile to them. After such a succession of constitutional irregularities, which political expediency alone could scarcely justify, Napoleon's own *coup d'état* was to seem altogether less shocking. No public outcry greeted the fall of the Directory. It had never been a popular regime in either an electoral or a sentimental sense.

All these developments *before* Brumaire should be taken into account when one assesses how far Napoleon usurped the 'liberties' of citizens purportedly established by the Revolution. As one authority has pungently remarked, 'if Bonaparte was the gravedigger of political liberty, the Directory had already presented him with the corpse.'[7] The Constitution of the Year VIII (13 December 1799) formally established the Consulate and legitimized his coup. Officially, it was drawn up by the three provisional consuls (himself, Sieyès, and Ducos) in collaboration with the legislative commissions chosen from the former councils of the Directory, but on all crucial points he made sure that it bore his own stamp, while keeping a substantial part of Sieyès' original proposals. If it reaffirmed the inviolability of private property in general terms, except in the case of émigrés still named on the proscribed list, it incorporated no declaration of rights and no clear provisions for its own amendment. These, perhaps, were its two most conspicuous omissions when compared with the earlier Revolutionary constitutions.

The new constitution was nevertheless in line with Revolutionary precedent in restricting the effective 'legal nation' from the start. Universal manhood suffrage was indeed conceded, nominally at least, but only at the lowest rung of the indirect electoral process. As one commentator has cogently observed, the requirement of successive rounds of selection by tenths had the effect of reducing an eligible primary electorate of some 6 million to 600,000 at communal level, then to 60,000 at departmental level, and finally to the 6,000 who formed the national list from which members of the central legislature were to be chosen.[8] This filtering-up process was to be reinforced by the electoral provisions of the Constitution of the Year X (4 August 1802), which introduced an explicitly plutocratic principle. Cantonal assemblies were to choose the arrondissement and departmental electoral colleges which were now to be set up, but henceforth the 200 to 300 members of each departmental electoral college *had* to be drawn from its 600 highest taxpayers (*plus imposés*) and were to serve for life. The first consul could reward distinguished public service by nominating up to 10 members of each arrondissement and departmental college himself, and he also had the right to add 10 members to each departmental college chosen from among the 30 highest taxpayers in the department.[9]

Now, it is true that Napoleon made a more direct appeal to 'the people' through his successive plebiscites on the Constitution of the Year VIII, on the life consulate of August 1802, and on the hereditary Empire of May 1804. The for votes far outnumbered those against by 3,011,007 to 1,562, by 3,568,000 to 8,374, and by 3,572,000 to 2,569, respectively. However, it is now widely accepted that such massive majorities were produced by a good deal of official manipulation in the face of what were already *faits accomplis*, more especially in the first exercise of 1800. It seems, too, that well over two million eligible electors may have abstained on all those occasions. In any case, the plebiscitary device was not used again until the hurried referendum on the 'Additional Act to the Constitutions of the Empire' during the Hundred Days, *in extremis*, when abstentions were again rather high.[10]

If we turn next to the central political structures, there seems no good reason to doubt the republican credentials of those who fashioned the Constitution of the Year VIII. And yet the elaboration of the legislative organs and executive offices of the Consulate soon produced a fundamental imbalance which was increasingly at variance with earlier republican principles. The exercise of hierarchical power, and of executive power in particular, was much more pronounced. Indeed, it was able to shape and then manipulate the legislature from the start.

The 'Conservative Senate', as it was defined in the constitution, was not at first intended to be a law-making body, although it was of course to have a major role in electing the members of the central legislature, and in due course it was actually given quasi-legislative functions of its own. Its first two members were to be the retiring provisional consuls, Sieyès (who became its first president) and Ducos. They were to consult with the new second and third consuls named in the constitution, Cambacérès (a former minister of justice) and Lebrun (a former member of the council of ancients), in choosing 29 colleagues to join them. These 31 were to select another 29, making an initial total of 60, who would then collectively co-opt two more annually for ten years from three candidates nominated by the legislative body, the tribunate, and the first consul respectively, so as eventually to constitute a body of 80 members. Senators had to be at least forty years of age, were appointed for life and declared inviolable, and were to be ineligible for any other public office. Among their constitutional functions, they were to elect the consuls (a theoretical nicety), tribunes, legislators, judges of appeal courts, and commissioners of accounts. They were also given powers to preserve the constitution, and, in order to ensure the high public prestige Napoleon always intended for them, were to receive an annual salary of 25,000 francs each.

The central legislature of the Consulate, strictly defined, was bicameral. The tribunate consisted of 100 members, aged at least twenty-five years, chosen by the senate from national lists of candidates emanating from each department. One-fifth of their number was to be replaced annually as from the Year X, although immediate re-eligibility was conditionally allowed. The tribunes were each to receive an annual salary of 15,000 francs and had the right to debate proposed laws, to recommend their immediate passage, or refer them back to the government for alteration, but could not themselves formally initiate, amend, or enact such bills. The official role of voting for or against proposed laws fell to the legislative body, by secret ballot, but without any right of debate. A bill thus receiving a majority vote was to be promulgated as law by the first consul ten days later, provided the senate had not declared it unconstitutional in the meantime. The 300 members of the legislative body, also chosen by the senate from national lists, had to be at least thirty years of age, and were to receive an annual salary of 10,000 francs each. One-fifth of their number was again renewable annually as from the Year X, and there was always to be at least one legislator for each department. Retiring legislators could be re-elected only after a year's interval, but might immediately assume other public office if so eligible. When it came to the initial elections to both of the above bodies, prior experience counted for much, and the continuity of personnel is at once conspicuous. Of the first 100 tribunes, 69 had served in the councils of the Directory, 5 others in earlier Revolutionary assemblies, and only 26 lacked such previous experience. Similarly, of the first 300 legislators, only 21 had never been members of a Revolutionary assembly, while no less than 240 were recruited directly from the defunct Directorial councils.[11]

The real break with the Revolutionary past came with the constitutional provisions for the central executive offices of state, or perhaps rather with the manner in which Napoleon implemented and then extended those provisions. He had already contemptuously rejected Sieyès' original idea of a grand elector, chosen by the senate and with power to nominate two consuls, conjuring up the image of a 'fatted pig' residing in pompous splendour in the palace of Versailles. Instead, Title IV of the Constitution of the Year VIII vested government in three named consuls, the first two for ten years and the third (in Lebrun's particular case) for five. Yet any suggestion of a balanced triumvirate was belied by the defining clauses, which were in fact widely permissive.

Article 40, on the one hand, seemed to denote restraint: 'the First Consul has specific functions and powers, in which he may briefly be replaced, when there is cause, by one of his colleagues'. Article 41, on the other, then specified his very considerable powers: to promulgate laws; to name and dismiss at his pleasure members of the council of state, ministers, ambassadors and other high diplomatic agents, officers of the land army and navy, the members of local government as well as government commissioners attached to the courts; and to appoint all civil and criminal judges other than justices of the peace and judges of the sovereign court of appeal, but without the power to dismiss them. The celebrated article 42 furthermore laid down that 'in other acts of government, the Second and Third Consuls have a consultative voice; they sign the register of acts to establish their presence and, if they wish, they may register their opinions, after which the decision of the First Consul suffices'.[12] In general terms, the government was given powers to propose laws and ensure their execution, to control all parts of the public finances, to safeguard the internal security and external defence of the Republic, to exercise the prerogative of war and peace, and to enter into treaties of all kinds with foreign states. As if to drive home the unequal demarcation of authority, the salary of the first consul was fixed at an initial 500,000 francs a year, while the others were each to receive three-tenths of that sum.

Granted such constitutional licence, Napoleon was able to concentrate more and more power in his own hands. One expression of his personal will took the form of the Consular *arrêté*, later the Imperial decree, and it was reinforced by strict State censorship from the start. What is more, he broke with the inherited republican principle of the separation of the powers in at least two other ways, both much more blatant than any such aberrations under the Directory. First, he intervened repeatedly in the affairs of the legislature. He carefully vetted elections to the pliant senate, to which he later added his own nominees by constitutional right. So, in effect, he could also influence the composition of the legislative body and the tribunate, whose limited annual sessions were in any case carefully controlled by the government. Moreover, by a procedure known as *senatus-consultum*, first adopted on 5 January 1801, and originally intended for only major constitutional changes on the proposal of the three consuls, he was increasingly able to bypass and override the wishes of the legislative chambers. In the early months of 1802, for instance, the constitutional provisions which required one-fifth of their members to be replaced gave him an early chance to get rid of his most troublesome critics there, with the senate's formal approval. One of those then 'purged' from the tribunate was P.-C. Daunou, a committed republican who among other things had been a member of the council of five hundred and the principal architect of the Constitution of the Year III.

Secondly, Napoleon altogether reorganized the relationship between the civil state and the army. The Directory, as we have seen, had tried to keep high military appointments in civilian hands. Under the Constitution of the Year III, there had been no one head of state, and no one commander-in-chief of the army. During the Consulate Napoleon preserved the fiction of such republican forms, but even this ceased with the proclamation of the Empire. Thereafter, he combined the supreme civil and military functions of state in his own person, and in an only too active sense. This was to be of enormous importance when it came to mobilizing resources for war, in which respect at least he had a distinct advantage over nearly all his foreign enemies.

The Constitution of the Year VIII allowed Napoleon a free hand to choose his own advisory councillors of state, through whom proposed laws were usually presented to the legislative chambers, as well as his ministers. In doing so, and as if to demonstrate his ability to command their common loyalty and obedience, he preferred men of often widely differing political backgrounds, including former regicides, royalist sympathizers, and republican trimmers. Many of them were competent professionals, who in the exercise of their functions more closely resembled dutiful technocrats than men of independent initiative. Each minister was served by an advisory administrative council, while the business of the dozen or so ministries established by Napoleon was orchestrated by a state secretariat. Its major co-ordinating role was duly recognized at the proclamation of the Empire, when it was given full ministerial status, under the faithful and long-serving Maret.

And yet, of all the ministries, two in particular had a still more pervasive influence on the nature of Napoleon's civil state. One was the ministry of the interior, whose burgeoning *Directions générales* and bureaux steadily acquired a wide-ranging jurisdiction. Apart from central, departmental, and local administration, their functions extended to certain branches of the public finances (especially at local level), to education, censorship, public works and welfare, prisons, food supplies, the arts and sciences, and the collection of official statistics. Until the creation of the new ministry of trade and industry in January 1812, the ministry of the interior also had a crucial role in the regulation of commerce, manufactures, and not least agriculture. It was, in all these respects, the central cog of Napoleon's executive machine. Not surprisingly, it underwent major internal reorganization over the years of the Consulate and Empire, and in the process its staff increased from the lowest level of 85 during Chaptal's tenure of the office (1800–4) to more than 220 at one point under Montalivet's (1809–14).[13]

The other body which stamped its mark on Napoleon's civil government, not least through its covert operations, was the ministry of general police. Although it usually employed a staff of around 120, its history was rather more chequered than that of most others. Its origins as an independent ministry in fact went back to the Directory's law of 2 January 1796, which had specifically separated its functions from the ministry of the interior. Its initial impact had been slight, however, and its role as an effective instrument of internal security and surveillance really dated from June 1799, when Joseph Fouché was appointed as minister, in which office he was confirmed after Napoleon's *coup d'état* a few months later. And indeed, it is with Fouché, a former terrorist and regicide, that the work of this ministry under Napoleon is associated above all. He served until September 1802, when the General Police was abolished and its functions temporarily transferred to the ministry of justice, and then again after its reconstitution from July 1804 to June 1810, when he was dismissed and replaced by Savary.[14]

Although Fouché's loyalty was often suspect and his opportunism notorious, he had an efficient system of informants, with well-established connections in the criminal underworld, and some of his techniques at least had a ruthless pedigree going back to the old regime. Assisted in his reconstituted ministry by four councillors of state, each presiding over a large police district which incorporated many Imperial departments, he passed on valuable information to Napoleon, not always heeded, and was adept at uncovering political plots against him. Subject himself to secret police surveillance, most notably by L.-N. Dubois, technically one of his inferiors in charge of the third district (prefecture of police for Paris), Fouché's public image seemed to many to symbolize the seamy side of the Napoleonic regime itself.[15]

The extension of Napoleon's authoritarian system of government to all the regions of the Consular Republic might be described as a tentacular process, one which also started early. While his own control of it was never as omniscient as has so often been claimed, it was nevertheless a much more thorough and uniform process than any which had gone before. If anything, his reform of provincial and local government was to prove more enduring than his reorganization of central government itself, and his major achievements here can be fully appreciated only by comparison with his faltering inheritance from the Revolution. During the Terror, the district had been the essential basis of Jacobin local government. The Directory, for its part, fearful of lingering Jacobin support in many of the major towns, had reacted by enhancing the status of the department as an administrative unit, though not to the level of 1790–92 under the constitutional monarchy. Between 1795 and 1799, the departmental administrations of five members each, elected by assemblies of 200 to 300 rich citizens, and renewable by one-fifth annually, had thus been given authority over the municipalities. But at the same time they had been subordinated to the ministries in Paris through resident central commissioners appointed by the Directory. The system had not worked well, least of all in its management of local finances, and in this respect its legacy was something of a mess. Political disputes had also undermined its stability, and in some areas order had been restored only by the intervention of the line army.[16]

The remedy, it seemed to Napoleon, again lay in more rigorous centralization. The organic law of 17 February 1800 created the new prefectures in the ninety-eight departments of the extended French Republic, along with their intermediate and local sub-divisions, and abandoned the elective principle altogether. The prefect, the general secretary (who also deputized in his absence), and the members of their advisory bodies, that is the prefectoral and general councils of each department, were now all appointed by the first consul himself. Although the prefect's own administrative role was wholly dependent on orders from the central government, he was nevertheless the crucial agent of its will throughout the provinces of France.

Jacques Godechot has likened him to 'a miniature emperor' in his department.[17] Each department in turn was sub-divided into arrondissements, newly formed units which resembled the original districts of 1790 in enlarged form. Except in the departmental capital itself, each arrondissement was administered by a sub-prefect. The latter, who was also appointed by the first consul, had an advisory arrondissement council to assist him, and his wholly subordinate role was clearly defined. At local level, finally, the municipalities regained their former administrative functions, under mayors assisted by advisory municipal councils, but were reduced in number. And, here again, the mayors and their deputies, as well as the local police commissioners who worked alongside them in the larger communes, were appointed by the first consul. The cantons, by contrast, were reduced in number and status to purely electoral and judicial units.

In his choice of the departmental officials and their more numerous subordinates, Napoleon again preferred men with some administrative experience. Of his first 98 prefects, for instance, 76 had served in the various Revolutionary assemblies, including several former ministers or other high executive officers. Many more had been employed in departmental administration or served as mayors of large towns before the establishment of the Consulate.[18] As a group, they were also significant property-owners. On the whole, the arrondissement and municipal officials also met this last criterion, though on a scale appropriate to their lesser status. In selecting the sub-prefects, Napoleon as a general rule favoured those who were known for their moderate political views. If the prefects were not usually appointed to their native departments, the mayors not surprisingly were very nearly always local men. As for the advisory councillors, the vast majority were drawn from the lists of 'notabilities', or *notables* as they were officially called as from 1802, who almost by definition had some landed wealth, especially at departmental level.

How far, then, does Napoleon's system of government justify the term 'meritocracy' which is sometimes attributed to it? If one looks beyond the specious claims of phrases like 'careers open to talents' so familiar in textbook coinage, one finds that certain talents actually mattered rather more than others. Napoleon laid down clear rules for the training of his public officials, especially by the law of 9 April 1803. Professional experience was the basis of his administrative recruitment, and seniority of service was also the criterion which most commonly applied in the promotion of officials, whose salaries and pensions were fixed on carefully graded scales. Even new professional groups, of which the *Auditeurs* attached to the council of state as from 1803 were the most important, providing roughly a fifth of the 300 or so prefects who served under Napoleon at one time or another, were strictly integrated into his administrative system. In his civil state at least, sudden leap-frogging into high office through precocious talent alone was certainly not normal, and there were many cases of official patronage and favouritism beyond the members of the Bonaparte family themselves. The possession of landed wealth also counted for much; indeed, from the inception of the life consulate it underpinned Napoleon's whole concept of 'notability'. The same plutocratic ethic later infused his elaborate system of social honours, as we shall see. In all these respects, his system of government was less 'open' to aspiring careerists of humble background than has often been supposed.

Stuart Woolf, in a substantial work, makes a strong case for viewing Napoleon's civil state as in some sense an administrative 'model' of forward-looking centralism and uniformity which could then be exported to all the lands brought under his rule. He repeats the idea in such terms as 'a French model of modernity', 'the French archetype', 'this massive experiment in modernisation', 'the suffocating administrative imposition of French uniformity', 'authoritarian centralism', and the like.[19] The optimistic notion that 'social utility' might be achieved through a perfectible 'science of administration' spawned a whole genre of statistical inquiries, which Woolf sees as 'a direct offshoot of the *Kameralwissenschaft*', that is of enlightened ideas of statecraft current in Germany during the eighteenth century.[20] We should, however, be wary of easy inferences here. In practice, the 'model' was much more successfully exported to some conquered territories than to others, as Woolf indeed allows. In 'old France', it may have been a relatively efficient 'model', but it was certainly never an egalitarian one. It was aimed almost entirely at the propertied and professional élites, including the old nobility to an increasing extent, with some significant success in the later years of the Empire. Taking a more global view of the underlying structures of the Napoleonic state, Louis Bergeron has concluded that 'France changed very little from 1800 to 1815. Paradoxically, Napoleon was both behind and ahead of his time, the last of the enlightened despots, and a prophet of the modern State.'[21]

We are now in a position to summarize the main features of Napoleon's civil government, taken as a whole, and to reach a conclusion on what it owed to and how far it departed from his Revolutionary inheritance. It should be clear that the Revolutionary reforms had done much to rationalize the civil functions of the French state, and in the process had produced an administrative élite on whose diverse professional skills Napoleon in his turn drew heavily. And yet, if the period of the Terror is excluded, attempts had also been made by the various Revolutionary regimes to preserve something – however imperfect – of the elective principle in appointments to executive office, especially at local level, which had first appeared late in 1789. By comparison, Napoleon's civil state came increasingly to be ruled according to precepts which, even before the Empire, had really ceased to be republican. The elective principle in appointments to central, departmental, and local office disappeared from an early stage. The principle of the separation of the powers, and in that sense of a balanced constitution, was in practice also discarded.

Notwithstanding its formal provisions for an elective legislature, as well as its pretensions to a 'popular' mandate, Napoleonic government was characterized by an assertive authoritarian principle. Power and responsibility devolved from the centre and from the top, intruding to a greater or lesser extent into all the public institutions and regions of the French State. They were concentrated in an executive which found ways of manipulating and muzzling the legislative chambers soon enough, and which in due course was also able to govern by decree. Official status, functions, salaries, promotions, and later even social honours were determined by more uniform and hierarchical rules than the revolutionaries had ever been willing to tolerate. The leading beneficiary of the Revolutionary Republic, Napoleon had in a sense contrived to undermine it from within, by first accepting and then abandoning its public forms.

This process was gradual rather than convulsive, pragmatic rather than based on any clear preconceived plan. More than two and a half years passed between the Constitution of the Year VIII and the life consulate of 4 August 1802, conferred by a *senatus-consultum* during the only brief interlude of general peace France ever knew under Napoleonic rule. The Constitution of the Year XII, which inaugurated the hereditary Empire, was proclaimed by a similar procedure on 18 May 1804, some twenty-one months later. It followed an even more convincing display of support from the senate, the legislative body, and the now more pliant tribunate alike. Formal use of the Republican calendar continued for more than a year and a half, but as from 1 January 1806 the French Empire was officially administered according to the Gregorian calendar. This transition had a mainly symbolical importance. Well before then, Napoleon had overturned perhaps the most fundamental republican principle of all: that power and authority, whether in the civil state or in the army, must not be concentrated in one man. The Napoleonic Empire was more like absolute monarchy under another name. Sovereignty, after its selective association with 'the nation' or 'the people' at different times during the Revolution, had once again become identified in a *person*.

. . . .

THE TREATMENT OF THE OPPOSITION

Napoleonic propaganda immediately presented the *coup d'état* of Brumaire as a return to strong, orderly government, and so also as providing the promise of political reconciliation in France, after the Revolutionary upheavals. This obviously had an important bearing on how the new first consul would react to groups whose political views and activities could still be construed as possible threats to his rule. During the course of the Revolution, the old Bourbon concept of '*lèse-majesté*', that is subversion of the kind amounting to or bordering on treason, and incurring the highest penalties, had been replaced by the new notion of '*lèse-nation*'. The latter, however, had in practice been much more freely extended to cover less extreme forms of resistance to a given political regime, most notably during the Jacobin Terror and the Thermidorian reaction which followed it. By the time of Brumaire, the revolutionaries had never naturalized any concept of an 'official opposition', in other words of *bona fide* and lawful opposition to one particular governing group by another which might take its place by peaceful means. On the contrary, successive Revolutionary regimes had been more inclined to view organized opposition *of any kind* as subversive in itself, and had sought to eliminate it, claiming that they represented the true wishes and interests of 'the nation'. In dealing with the real or imagined 'plots' which proliferated during the 1790s, they had often resorted to punishments of varying severity: execution by extraordinary judicial processes, military reprisals (which often had the same lethal effect), punitive exile, or merely imprisonment.

Napoleon therefore inherited a state in which political scores had often been settled by violent or at least irregular means, and on occasion indeed he had himself participated in them. After his coup, however, he gave an early indication of his wish for a new kind of reconciliation, by removing power from those who had been unable to bury their old enmities, and by projecting himself as the great pacifier of all his subjects. Napoleon hoped that if all groups rallied to his regime, the destructive political factionalism of the Revolutionary years would naturally give way to a loyal and orderly consensus, an aim which has sometimes been called his 'politics of amalgamation'. Before we examine the practical details of this policy, it may be helpful to consider the nature of his *potential* opposition in the immediate aftermath of Brumaire, given that relatively few subjects had actually taken an active part in his coup.

The threat of mutiny within Napoleon's army may be discounted at once. He clearly commanded its loyalty even before the victorious Marengo campaign of June 1800, while General Hoche, once seen as his main military rival, had died in 1797. Still, apart from the Allied armies themselves, he faced at least three other sources of possible opposition. First, resistance might have been expected from royalists and refractory priests, whether resident in France or in exile, on the assumption that they favoured the restoration of the legitimate monarch, who had already proclaimed himself Louis XVIII, initially with papal approval. Sporadic insurgency among the Chouans in the west country of France, scene of the wider Vendean civil war of 1793, had never been wholly eradicated by the National Convention or the Directory. Late in 1799, this area provided a possible regional base and its political malcontents the main ideological cause for armed resistance to the Consulate. Secondly, opposition might also have been anticipated from Jacobin diehards, on the grounds that their annulled electoral gains of 1798 had demonstrated the unpopularity of the Directory as well as wider support for a more radical republicanism, which the Constitution of the Year VIII plainly did not offer them.

On the other hand, these were both marginal and rather poorly co-ordinated groups, whose real threat to Napoleon is easily exaggerated. More effective opposition might therefore have been expected from a third source: the political élite itself. It included several of the men who at first served in Napoleon's central institutions, the tribunate most notably, and who could thus claim at least some constitutional right to challenge his policies. They found common cause with others among the liberal intelligentsia who themselves had no direct part in official politics.

In the event, Napoleon's initial reaction to all those groups clearly showed that he took their real or potential opposition seriously enough. His early gestures of conciliation were aimed at French dissidents beyond as well as within the home frontiers. He was thus willing to allow former exiles, both noble émigrés and the Jacobins who had been deported in the Year III, the chance to return to France, on condition of their political obedience and good behaviour. Having repealed the law of hostages against the families of royalist émigrés on 13 November 1799, he granted amnesties to many émigrés themselves on 2 March and 20 October 1800, and later to others on 26 April 1802. Under such measures, the vast majority of those counter-revolutionary exiles were repatriated. At the same time, Napoleon was quick to deal with the lingering sore of *Chouannerie* in the western provinces, chiefly north of the Loire. He saw the mere existence of the guerrillas there as a challenge to his authority, or to what his propaganda was already presenting as a sort of '*Pax Napoleonica*' across the whole of France. Their traditional resistance to military conscription, as well as their endemic banditry and traffic in contraband goods, seemed wholly incompatible with his own vision of law and order.

Political insurgency among the Chouans had a history of sporadic outbursts interspersed with periods of inactivity. It had, however, revived significantly during the course of 1799, aided by Britain and the exiled Bourbons, as the Second Coalition sought to mobilize all possible resources against the French Republic. As things turned out, Napoleon used more than conciliatory words and promises to persuade the Chouan leaders to negotiate with him; in some cases brutal force was his preferred method. One of those leaders, the vicomte Louis de Frotté, who believed he had surrendered on terms, was promptly murdered on 18 February 1800, although there is no evidence that Napoleon had given the direct orders for this atrocity. It served nevertheless as an exemplary deterrent, and in the course of that year, by a series of amnesties or field 'treaties', most of the Chouan commanders ceased their hostilities. This enabled Napoleon to claim that he alone, after so many failures before Brumaire, had been able to 'pacify the Vendée'. He followed up his initiative by what at first seemed a much more important reconciliation with the Catholic Church, the Concordat of 1801, which probably did more than anything else to pacify the western provinces in the early years of the Consulate. Its details form the next sub-section of this chapter.

The amnesties to the Chouans and noble émigrés did not of course eliminate the threat of hostile royalists altogether. On Christmas Eve 1800, while Napoleon was on his way to the Opéra, a bomb (the legendary *machine infernale*) exploded in the Rue Saint-Nicaise, narrowly missing him. Fouché's best police intelligence plainly indicated that the principal culprits were Pierre de Saint-Réjeant and François Carbon, agents of Georges Cadoudal, an implacable royalist and former Chouan leader, who after spurning all offers of peace had taken refuge in England under the protection of the comte d'Artois earlier that year. Napoleon, perhaps too secure in the belief that he *had* finally neutralized the royalists, insisted that the attempted assassination was the work of Jacobins. His somewhat indiscriminate and irrational reaction was to deport 130 innocent men allegedly implicated in the affair on 5 January 1801.

And so, Cadoudal could live to fight another day. His more complicated conspiracy of 1803–4 to kidnap and kill Napoleon, then to invade France with royalist allies and effect the restoration of Louis XVIII, certainly implicated Pichegru, and allegedly other military commanders as well. But on this occasion Fouché's police had uncovered the plot in time. After the arrest of the ringleaders, Pichegru was found on 5 April 1804 strangled in his cell in suspicious circumstances, Cadoudal was executed in June, and General Moreau (although probably innocent) was exiled from France. Earlier still, on 20 March 1804, Napoleon had ordered the execution of the duc d'Enghien after a summary court-martial at Vincennes. The victim, a grandson of the prince de Condé and indeed the last of his famous Bourbon line, had been captured beyond French frontiers in Baden. A former commander in the émigré armies, he now stood accused of fostering royalist plots in Germany, but was given no chance to defend himself. This notorious affair, which shocked foreign courts and had an adverse reaction in France as well, has sometimes been regarded as Napoleon's most gratuitous atrocity, in spite of his claim that it was a necessary act of state to deter his enemies. It did not delay the proclamation of the Empire two months later, but it hardly enhanced his dynastic pretensions. It was later to cause him considerable embarrassment, although not it seems much bad conscience.

Clearly, Napoleon could not use such brutally crude methods in dealing with opposition among the political élite in France itself. One classic way of silencing his critics was of course through censorship of the press. This started early with his highly restrictive executive order of 17 January 1800, the first of several increasingly draconian measures. These latter, along with his harsh treatment of prominent writers like Madame de Staël and of the 'Ideologues' at the Institute, are more fully discussed in chapter 6 of the present volume. Now, censorship might be seen as the knuckle-end of a blanket policy, as an attempt to stifle the expression of any adverse public opinion, from whichever source it might come. On the other hand, Napoleon could react to public opposition in a much more particular way, directing his personal wrath at certain figures active in politics who were themselves only too clearly identifiable. As Martyn Lyons has shrewdly observed, 'it may be true that while counter-revolutionary royalism tended to be an army without a leader, the liberals were all generals with no army'.[22]

Nowhere is this better illustrated than in Napoleon's dealings with the tribunate, the official forum in which most of his early liberal critics were concentrated. Under the constitution, the tribunes were supposed to remain in permanent session, a provision quickly and drastically curtailed in practice, and to conduct their debates in public. All had accepted the coup of Brumaire, officially at least, but the bolder spirits among them soon took issue with several of Napoleon's policies during the early Consulate. These ranged from purely internal matters, such as their own nominations for the senate and the procedures for enacting or rejecting bills, to much wider issues like the independence of the judiciary, the introduction of special courts to deal with brigandage, attempts to revise the Revolutionary land laws abolishing 'feudal' dues or establishing property division more equally among male heirs, the Concordat itself, and even early draft bills of the Civil Code.

There had then been a steady accumulation of anger and distrust on Napoleon's part when, as he put it, he sought to root out the 'Medusa's head' by his 'purge' of the legislative chambers early in 1802. The sixty replacements in the legislative body raised comparatively little fuss, but the twenty carried out in the tribunate removed some of his most distinguished and persistent public critics there: Daunou (for whom he had a particular dislike), Constant, Ginguené, Thiessé, Chazal, Ganilh, Marie-Joseph Chénier, Garat-Mailla, and Bara. These men, along with some others axed at the same time or during the years which immediately followed, have sometimes been referred to as 'the committee of the Enlightenment in the tribunate'. In spite of his contemptuous dismissal of them as troublesome 'metaphysicians', Napoleon was anxious to avoid giving the impression of sheer vindictiveness in this first replacement exercise. At least half of the outgoing tribunes and a third (probably more) of the legislators received other official posts, mostly in politically innocuous services such as customs and excise.[23]

The same *senatus-consultum* of 4 August 1802 which proclaimed the life consulate also stipulated that the membership of the tribunate would be reduced to fifty by the Year XIII. Moreover, its deliberations were henceforth to be conducted in three separate sections (interior, legislation, and finance), into which it had already been divided, each placed under the supervision of a corresponding section of the council of state. The writing was on the wall. On 19 August 1807 the tribunate was abolished altogether, characteristically again by the procedure of *senatus-consultum*, and its muted rump transferred to the legislative body. The latter, incidentally, continued periodically until its last gathering in 1813, but throughout it remained an undistinguished assembly, manned for the most part by docile provincials who came to Paris for its short-lived sessions each year.

Finally, for reasons which had much to do with tenable food prices during most of his rule, Napoleon did not have to face major artisan or peasant unrest until quite late in the Empire, when emergency relief measures were enough to quell popular disturbances in several regions. Only the harvests of 1801–3 (which partly coincided with a time of peace) and that of 1811 were widely deficient, while the four-year cycle of 1806–9 was especially plentiful. In this respect, not least, Napoleon was a good deal more fortunate than Louis XVI and some of the Revolutionary governments had been. It is true that he took additional steps to keep the artisans and industrial workers in their place, just as he was determined to deal (though by no means always successfully) with the chronic problem of resistance to military conscription among the peasantry. The Revolutionary laws against workers' coalitions or strikes were reaffirmed in April 1803, and then toughened by the Penal Code of 1810. A law of December 1803 furthermore required each industrial worker to possess a work record-book (*livret*), and he also needed a police pass before being allowed to change employers. Such measures may have played their part in damping down unrest among the popular classes, so far even as to allow Napoleon to claim their acquiescence in his regime. And yet, if he was right in this assumption, then he probably owed more to the 'luck factor' of harvest sufficiency during most of the Empire than to anything else.

. . . .

THE CONCORDAT

Napoleon's Concordat with the pope in 1801 has often been seen as one of his more conciliatory and popular acts during the early Consulate. Just how popular that agreement was can be gauged only in relation to the deep crisis which had engulfed the French Church since the conflict over the Civil Constitution of the Clergy (July 1790). That reform, with its new provisions for higher and more regular salaries for parish priests, would perhaps have been welcome to most of them, *de facto*. But the requirement of an oath to the Civil Constitution (November 1790) had soon confronted them with a major crisis of conscience, especially once Pius VI had outlawed the measure and instructed the French clergy to refuse the oath in March and April 1791. All but seven bishops had obeyed the pope, while the lesser clergy as a whole had divided roughly evenly on the issue, although the incidence of non-jurorship was very high in several departments. Many of the refractory clergy had thereafter joined forces with royalists in the counter-revolutionary movement, again chiefly in the western provinces.

One of the Revolution's legacies to Napoleon was thus a schismatic Church and total alienation from Rome, and the problem had been exacerbated by successive regimes in various ways.[24]

Appalled by the excesses of the 'dechristianization' campaign launched by Jacobin militants in 1793–94, the Montagnard government had turned against and eventually eliminated its main perpetrators, but without placating the millions of Catholic faithful. The Thermidorian regime, for its part, had in effect admitted its inability to establish the constitutional church when, on 21 February 1795, it proclaimed 'the liberty of cults' and at the same time refused State subsidies to any of them. While maintaining the same official neutrality, the Directory had nevertheless asserted its secular republican principles in a new wave of repressive measures against non-jurors in 1798.

In spite of this confused and uneasy backdrop, it now seems that the refractory church had come through the years of the Directory spiritually and in some ways materially stronger than the rump of the constitutional church. Although estimates vary, it is likely that a few thousand of its clergy had perished at the hands of revolutionaries and many more had been driven into exile, while its buildings had frequently been ransacked for precious metals and other useful materials. Yet a large number of non-juror priests had somehow managed to survive those troubles without physical mishap or prolonged exile, finding food and shelter in clandestine retreats, usually among rural communities, which they continued to serve through the old Catholic rites. Thus encouraged, the response of the Catholic laity had also become stronger and more open. Olwen Hufton, in a fascinating study of the question during the years 1796–1801, its time of greatest obscurity in texts published hitherto, shows that there was then not only a religious but indeed a clerical revival in many regions where Catholicism had deep roots. It was (so to speak) 'unofficial', it was also more pronounced among French women than their menfolk, and it worked in favour of the refractory clergy almost entirely. All this, Hufton argues, 'is the story of religious survival and of how a church was re-established from below long before the Concordat, which merely restored and placed a hierarchy on a legal footing, made peace with Rome and allowed the people to commit their spiritual well-being into professional hands'.[25]

Now, while it may be going rather too far to say that the Concordat merely recognized a *fait accompli*, as Hufton claims in the same place, there is no doubt that Napoleon had an acute sense of this growing religious mood among Catholic communities. Pius VI had died in French hands at Valence in

August 1799, and the election in March 1800 of a new pope, Cardinal Chiaramonti, a Benedictine monk and archbishop of Imola, who assumed the name Pius VII, offered the first consul a favourable opportunity for reconciliation with Rome. It is well known that his motives were not spiritual but pragmatic. 'In religion,' as he once famously remarked, 'I see not the mystery of the Incarnation, but the mystery of the social order.' He was also keen to secure papal recognition of his coup, which he reckoned would help him to pacify the Vendée, detach the émigrés from the cause of the exiled Bourbons, and facilitate the assimilation of annexed or occupied areas like Belgium, the Rhenish left bank and Piedmont, all strongly Catholic.

As soon as he was free from the military commitments of the victorious Marengo campaign of 1800, Napoleon made his first overtures to Rome. Pius VII could see obvious advantages for the Church in an agreement, but his initial reaction was nevertheless both suspicious and cautious. It was his fear of a French occupation of the Papal States which chiefly persuaded him in September that year to send Spina and Caselli as special plenipotentiaries to Paris. Napoleon was represented at first by the abbé Bernier, who as a former Chouan seemed a shrewd choice, and at the same time d'Hauterive, one of Talleyrand's collaborators, was instructed to draw up the project of a Concordat. This, however, was only the start of what proved to be a difficult, laborious, and prolonged process of secret negotiation. As his impatience grew, Napoleon decided to take advantage of his peace with Austria at Lunéville (9 February 1801), which strengthened his position in Italy and obliged the pope to be more pliant, by adopting rougher tactics. He sent Cacault, a diplomatic agent, to put direct pressure on Pius in Rome, and in May 1801 delivered a virtual ultimatum to him. But still there was no real progress, and when Cacault was recalled, the pope thought it best to send his secretary of state, Cardinal Consalvi, to Paris in an attempt to avoid a total rupture. Even then, in spite of Napoleon's repeated insistence on a prompt agreement, none was forthcoming until Bernier, Joseph Bonaparte, and Crétet (for the French Republic) and Consalvi and Spina (for the papacy) finally signed the Concordat at 2 a.m. on 16 July 1801. It was ratified in Rome on 15 August and in Paris on 10 September that year.

In view of its long and troubled gestation, the Concordat was a surprisingly brief document. Its terms, as originally agreed, and in spite of some deliberate vagueness, gave the first impression of a reasonable enough compromise on both sides. Napoleon did not want an official religion of state nor an established Church with exclusive constitutional privileges. Instead, he recognized that Roman Catholicism was 'the religion of the vast majority of French citizens'. As such, it was to be freely and openly practised in France, in conformity with police regulations considered necessary for public tranquillity. Pius VII, for his part, formally recognized the legitimacy of the Consular Republic. The French dioceses were to be reorganized with the agreement of both contracting parties, and incumbent bishops would if necessary be required to resign, pending their renomination or the appointment of new ones. The first consul was to make all nominations to archbishoprics and bishoprics, while the pope's right of canonical investiture was recognized in return. A new oath of loyalty to the Consular government would be required of all bishops and lower clergy. The bishops were to make a new delimitation of the parishes of their dioceses, but it could not take effect without the government's consent. The appointment of the parish clergy, now also entrusted to the bishops, similarly had to meet with the government's approval. Bishops might establish a cathedral chapter and a seminary in their dioceses, but with no guarantee of State subsidies. 'A suitable salary' for bishops and parish priests would, however, be guaranteed by the government.

The Concordat also included important statements on the Revolutionary land settlement, and these need particular attention, since they affected a large number of French citizens. The rather vague terms of article 12, which put at the bishops' disposal all metropolitan churches, cathedrals, parish and other churches not yet alienated and which were 'necessary for worship', almost invited disputes over their proper definition. By the far more crucial article 13, and in terms which left no such doubt, the pope gave a solemn undertaking that neither he nor his successors would disturb in any way those who had acquired alienated Church lands and now enjoyed the revenues attached to them, and that the proprietary rights of their heirs would be similarly respected.

We can only surmise how the Concordat might have worked if its original terms had been duly honoured in its implementation. It was not in fact formally published in Paris until Easter

Sunday (8 April) 1802, seven months after its ratification. In the meantime Napoleon had established a general directory of cults within the ministry of the interior on 7 October 1801 and appointed Portalis, a councillor of state, as its head. Much more provocatively, he had also had a whole series of so-called 'Organic Articles' drawn up, and these were simply added to the Concordat unilaterally and published at the same time. So far from giving his prior approval to them, Pius VII had not even been consulted on their details, and he was understandably offended by them. Not least, they complicated the position of his special legate to Paris, Cardinal Caprara, from the start.

The Organic Articles, a detailed code of seventy-seven articles in fact, greatly restrained the rights and powers the pope believed he had been given in the preceding July, and at the same time subjected the whole ecclesiastical establishment to much stricter control by the government. They amounted, in effect, to a comprehensive reformulation of caesaro-papist principles. By such measures, Napoleon clearly reaffirmed and extended the old 'Gallican Liberties' of the French Church, now under the auspices of the secular state, and signalled his determination to hold all forms of ultramontanism in check. On this basis, then, the Concordat was implemented in France. The ecclesiastical hierarchy of archbishops, bishops, parish priests (*curés*), vicars, and subordinates (*desservants*) was indeed reconstituted, but it was now grafted into the administrative structures of the civil state, and in diminished form at that. France was divided into 10 archbishoprics, 60 bishoprics, and only about 3,000 parishes whose area roughly corresponded to that of the cantons. Strict conditions were laid down for the nomination to bishoprics of Frenchmen only, aged at least thirty years, and non-residence was specifically outlawed.

As first consul, and then emperor, Napoleon also assumed authority over a whole range of internal ecclesiastical business. It is worth noting here that the Church's former role in the registration of births, deaths, marriages, and other vital statistics had already been taken over by the civil state during the 1790s. This might be seen as a largely administrative process, following logically from the various Revolutionary policies aimed at secularizing the government of France and reducing clerical influence in public life. Napoleon not only maintained that system but went much further. He claimed the right to intercept and inspect papal communications with France, and even to interfere in the training of its clergy. The deliberately vague police regulations to which the French Church was subject gave an ominous foretaste of things to come, and they not surprisingly alarmed the pope from the earliest days.

The Organic Articles provided for the payment of clerical salaries, though not of the maintenance costs of church fabrics, by the State. Here again, the element of hierarchy was quite conspicuous. An archbishop was to receive 15,000 francs a year, a bishop 10,000, and a parish priest 1,000 or 1,500, depending on his station. In practice, however, there was very little financial security for most of the lower clergy. Under the Organic Articles, only the *curés* appointed to the chief towns of cantons were assured of tenure. All the rest, about four-fifths of the parish clergy, were considered removable and were to serve in subsidiary stations (*succursales*) at the bishops' pleasure. In this way, from top to bottom, the concordatory clergy in effect became either fully salaried officials or provisional servants of the State. On an analogy with their civil homologues, the bishops have been likened to 'prefects in purple' and the tenured priests to 'mayors in black'.[26] Clerical careerism, which the Revolution had done much to destroy, could revive only with the government's approval.

One might then ask how far the concordatory regime actually helped to boost new recruitment into the priesthood. Clearly, the question can be answered only in the longer term. We should note, first, that it relates essentially to the *secular* clergy, since the Concordat did not revoke the Revolutionary laws which had suppressed the old regular orders, and officially at least it made no provision for their restoration. On the eve of the Revolution, the French clergy had totalled some 130,000, of whom 60,000 were seculars and 70,000 regulars; at the time of Napoleon's first abdication in April 1814, there were barely 36,000 seculars. The number of new ordinations in France between 1802 and 1814 was only around 6,000, somewhat fewer than deaths among priests during those years, and only slightly more than the *annual* average number at the end of the old regime.[27] Napoleon himself made no particular effort to encourage new ordinations. Potential young ordinands were not exempt from military service, and were also subject to an age restriction for their vocation. The result was that the secular clergy tended to become an ageing group, while the progressive 'ruralization' of the concordatory church actually accentuated an older trend in France, as Claude Langlois has shown in his detailed study of a Breton diocese.[28] Furthermore, the Concordat itself provoked a minor schismatic movement, which came to be known as '*la petite église*', composed of Catholic recalcitrants who believed that the pope had acted beyond his personal authority in agreeing to certain of Napoleon's demands.

It is clear that Napoleon regarded the Concordat in its published form as a part, albeit much the most important part, of a more general reorganization of the religious life of his subjects. Officially at least, the Civil Code of 1804 was to grant religious freedom to all of them. There were in France at that time around 480,000 Calvinists and 200,000 Lutherans. Having promulgated Organic Articles for the public regulation of these Protestant communities in April 1802, Napoleon decided that the State would assume responsibility for the salaries of their pastors as from 1804. He was unwilling to extend this last provision to the much less numerous Jewish communities, but by a series of measures issued in 1806 he assimilated their newly formed consistories into his religious organization, once again under centralized control, and then established the Grand Sanhedrin of European rabbis in 1807. Even so, the civic status of the Jews under Napoleon was rather more ambivalent than they might have hoped for after their notional emancipation by the Revolutionary laws of 1790 and 1791, which in fact had never been fully honoured. French Protestants, by contrast, were free to take a much more active part in the public life of the Consulate and Empire, especially in areas of the south and east where their population was relatively dense, and their traditional foothold in banking and trade also remained firm.

In all, Napoleon clearly conducted his religious policy as an integral function of his executive authority. Although deeply concerned by the terms of the Organic Articles and the manner of their publication, Pius VII thought it best to steer clear of a major quarrel over their implementation in the early years. He accepted the nomination of Joseph Fesch, Napoleon's uncle, as archbishop of Lyons, and even made him a cardinal in 1803. After much initial hesitation, not helped by Fesch's ineptitude during a brief term as ambassador to Rome in 1804, the pope finally agreed to travel to Paris for the Imperial coronation in December that year. But the public presentation of Church–State relations as a master-stroke of Napoleonic statesmanship could not be continued indefinitely. Those relations worsened steadily as from 1805, and the great rupture which ensued is fully discussed in the next chapter.

. . . .

THE REORGANIZATION OF FRENCH FINANCES

So much has been made of the disarray of public finances under successive Revolutionary assemblies that one can easily overlook the first signs of a return to a saner monetary policy during the Directory. It suited Napoleon's propaganda to construe the whole of the decade preceding Brumaire as a time of financial recklessness and chaos. And indeed, it must be said that the effects of the paper money (*assignats*), whose compulsory circulation dated from April 1790, had been widely disruptive. Its fast depreciation and the corresponding rise in prices had been at the root of recurrent subsistence crises and the popular disturbances these provoked, especially in the years 1792–95. Successive and increasingly profligate issues of *assignats* had certainly fuelled the sales of the national lands (*biens nationaux*) confiscated from the Church in November 1789 and then from the émigrés in July 1792, with which the paper money was supposed to be organically linked. But the terms of the sales, staggered over twelve-year instalments, would have been favourable to buyers even without the additional benefit of meeting payments in depreciated paper, and the State had ended up by selling itself grossly short. Seen by many as a universal panacea, at a time when collection of the new regular taxes had fallen notoriously into arrears, the *assignats* had also been used as a sort of fiscal device to meet the immediate running costs of the State. That policy, already evident earlier, had become more or less routine practice as the costs of war steadily mounted after April 1792.

It had taken the hyper-inflation of 1795, also a year of terrible famine in France, to concentrate minds on a sounder monetary policy. The early Directory had abolished the *assignats* in February 1796, but even then had prolonged the ruinous experiment in paper money by means of an interim substitute known as the 'territorial mandates'. The latter, so named because they too were nominally secured on anticipated receipts from further sales of the national lands, had ended in the scandalous affair of the *Compagnie Dijon* (1796–97). The so-called 'bank-ruptcy of the two-thirds' (September 1797) had marked another notorious repudiation of remaining obligations on the public debt. None of this had helped to restore confidence in the solvency of the State, or to remedy the chronic problem of tax arrears, and the later Directory had come to rely increasingly on shady deals with wartime contractors and profiteers to pay its way. In all, it is not difficult to see why the financial policies of different Revolutionary regimes have had a generally bad press, and why the unhappy experience of the paper money has attracted particular criticism.[29]

On the other hand, it is also significant that France had returned to a metal money policy by the end of 1797, officially at least. On 7 April 1795 indeed, some ten months before the abolition of the *assignats*, the Convention had replaced the old *livre tournois* with the silver franc as the official unit of currency. A law of the following 15 August had laid down that its silver content would be 5 grammes, that it would be minted in denominations of 1, 2, and 5 francs, along with denominations of copper centimes, but without fixing the ratio of silver to gold as such. Though necessary, these deflationary measures had intensified the economic depression of the years 1797–99, not least in the rural areas, where debased and foreign coins were often still in circulation, since the new specie was in short supply. All this had eclipsed the Directory's formal commitment to stricter monetary discipline, and no doubt had also added to its growing unpopularity. On balance, then, it would be fair to conclude that the Directory's financial legacy was generally poor, but that some at least of the disagreeable spade-work for a 'hard' money policy had been done *before* Brumaire. It was a base on which the Consular regime could build.

If we turn now to the major financial reforms achieved under Napoleon, the contrast with what had gone before seems plain enough, even if the appearance of smoother co-ordination is sometimes deceptive. There was, for instance, a clearer functional division between the ministry of finances (the central revenue office) and the treasury (the central expenditure office). Monetary reform was extended and consolidated. Tax collection, both direct and indirect, was reorganized, and a greatly improved system of public accounting was introduced. The first important steps in public banking also dated from the early Consulate. A prominent feature of the whole system was stability of service at the top of the key financial departments. Gaudin, having rejected an overture from the ailing Directory to serve as minister of finances, accepted that office on Napoleon's invitation (10 November 1799) and was to hold it until the first abdication in April 1814, and again during the Hundred Days. The treasury, upon its elevation from a dependent directory to ministerial status, was entrusted first to Barbé-Marbois (1801–6) and then to Mollien, who held the office for the rest of the Empire and also during the Hundred Days. These were the men chiefly responsible for providing the financial expertise Napoleon himself lacked, and they were assisted by a number of able and similarly long-serving subordinates.

Gaudin's foremost achievement lay in an improved system of tax collection. The main direct taxes all dated from the Revolutionary reforms of 1790–92 but had never worked efficiently before Brumaire. Improved collection and a more equitable apportionment of the staple land tax (*la contribution foncière*), assessed on agricultural incomes, ensured that its value in the Year XII (1803–4), as the Consulate came to an end, was around 206 million francs within the 1792 frontiers of France. The introduction of more efficient land registers (*cadastres*) in 1802, which were later more widely extended under Delambre's presidency as from September 1807, helped to stabilize its yield, until mounting war costs in 1812–14 undid much of the earlier work. The tax on personal or industrial incomes (*la contribution personnelle-mobilière*) fell mostly on the towns but remained, as before, difficult to define and collect. From a notional 60 million at the start of the Consulate, its yield declined noticeably after September 1803, as stiffer consumer duties (*droits d'octroi*) gradually replaced it in the larger cities. The smaller levy on trades and services (*la patente*), initially reckoned to raise 12 million, worked little better under Napoleon than during the Revolution. Fiscal surcharges, the so-called '*centimes additionnels*', dated from 1 December 1798 and were continued, indeed increased, during the Consulate and Empire. Their main purpose was to meet rising expenditure in the localities, where they were collected, and they were charged at a partly fixed and partly variable rate within each department.

The most unpopular indirect taxes of the old regime had been abolished by the Constituent Assembly, but its optimistic assumption that compensatory levies could be integrated with the new direct taxes had simply not worked out in practice.

Customs receipts had also been hit by foreign trade losses during the maritime wars of 1793–99. Faced with mounting deficits in local finances, the Directory had authorized the reintroduction of urban *octrois* on certain goods in October and December 1798. Yet in spite of such expedients, the indirect taxes were hardly in a flourishing state when Napoleon seized power. His own early reforms in this field were reinforced when a new central excise office, the *Régie des droits réunis*, was set up in 1804 to consolidate the collection of duties on tobacco, alcoholic drinks, playing cards, public transport, gold and silver ware, and a number of other commodities or services. Salt was added to the list in 1806, reviving old memories of the widely detested royal *gabelle*, and in December 1810 the manufacture of and all trade in tobacco products were also placed under a separate State monopoly. As shortfalls in the direct taxes continued to upset the public revenue, so the *droits réunis* gained in relative importance. According to one estimate, their value quadrupled between 1806 and 1812. By 1813, they accounted for perhaps 25 per cent of the State's total revenue, compared with the 29 per cent then deriving from the direct taxes.[30] The collection of customs duties and of the various stamp and registry charges, taken together, constituted a third major source of public income.

Napoleon's fiscal apparatus was of course an integral part of his whole administrative system and, as such, it bore the characteristic stamp of centralized controls. It had the same well-defined hierarchy of authority evident in all the other branches of government. Inspectors general worked under the immediate supervision of the ministries in Paris. A new *Direction* for collecting the direct taxes was set up in each department as early as 24 November 1799. In the same way, a receiver general was appointed to each department, a receiver particular to each arrondissement. The former was required to make prompt payments to Paris, at first on a monthly basis, but after the Bank crisis of 1805 every ten days. For this purpose, a central service fund (*Caisse de service*), in effect a more elaborate version of the Consular *Caisse de garantie*, was created under Mollien's supervision on 16 July 1806.

The reform of the treasury followed the same principles. During his ministry there, Barbé-Marbois had to ensure the prompt receipt of all taxes due, and was then also responsible for the transfer and payment of public funds. He therefore insisted on detailed and certified accounts from each ministry, established the practice of their regular publication, and secured the necessary authorization for all payments. When Mollien succeeded him, steps were taken to refine the whole system of accounting. The result was a new central accounts office, the *Cour des comptes*, set up in September 1807 to audit State finances more efficiently, and double-entry bookkeeping was progressively extended throughout the treasury. Mollien indeed had already introduced that practice to the sinking fund (*Caisse d'amortissement*) during his term as its director (1800–6). This fund had itself been created on 27 November 1799 and, initially at least, its main purpose was to assist the treasury in meeting obligations on the public debt. Later, its functions were widened to boost the credit of the State in other ways, for instance through the issue of its own short-term bonds at 6 to 7 per cent interest as from 1806.

Better order in public finances presupposed a sound currency, and, as we have seen, this was the area where Napoleon's debt to the Directory was most material. His own hostility to paper money and heavy State borrowing is well established. Everything he had learnt from the lamentable history of the *assignats* reinforced his neo-mercantilist prejudices against credit financing through fiduciary paper. Although his notions on the matter are often seen as crude, they were the inspiration behind the crucial measure of 7 Germinal Year XI (28 March 1803), which formed the basis of his monetary system. The so-called '*franc de germinal*' was thereby established as a bimetallic standard, fixing the ratio of gold to silver at 1 : 15.5. It strictly regulated the metal content of the new coins, now issued in high denominations of gold, in lower and more numerous ones of silver, and in various small denominations of pure copper centimes. Primarily a silver standard, the '*franc de germinal*' at last brought the circulating medium into line with the official unit of account. It strengthened the French currency in relation to its European counterparts, not least to the pound sterling, and it was to last as a monetary standard for over 120 years.

Another of Napoleon's financial innovations which was to be of monumental importance, and which indeed survives to this day, was the creation of the Bank of France on 6 January 1800. There was no Revolutionary precedent on which he could build here, nor any from the old regime which could serve as a model.

On the contrary, hostile reaction to the collapse of John Law's *Système* back in 1720 had discredited the whole idea of a central bank in France, and no attempt had been made to found one during the next eighty years. Since Napoleon's aim was to establish such an institution as essentially a private stock company, the State providing the enabling legislation but confining its own direct participation to a minority holding, the main initiative was taken by J.-F. Perregaux. He assembled the group of financiers in Paris who raised the Bank's founding capital of 30 million francs, in shares of 1,000 each. Since the 200 largest shareholders of the Bank also elected its board of fifteen directors, the cream of the financial élite became materially involved in its management and fortunes.[31] On 14 April 1803 the Bank was allowed a monopoly over the issue of paper notes of 500 and 1,000 francs, which in turn necessitated the buying out and inclusion of two other issuing banks, an operation which at the same time increased its sharehold capital to 45 million.

The Bank worked well enough as a private venture, albeit within a still rather modest portfolio, until the combination of imminent hostilities and the repercussions of the Ouvrard affair in 1805 precipitated a run on funds and a sharp shock for shareholders, whose holdings fell by an estimated 10 per cent. It was a classic case of over-extension through a risky business escapade. Ouvrard's group, the *Négociants réunis*, had at first enjoyed Napoleon's support in their venture to break the British naval blockade by importing Mexican bullion – the legendary '*piastres*' – to Spain, and so to raise valuable funds for the military campaign of 1805. The collapse of the *Négociants réunis* was unavoidable, but the threatened insolvency of the Bank at least was staved off by the victory of Austerlitz at the end of the year.[32] All this prompted Napoleon to abandon such deals with merchant adventurers and to return to more orthodox methods of military provisioning. Barbé-Marbois, a convenient scapegoat, was dismissed from the treasury in January 1806. Stricter governmental control of the Bank itself was achieved when Crétet (later to become minister of the interior, 1807–9) was appointed as its first governor on 22 April 1806, and at the same time its capital was doubled to 90 million francs. Even then, as has often been remarked, it more closely resembled a 'Bank of Paris' during the rest of the Empire. Its notes continued to circulate in such large denominations that their transaction was almost exclusively confined to the business élite of the capital. Dealings at its branches in Lyons, Rouen, and later Lille were of comparatively minor importance.

How far, then, may one speak of lasting financial stability under Napoleon? By comparison with the rather chaotic finances of the old regime, or with the upheavals of the Revolution, his reforms certainly seem orderly and effective. Public debts were duly honoured on the whole, as were official salaries and pensions, and in a currency which kept its value. The State was able to avoid large loans, and its bonds generally rose in value until the end of 1807, when the prospect of war in the Iberian peninsula had an adverse impact on the market. One wider economic effect of Napoleon's 'hard' money policy was that prices, although on a generally upward trend during this period of prolonged wars, remained tolerable in the critical consumer markets. Institutionally, too, many of Napoleon's financial reforms survived his fall.

There is, however, another side to this coin. If Napoleon dealt effectively with the problem of the public debt, as previous regimes had singularly failed to do, he was not above repudiating nearly all the unpaid debt of the Directory, estimated at 90 million francs. There were dubious technical reasons for this decision, of course, but foremost in his mind perhaps was the symbolical importance of a high-handed act designed to break (and to be *seen* to break) with a discredited past. When Holland was annexed to the Empire in 1810, its unpaid debt of some 78 million francs was similarly repudiated. The sinking fund, originally conceived of as a guarantee against the State's resort to a fiduciary paper money, ended the Empire in some disarray. Its right to issue paper bonds in its own name got out of hand in 1813–14, when high flotations secured only on anticipated receipts from the sale of the communal lands (*biens communaux*) failed to attract the expected response from the public. Moreover, as the State's expenditure steadily mounted from an estimated 700 million francs in 1806 to well over 1,000 million in 1812 and 1813, at which latter point war costs alone made up at least 80 per cent of the total, compared with 60 per cent in 1807, so its revenue fell progressively short.[33] The last budgets of the Empire had lost the semblance of balance advertised, and up to a point achieved, during the earlier years. Among Napoleon's expedients to raise ready cash in these more troubled years was the issue of special 'licences' for trade with the enemy, which further undermined the official rigour of his Continental Blockade against Britain.

It would be equally misleading to conclude that Napoleon's financial achievements, such as they were, always stemmed from a more efficient use of home resources alone. As his Imperial vision became more grandiose, he came to rely increasingly on extraordinary income from conquered enemies and from the subject states to help pay France's way through the wars. Military victories gave him the chance to impose indemnities on his continental enemies, most notably during and after the successful campaigns of 1805–7. In this way war came to be seen as 'a good thing' – '*une bonne affaire*' – to be waged at the expense of defeated foes. In 1805, for example, 118 million francs was demanded of Austria, of which at least 75 million seems to have been received. In 1809, similarly, Austria paid 164 of the 250 million imposed on her after the Wagram campaign. Following the defeat of Jena–Auerstädt, Prussia was saddled with an indemnity of 311 million, to be settled in specie, while her total payments to France over the whole period 1806–12 have been estimated variously at between 470 and 514 million.[34] If Gaudin's own estimates are to be believed, punitive levies of this sort may have accounted for as much as a third of Napoleon's revenue in the years 1806 and 1807.[35] Moreover, the so-called '*Domaine extraordinaire*' which he set up early in 1810 had the precise purpose of raking off the fiscal resources of the subject states for his own use. In short, the final verdict on his financial achievements, taken as a whole, will never be complete unless allowance is made for his ruthless exploitation of the satellites and the defeated enemies of France during the ascendant years of the Empire.

. . . .

THE JUDICIAL SYSTEM

None of the judicial institutions of the old regime, from the lowest courts of first instance to the sovereign appeal courts, had survived the fundamental reforms of the Revolution. If the extraordinary measures adopted during the Terror are again excluded as an aberration, the guiding principles of the reorganization of French justice during the 1790s had been the uniformity of the criminal and civil courts across all the new administrative departments and the professionalization of their functions. And that, whatever its practical deficiencies, was the system in place at the time of Brumaire. Much of its basic structure was retained by Napoleon, in formal deference to the two principles of legal equality and the independence of the judiciary itself, but he also introduced some important changes under both the Consulate and the Empire. The main general features of these changes were an increasing intrusion of the government into French judicial procedures and the appointment of their personnel, a steady accentuation of repressive measures in the operation of the criminal courts and of what was also called 'correctional justice', and a reduction of the legal status of women after several significant advances during the Revolution.

Under the Constitution of the Year VIII, only the justices of the peace (in effect local magistrates) in all the communal arrondissements were to be elected directly by the citizens, and for a term of three years (article 60). They had no real powers of constraint; their role was confined to arbitration and conciliation in settling legal disputes. All other judges of the criminal and civil courts (including the appeal courts) were to be appointed by the first consul from the lists of departmental 'notabilities', while those of the single sovereign court of appeal (*Tribunal de Cassation*, later the *Cour de Cassation* under the Empire) were initially selected by the senate from the lists of national 'notabilities'. All judges other than the justices of the peace were to hold office for life, unless they were found guilty of negligence, or failed to be maintained on the list of eligibles, a condition which ceased with the abandonment of the lists in August 1802. On the other hand, the direct intrusion of the State into the criminal courts was assured, since article 63 of the constitution laid down that the functions of public prosecutor were to be carried out by government commissioners in those courts at all levels.

There was then, from the start, a formal judicial structure potentially exposed to interference by the State, and this caused liberals some concern. Two further measures during the early Consulate, not specifically provided for in the constitution, aroused greater public opposition, most notably in the tribunate. One was the law of 28 January 1801 which, in matching the number of justices of the peace to their cantonal jurisdictions, consequentially reduced the total to a minimum of 3,000 and a maximum of 3,500, compared with some 6,000 under the Directory. In spite of its administrative logic, critics of this law considered it an unwarranted limitation of the legal rights of the people at local level. The other measure which caused concern was the law of 7 February 1801, hotly disputed in the tribunate, which introduced a number of 'special courts' for the suppression of brigandage, especially in some western departments. Working without juries, and with powers to impose the death penalty, these courts were denounced by liberal critics as quasi-military tribunals and as an attack on the independence of the judiciary. And indeed, their jurisdiction eventually extended well beyond brigandage to include a whole range of other criminal allegations, which in turn removed such cases from the ordinary criminal courts.

As the Napoleonic state became more hierarchical and the executive authority of its head more pronounced, so the judicial system, indeed its very nomenclature, reflected the same process.[36] The elective principle in the appointment of justices of the peace was gradually phased out with the life consulate, as Napoleon increasingly restricted the choice of the eligible cantonal electors, while the term of the justices was extended to ten years. It must be said that the government's intervention here to some extent reflected the rather feeble operation of the elective principle itself in most departments during the early years, and that cases of local favouritism and corruption had also been quite common. In any case, all this marked an intrusion into the local magistrature, the lowest level of the judicial system. As from August 1802, Napoleon saw fit to assert his influence on its highest level as well. While the senate exercised its formal procedure for selecting the judges of the sovereign court of appeal, it was now required to do so from candidates he had himself presented. As emperor, he was also given the exclusive right to appoint the first president and the presidents of all the sections of the *Cour de Cassation* for life. So, too, the appointment and dismissal of the government commissioners to the criminal courts were entirely at his discretion, and after 18 May 1804 these men were styled 'Imperial prosecutors' (*procureurs impériaux*). A similar progression in the status of the original 'appeal tribunals', each of which served an average of three to four departments, also took place. As from 1804 they were redesignated as 'appeal courts', and in April 1810 as 'Imperial courts'. Here again, Napoleon had had the constitutional prerogative of appointing their judges, whom in theory he could not dismiss, since December 1799.

In his choice of judges, Napoleon does not appear to have acted despotically or indiscriminately. Throughout his rule, he relied heavily on the legal advice of the distinguished jurist Cambacérès, who after serving as second consul was appointed arch-chancellor during the Empire. He had also served briefly as minister of justice under the provisional Consulate and was to do so again at the very end of the Empire and during the Hundred Days. The longer-serving titular ministers of justice, A.-J. Abrial (1799–1802) and especially C.-A. Régnier (1802–13), were themselves always inclined to defer to him. Given such advice, Napoleon seems to have chosen the magistrates and higher judges sensibly, preferring men of sound professional training, which again provided an important link of continuity with the legal personnel of the Revolution. There were times, however, as on 12 October 1807, when a *senatus-consultum* which modified the terms of service in the magistrature enabled him to conduct something like a 'purge' of its members. On this occasion, apart from those of reputedly loose personal habits, most of the victims were men regarded as former Republican partisans.

Napoleon's obsession with proper authority, order, and uniformity had a major extension into the definition of the laws themselves, and the result was the most comprehensive work of codification France had ever known. Some historians have seen this as the most monumental and ultimately the most enduring of all his achievements, and the evidence suggests that he too regarded it as a crucial part of his legacy. The process started early with the successive appointment during the years 1800–2 of five commissions to draw up a civil code, a criminal code, a commercial code, a rural code, and a code of civil procedure. Of these, the Civil Code, which from 1807 was also called the *Code Napoléon*, mainly for 'export' purposes, was the most important. A number of legal experts at different times helped to draft it, in regular communication with the council of state: Cambacérès of course, Tronchet, Bigot de Préameneu, Malleville, Portalis, among others. Napoleon himself took a keen interest in the commission's deliberations, frequently intervening personally to shape particular drafts, and generally putting pressure on its members to hasten the completion of their work.

The Civil Code (*Code civil des Français*) was officially promulgated on 21 March 1804. It reaffirmed the principle of legal equality, a whole section being devoted to the rights of persons, and it marked the final, definitive extinction of feudalism and any surviving traces of seigneurial justice in all their forms. Its two other sections dealt with the rights of property and of the acquisition of property. In this respect, none of its provisions were more important than those, numerous in fact, which formally recognized the legal title of all earlier sales of national lands confiscated from the Church and the émigrés. In doing so, it bound the material interests of a great many beneficiaries, the 'acquéreurs des biens nationaux', more closely to the new political and social order in France. It also went some way towards upholding the Revolutionary principle of *partage*, which had suppressed the old rights of primogeniture in favour of a more equal division of estates among all male heirs, although many of its clauses were regressive on this point and subject in practice to numerous legal disputes. Similarly, while reaffirming the rights of civil marriage and divorce in general terms, its particular clauses had a strongly patriarchal bias. The legal rights of women in inheritance and divorce were significantly reduced from what had seemed a partial emancipation under the Revolutionary laws, more particularly those of 1792.

On these last two points, inheritance and divorce, the provisions of the Civil Code were often to be referred to as '*la puissance paternelle*' (the rights of fathers over their children) and '*la puissance maritale*' (the rights of husbands over their wives) during the course of the nineteenth century. Taken as a whole, the Civil Code should be seen above all as a great work of consolidation rather than of major innovation. Its 2,281 articles were a grand recapitulation of no less than thirty-six laws which had been passed severally during the years 1801–3. As such, the extension of the *Code Napoléon* to all the overseas dependencies of France after 1815 ensured its wider global influence, which indeed survives to this day in many Francophone lands.[37]

The work of all but one of the other legal commissions appointed in 1800–2 in due course also bore fruit. The Code of Civil Procedure was promulgated in 1806, and the Commercial Code in 1807. They were followed by the Code of Criminal Instruction in 1808, which in fact incorporated both a Criminal Code and a Code of Criminal Procedure, and by the Penal Code in 1810. These last two codes marked the start of a major reorganization of repressive justice and its related police apparatus, which had its full effect as from 1810–11, and is sometimes seen as a defining characteristic of the Empire at its height.[38] The jurisdiction of what were now called the *cours d'assises*, which had replaced the criminal tribunals, was considerably widened. Apart from facilitating another 'purge' of the magistrature, the Code of Criminal Instruction also introduced two new types of judicial official whose importance soon became clear. These were the examining magistrates (*juges d'instruction*), with powers to give initial verdicts on accused persons quickly and in secrecy, and the Imperial prosecutors general (*procureurs généraux impériaux*), whose job it was to seek out and follow up crimes. The Penal Code, for its part, formalized and toughened the whole system of legal punishments for criminal offences, themselves now more broadly defined, and had an especially reactionary impact on the urban industrial workforce. As for the Rural Code, finally, nothing definite came of it. The complexities of rural life defied uniform legal definition. Such a code had already been discussed at length before Brumaire, and was to be pursued many a time after 1815. But it continued to frustrate all subsequent regimes, just as it had eluded the jurists of the Napoleonic Empire.

. . . .

NOTES AND REFERENCES

1. Eric A. Arnold, Jr, ed. and trans., *A Documentary Survey of Napoleonic France*, Lanham, Md, 1994, pp. 34–5.
2. *Letters of Napoleon*, selected, trans., and ed. by J.M. Thompson, Oxford, 1934, p. 70.
3. George V. Taylor, 'Revolutionary and Nonrevolutionary Content in the *Cahiers* of 1789: An Interim Report', *French Historical Studies*, vol. 7, Fall 1972, pp. 479–502.
4. C. Ramsay, 'Constitution of 1793', in Samuel F. Scott and Barry Rothaus, eds, *Historical Dictionary of the French Revolution, 1789–1799*, 2 vols, Westport, Conn., 1985, vol. 1, pp. 238–42.
5. E.J. Knapton, 'Constitution of 1795', in Scott and Rothaus, eds, *Historical Dictionary*, vol. 1, pp. 242–5.
6. Ibid.
7. Martyn Lyons, *Napoleon Bonaparte and the Legacy of the French Revolution*, Basingstoke and London, 1994, p. 41.
8. E.J. Knapton, 'Constitution of 1799', in Scott and Rothaus, eds, *Historical Dictionary*, vol. 1, p. 246.

9. Irene Collins, *Napoleon and his Parliaments 1800–1815*, London, 1979, pp. 90–1.
10. Frédéric Bluche, *Le plébiscite des Cent-Jours, avril–mai 1815*, Geneva, 1974.
11. Collins, *Napoleon and his Parliaments*, pp. 19–20.
12. Text as cited in Arnold, ed., *Documentary Survey*, p. 28.
13. Clive H. Church, *Revolution and Red Tape: The French Ministerial Bureaucracy 1770–1850*, Oxford, 1981, p. 268.
14. Arnold, ed., *Documentary Survey*, pp. 1–3, 205–7.
15. Eric A. Arnold, Jr, *Fouché, Napoleon, and the General Police*, Washington, DC, 1979.
16. Jacques Godechot, *Les institutions de la France sous la Révolution et l'Empire*, 3rd revised and expanded edn, Paris, 1985, pp. 470–2.
17. Ibid., p. 589.
18. Ibid., p. 588.
19. Stuart Woolf, *Napoleon's Integration of Europe*, London, 1991, pp. 31, 116, 127, 222, 242.
20. Ibid., p. 4.
21. Louis Bergeron, *France under Napoleon*, Eng. edn, Princeton, 1981, p. xiv.
22. Lyons, *Napoleon Bonaparte*, p. 141.
23. Collins, *Napoleon and his Parliaments*, pp. 63–7.
24. J.M. McManners, *The French Revolution and the Church*, London, 1969.
25. Olwen Hufton, 'The Reconstruction of a Church 1796–1801', in Gwynne Lewis and Colin Lucas, eds, *Beyond the Terror: Essays in French Regional and Social History, 1794–1815*, Cambridge, 1983, p. 26.
26. Jean Godel, 'L'Église selon Napoléon', *Revue d'Histoire moderne et contemporaine*, vol. 17, 1970, p. 841.
27. Bergeron, *France under Napoleon*, p. 193.
28. Claude Langlois, *Le diocèse de Vannes au XIXe siècle, 1800–1830. Un diocèse breton au début du XIXe siècle*, Paris, 1974.
29. Florin Aftalion, *The French Revolution: An Economic Interpretation*, Eng. edn, Cambridge, 1990; and François Crouzet, *La grande inflation. La monnaie en France de Louis XVI à Napoléon*, Paris, 1993.
30. Bergeron, *France under Napoleon*, p. 39.
31. Romuald Szramkiewicz, *Les régents et censeurs de la Banque de France nommés sous le Consulat et l'Empire*, Geneva, 1974.
32. Jean Bouvier, 'A propos de la crise dite de 1805: Les crises économiques sous l'Empire', *Revue d'Histoire moderne et contemporaine*, vol. 17, 1970, pp. 506–13.
33. Bergeron, *France under Napoleon*, pp. 39–40.
34. Godechot, *Les institutions*, p. 647.

35. Jean Gabillard, 'Le financement des guerres napoléoniennes et la conjoncture du premier Empire', *Revue économique*, no. 4, July 1953, pp. 558–9.
36. Godechot, *Les institutions*, pp. 615–24.
37. B. Schwartz, ed., *The Code Napoleon and the Common-Law World*, New York, 1956.
38. Godechot, *Les institutions*, pp. 630–8.

Chapter 4

THE TERRITORIAL AND DYNASTIC EXTENSIONS OF POWER:
FROM EMPIRE TO 'GRAND EMPIRE'

A central theme of this book is that Napoleonic imperialism was a gradual and pragmatic process, in which the momentum of outward expansion closely followed the chronology of military conquest. As such, its dynastic, political, economic, and other embellishments all ultimately depended on the continuing superiority of French arms. The spoils of conquest offered opportunities which had not always been foreseen, and in his attempt to exploit them, Napoleon aimed not only to secure his enlarged military hegemony, but also to reorganize the civil life of the annexed territories and the subject states in a more comprehensive way. Believing as he did that what was good for Napoleon must be good for France, and so in turn good for conquered Europe as a whole, his wider Imperial vision became a natural extension of his personal dynastic ambition.

This chapter covers four main aspects of that wider Imperial ambition: the expansion of the annexed departments and the creation of the satellite states within a new dynastic system; the structure of the Grand Army and its role in forging the 'Grand Empire'; the aims and effects of Napoleon's attempt to reduce British economic power through his Continental Blockade; and his worsening relations with Pope Pius VII, which eventually led to a total rupture. In the first two of those developments, he had things more or less under control until his military reverses of 1812–14. But in the latter two, the limitations of his physical power had become evident rather earlier.

. . . .

CONQUEST, ANNEXATION,
AND THE SATELLITE STATES

The extension of the territory of 'old France' had been completed relatively early during the Revolution with the formal
annexation of Avignon and the Comtat Venaissin (formerly
papal enclaves) on 14 September 1791, of Savoy on 27 November 1792, and of Nice on 31 January 1793. The military dynamic
of expansion to the 'natural frontiers' of France (the Pyrenees,
the Alps, and the Rhine) had begun with the conquests of the
Republican armies in the years following the battle of Fleurus
(26 June 1794). Belgium and Luxemburg had been annexed
to form nine new departments on 30 September 1795. The German left bank of the Rhine, while technically still only occupied
lands until their full annexation early in 1802, had been turned
into four new French departments in January 1798. Geneva
and its environs had become a French department on 26 April
1798. Piedmont had been brought under a French military
occupation, although this was not altogether secure before the
Marengo campaign of June 1800, and other parts of Italy had
also been transformed by Napoleon's victories there.

Following in the wake of her military expansion, furthermore,
a whole crop of satellite republics had been formed in the
lands around France, some of them admittedly short-lived. The
Batavian (Dutch) Republic (May 1795), the enlarged Cisalpine
Republic (June 1797), the reconstituted Ligurian Republic
(June 1797), the Helvetic Republic (May 1798), the Roman Republic (1798–9), the Parthenopean Republic centred on Naples
(January–June 1799) – these, among others, had all preceded
the *coup d'état* of Brumaire, and all in some way had been constitutional imitations of the French model of 1795. As Stuart
Woolf has observed, 'of the thirteen constitutions promulgated
in the "sister republics", eleven were modelled on the thermidorian constitution of the Year III, with its elaborate, rigid and
ultimately unworkable separation of powers and graduated system of election'.[1]

In that sense, one may say that Napoleon also inherited a
republican legacy *beyond* French frontiers. Successive conquests
later allowed him to reconstruct it through what increasingly
resembled a dynastic policy of 'imperialism in one family'. At
first this was fanciful, born perhaps of his inflated vision of a

far-flung empire stretching to the waters of the Nile during his Egyptian campaign of 1798–9. But it became more practicable and more real as his focus steadily concentrated on *continental* Europe, where the land campaigns of 1805–7 had a critical importance. Throughout the years from the rupture of the Peace of Amiens in May 1803 to 1812, when he embarked on his ill-fated Russian campaign, Napoleon extended the official territory of France in ways that eventually made the 'natural frontiers' look decidedly *un*natural. He also brought the constitutional forms of all his dependencies more in line with his own expanding Imperial vision.

After the establishment of the formal French Empire, the 'Grand Empire' was conceived. The Swiss Confederation, of which Napoleon was the 'Mediator', had already been formed in February 1803. The Republic of Italy, which had succeeded the Cisalpine in December 1801, became a kingdom in March 1805. Centred on Lombardy, its crown was assumed by Napoleon himself, but soon afterwards he appointed Eugène de Beauharnais, his stepson, to rule as his viceroy there. Its territory, which already included the papal Legations of Bologna, Ferrara, and Ravenna, was set to incorporate the whole of Venetia by the end of 1805, following Napoleon's victories over the Austro-Russian forces at Ulm (20 October) and Austerlitz (2 December) and his ensuing peace treaty with Austria at Pressburg (26 December) that year. In March 1806, after the deposition of Ferdinand, the former Bourbon ruler, Joseph Bonaparte became the monarch of the new satellite kingdom of Naples, even if Sicily itself was still cut off by the British navy. Having engineered the demise of the Batavian Commonwealth in May, Napoleon similarly appointed Louis Bonaparte as king of Holland in June 1806. His queen, whom he had married in 1802, was Hortense de Beauharnais, daughter of the empress Josephine.

During the next year or so, Germany east of the Rhine underwent an equally important political reconstruction. Its more immediate origins lay back in the 'recess' of the German Diet in February 1803, when over a hundred ecclesiastical principalities had been secularized and 'mediatized', that is severed from their traditional affiliations in the old *Reich*. Their political realignment, along with that of many larger German states, was subsumed in the Confederation of the Rhine, created by a constitutional act of 12 July 1806, with Napoleon as its official 'Protector'. It consisted initially of sixteen states, including the newly created kingdoms of Bavaria and of Württemberg, which Napoleon had himself promoted under native sovereigns, and the grand duchy of Berg, a French subject state formed in March 1806 and entrusted to the rule of Joachim Murat, one of his marshals and the husband of Caroline Bonaparte. Its very formation struck a lethal blow at the historic Holy Roman Empire, which was formally abolished on 6 August 1806 by the Emperor Francis II, who now became Emperor Francis I of Austria.

Any prospect that Prussia might overthrow Napoleon's new confederation of German satellites was soon shattered by her catastrophic defeats at the hands of his armies in the twin battles of Jena and Auerstädt on 14 October 1806. The continuing Russian challenge inflicted heavy losses on the French at the inconclusive battle of Eylau (7–8 February 1807), but then foundered with Napoleon's decisive victory at Friedland on the following 14 June. Alexander I came to terms with Napoleon shortly afterwards in the first Treaty of Tilsit on 7 July, by which the French emperor was allowed a more or less free hand in his reconstruction of western and central Europe, while the tsar was given leave to pursue his own territorial aggrandizement further east, and at the same time agreed to apply Napoleon's Continental Blockade against British trade. Tilsit delivered the final blow to the faltering Fourth Allied Coalition, and for a time Britain was left to continue the fight against Napoleon alone, at sea of course, but before long in the Iberian peninsula as well.

The military context had thus been set for the important accessions to the Rhenish Confederation which also followed during the course of 1807. On 1 January Saxony, a former electorate which Napoleon had raised to a kingdom by his Treaty of Posen with Frederick Augustus on the preceding 11 December, became a member. With the dismemberment of something like half the Prussian lands by the second Treaty of Tilsit on 9 July, he could augment it still further. In the same month, the territorial spoils from Prussia west of the Elbe were amalgamated with Hesse-Cassel, Brunswick, Wolfenbüttel, southern Hanover, and some smaller principalities to form the new satellite kingdom of Westphalia, which now also joined the Rhenish Confederation. Napoleon's choice of monarch fell on his youngest brother, Jerome, who was back in favour after the annulment of his first marriage to Elizabeth Patterson in 1805. Jerome was now persuaded to contract a much more strategically useful marriage with Catherine, daughter of King Frederick I of Württemberg. His subsequent correspondence with the emperor seemed to promise that the new kingdom would be governed as a 'model state', a sort of functioning paradigm of Napoleonic civil reform under its constitution of the following November, but in the event this vaunted aim was not to be fulfilled.[2] On 22 July 1807 Napoleon also created the duchy of Warsaw from Prussian lands in Poland ceded at Tilsit, and placed its government under his Saxon ally, King Frederick Augustus.

During 1808 and 1809 Napoleon's imperial ambitions took a different direction south of the Pyrenees, south of the Alps, and into the Adriatic hinterland. General Junot had already been sent to subjugate Portugal at the end of 1807, and in February 1808 was proclaimed governor general of that country, an act which soon met with a concerted British reaction there. During the following months Napoleon devised a stratagem to depose Ferdinand VII, the Bourbon monarch of Spain, who had forced the abdication of his father, Charles IV, in March 1808. The plan was duly carried out by a special Spanish National Assembly, or Junta, which met at Napoleon's behest in Bayonne in the following May to July, and whose members he had carefully selected for the purpose. This enabled him to appoint his brother Joseph to the throne of a new satellite kingdom of Spain, and in due course Murat and Caroline Bonaparte were transferred from Berg to rule in the kingdom of Naples. In the same year the Papal States of Urbino, Macerata, Ancona, and Camerino were officially incorporated into the Kingdom of Italy. Its territory was further enlarged by the Trentino and south Tyrol, after Napoleon's victory over the Austrians at Wagram on 5–6 July and the Treaty of Schönbrunn which ensued on 14 October 1809. At the same time, he reinforced his partial gains of 1805 by detaching the whole of Istria (along with Trieste and Fiume) and Dalmatia, as well as parts of Carniola, Carinthia, and Croatia, from the Habsburg Empire. All these now formed the so-called 'Illyrian Provinces of the Empire' and were formally ruled as an integral part of it until the beginning of 1814, although their effective status as directly annexed lands under the governance of Marshal Marmont and later Generals Bertrand and Junot has sometimes been doubted.

All this, moreover, is to say nothing of the territorial expansion of the formal French Empire itself. At its inauguration on 18 May 1804, it consisted of 108 departments, including four on the left bank of the Rhine which had been fully incorporated early in 1802, and six in Piedmont (later reduced to five) annexed in September that year. Three more were formed on 30 June 1805 from the lands of the reconstituted Ligurian Republic, which included the port of Genoa. Parma and the kingdom of Etruria were similarly turned into four annexed departments in May 1808. When Tuscan patriots protested, Napoleon's response was to appoint his sister Elisa and her husband, Prince Bacciochi, as rulers of a new grand duchy of Tuscany in 1809, but he still treated those lands as an integral part of the Empire. The remnants of the truncated Papal States, having been exposed to a French military occupation as from February 1808, were officially annexed on 17 May 1809. The process was completed on 17 February 1810, when Rome itself was proclaimed 'the second city of the Empire'. Later that year Louis Bonaparte was deposed as king of Holland, which was then directly annexed in two stages during April and July; and part of Hanover, which had been occupied by the French since 1804, followed suit. The last annexations came in December 1810 and January 1811, when the Hanse towns (Hamburg, Bremen, Lübeck) and the grand duchy of Oldenburg were also incorporated.

At its territorial height in 1811, the Empire's official frontiers included 130 departments, with a total population of around 44 million. If one counts all the other states which under various constitutional arrangements then comprised the 'Grand Empire', Napoleon held sway over more than 80 million subjects. His potential influence (and as things later turned out it did not even amount to that) seemed to have an extension north of the Baltic as well. With his approval, Marshal Bernadotte, who had married Desirée Clary, was elected crown prince of Sweden, heir to the childless Charles XIII, on 21 October 1810. All this, however, was of really only marginal interest to Napoleon, who by then had a new empress, following his divorce from Josephine at the end of 1809. After being cold-shouldered by Alexander I in his initial pursuit of the Archduchess Anna, sister of the tsar who was then only fourteen years old, Napoleon had turned his attention to the eighteen-year-old Archduchess Marie-Louise of Austria, daughter of Emperor Francis I, and received a much more favourable response. With the good offices of Count Metternich, then the Austrian ambassador to Paris, an alliance was concluded, and the marriage itself was solemnized in Paris on 2 April 1810. Napoléon-François-Charles-Joseph was born on 20 March 1811, was immediately graced with the title 'King of Rome', and the Empire had an heir at last. This, it seemed, was the moment of Napoleon's greatest dynastic triumph of all.

However one interprets the whole process of empire-building in the years 1804–11, whether it is seen as the systematic fulfilment of a 'master-plan' for which Napoleon believed Destiny had always intended him, or as the improvised results of pragmatic opportunism, or perhaps as a combination of the two, one conclusion at least is not in doubt. The 'Grand Empire' was forged by the conquests of the Grand Army, and the victories of 1805–7 (Ulm and Austerlitz, Jena and Auerstädt, and Friedland if not Eylau) were the critical point of departure. The policies, organization, and mobilization of resources which together shaped this crucial instrument of conquest now need closer analysis.

. . . . . .

THE GRAND ARMY

The phrase 'Grand Army' seems to have been coined by Napoleon himself while he was in Boulogne before the campaign of 1805. The fighting force to which it referred will surely be most familiar to readers for its celebrated exploits under his command in the field. Important recent research enables us to measure just how 'grand' it actually was, in broad statistical terms, during most of the Napoleonic wars, how far it was troubled by the endemic problem of desertion and draft evasion, and further weakened by the mounting toll of war dead and wounded. All these issues have a major bearing on the whole relationship between the army and Imperial society at large, not least at local level. In this respect, the Grand Army can be seen as very much more than an instrument of war on the battle-field itself, a mobile force unleashed on enemies beyond the Imperial frontiers, until the last desperate campaigns of 1813–14 brought the attrition all the way back to Paris. Its problems of conscription were always present within the home frontiers, and the militarization of society throughout the long wars of 1792–1815 reached a pitch France had never known under the old regime, and was not again to know during the century which followed the fall of Napoleon.

It is not my present purpose to attempt a potted history of the Napoleonic campaigns, which are well covered in several accessible textbooks cited in the Bibliographical Essay at the end of this volume. My own discussion of the subject here is therefore confined to a few more general observations. It is clear, first of all, that Napoleon quickly learnt how to harness and exploit the cult of personality which developed around him from his earliest campaigns. He possessed natural gifts which seemed to mark him out as a born military commander. These included what was by all accounts a phenomenal memory, an extraordinary capacity for work, often without much sleep, and a personal presence which struck awe in all around him. He had a genius for brilliant improvisation on the field of battle, a sense of timing which could spread sudden panic in the enemy at critical 'moments', as he called them, and a unique ability to inspire his own troops to feats of bravery. His Imperial Guard, although rarely exposed to the heat of battle, and then only as a last reserve to add lustre to the hour of victory, has always had a special place in the heroic annals of the Grand Army, most memorably perhaps for its fearless loyalty to him during the Hundred Days. Its legacy was held in almost 'religious' reverence by the surviving *grognards* of the Old Guard after 1815.

And yet, if one looks more closely at Napoleon's tactics, battle formations, and weaponry, it seems equally clear that his main achievement lay more in the improvement and consolidation of well-tried practices than in radical innovation. As noted in chapter 2, his own earlier training in the military academies of the old regime had thoroughly acquainted him with the teachings of men like Gribeauval and the Du Teil brothers in new artillery techniques, and of Bourcet and Guibert in infantry tactics. What was known as the *ordre mixte*, for instance, combined the older formation of serried battle-lines (the *ordre mince*) with the newer deployment of detachable mobile columns (the *ordre profond*), whose stunning force could be quickly directed at the enemy flank or rear. The efficacy of such tactics had already been demonstrated by the French armies during the Revolutionary wars, not least by Napoleon himself in his first Italian campaign of 1796–97, and their improved weaponry (muskets, carbines, pistols, the guns and howitzers of the field artillery) had also proved their worth. In short, all such military craft was well established in the infantry divisions, regiments, and battalions, in the heavy and light cavalry brigades, and in the companies of artillery and engineers before Brumaire.

After becoming supreme commander, Napoleon increased the use and efficacy of mobile skirmishers (fusiliers, grenadiers, and light infantrymen alike) and often employed the cavalry for scouting or screening and sometimes as shock troops to rout the enemy, once the decisive break in its front lines had been achieved. These tactics, reinforced by his improved fire-power, were brought to a particularly devastating effect in the operations of the *corps*, his largest military units, and certainly also his major innovation in the field. The latter consisted of relatively self-contained formations of between 20,000 and 30,000 men each, usually under the command of a marshal, capable of moving quickly and independently, almost like small armies on their own, and of converging at a given place and time to ensure local superiority. The *corps* formed the basis of the so-called '*bataillon carré*', a quadrilateral formation in which several units could march independently of one another but within mutually supporting distance. They were a key factor in Napoleon's much-acclaimed flexibility and speed of manoeuvre on campaign. Their role was well adapted to his 'classic' tactics of stunning and overcoming enemies in short, sharp campaigns, which brought an older style of warfare to its highest art in the pre-railway age. Such tactics were played out with spectacular success against the Austro-Russian forces at Ulm and Austerlitz in 1805 and against the Prussians at Jena and Auerstädt in the following year. But they were much less effective in the Iberian peninsula, where the mountainous terrain in many places was unsuited to rapid manoeuvres, and they came sadly to grief in Russia, where the sheer vastness of the enemy territory and the hazards of the weather created unforeseen obstacles for the Grand Army.

Napoleon was loath to admit his own mistakes as a military commander and strategist, even in his more reflective years on St Helena, but others have since spelt out the painful lessons for him. His chief fault was an instinctive reluctance to delegate command. Apart from the Imperial Guard, which grew enormously in number from an initial *corps d'élite* of only a few thousand strong to something resembling a cosmopolitan army of over 112,000 infantry, cavalry, artillery, service, and medical units at its height early in 1814, he insisted on keeping personal command of the army cavalry and artillery reserves. Some of his commanders could certainly rise to the occasion with independent flair, or else play a decisive supporting role, as Masséna so often did in the early campaigns and Davout later at Austerlitz, Auerstädt, Eylau, and Wagram. Yet too many others, including several marshals, were found wanting in skill and judgement when they were removed from his proximity and forced to act on their own initiative. This was again especially evident in the Iberian peninsula, where Junot, Soult, and Marmont at different times made serious miscalculations, and where even Masséna was eventually disgraced.

In view of the ultimate cost, Napoleon's failure to devote enough of his own time and energy to Spain proved a major strategic blunder. He always underestimated the national pride and ferocity of the guerrillas there. Murat's notorious fusillade of 1808, whose victims were immortalized in Goya's great paintings *The Second of May* and *The Third of May*, which might be seen as the '*Guernicas*' of their time, although they were made public only after Napoleon's fall, was one of the atrocities his troops in Spain paid for dearly. The French defeats at Baylen in Spain (21 July) and Vimiero in Portugal (21 August) that same year, though not decisive in themselves, were psychologically important for the Allies in dispelling the myth of French invincibility. And indeed, comparative figures for Napoleon's war casualties alone suggest that his superiority over enemy commanders was less marked as from 1808 than in the earlier campaigns. Wellington, whose skills he also consistently underestimated, quickly learnt the tactics of his enemy, and these he used to good effect himself in his more successful campaigns of 1812 and 1813. The British commander was to do so again, and even more dramatically against Napoleon's own army, at Waterloo on 18 June 1815, which finally decided the conflict.

With the Peninsular War thus far from won, Napoleon's whole strategy in the Russian campaign proved a composite failure, and it was without doubt his greatest single miscalculation, one from which he never fully recovered. He sacrificed too many men in the Pyrrhic victory at Borodino (7 September 1812), as he had through crude massed charges against the Austrians in the battle at Aspern–Essling (21–2 May 1809), and this time no

Wagram followed to put things right. Instead, he exposed his advancing army to serious complications in commissariat supplies as the retreating Russians adopted a 'scorched-earth' policy. He waited too long in Moscow, assuming that Tsar Alexander I would oblige him with the decisive showdown that never came, while the snows did. In 1812, he was over-stretched on two major fronts, themselves too far apart, and that year certainly marked a turning point for the Grand Army, as the firmer Russian resolve to take the war west in due course gave hope of a new and bigger Allied Coalition. During 1813 many of his German allies deserted him, especially after the battle of Leipzig on 16–19 October, 'the Battle of the Nations', and he was increasingly thrown back on resources nearer home.

Now, in assessing the organization and mobilization of those resources during the earlier years of the Empire, we need to look well beyond the evolving trail of Napoleon's campaigns. The Grand Army in the field was only the spearhead of a much greater military establishment, which entrained an elaborate command-centre for wartime planning and many subordinate back-up services. The expanded ministry of war, for instance, was much the largest of all Napoleon's ministries, and for most of the period actually consisted of *two* ministries. In 1802 he divided it into a 'core' ministry of war and a new ministry of war administration. The former kept its central responsibilities over the running of the combat forces, most notably over conscription, troop movements, artillery operations, promotions, salaries, and pensions. Continuity at the top was assured by the long service of two ministers throughout the Consulate and Empire: Berthier from 1800 to 1806, and Clarke from 1807 to 1814. Davout's appointment during the Hundred Days was, by definition, brief. The ministry of war administration was given charge of the commissariat service and the organization of military transports and hospitals. It too enjoyed some continuity at the top under the ministers Dejean (1802–9), Lacuée de Cessac (1809–13), whose influence on the formulation of military policy was more than usually important, and finally Daru (1813–14, 1815), who had previously served as intendant-general of the Grand Army as well as of the conquered territories during the formative years of the 'Grand Empire'. In addition, Napoleon could turn for advice, *when* he saw fit to seek it, to a special war section within the council of state. By the end of the Empire, the two ministries had a combined staff of around 1,500, compared with not quite 500 in the old ministry of war before the division of 1802.[3]

From these central controls, the military establishment extended over all the departments of the expanding Empire. Paris itself had a military governor from as early as 1804, the honour falling initially to Marshal Murat, and also formed the base of the large first military division. Farther afield, the official military divisions were placed under the authority of divisional generals, who were assisted by resident commandants and adjutants. Each of these divisions was centred on a major town and, although of variable size and importance, generally covered several adjacent departments. Their number rose to thirty-two at the height of the Empire in 1811, including those in all the directly annexed departments, while the Kingdom of Italy then had six more of its own.[4]

Within that wider administrative structure, the Grand Army could also draw on a number of supplementary services, some of them highly specialized. The Imperial headquarters itself consisted of three divisions: the emperor's personal staff, or *Maison*, whose military functions increased in importance; the general staff of the Grand Army, headed by Berthier; and the staff of the commissary general. The technical improvements introduced after the campaigns of 1805–7 included nine new transport battalions and a whole network of staging posts. Military training itself owed something to major innovations during the Revolution. The École Polytechnique dated from 1795 and, in its reconstituted form under Napoleon, continued to play a crucial role in the instruction of artillery officers and engineers. The school of Saint-Germain, among other Napoleonic foundations, fulfilled a similar function for the cavalry. A new École Spéciale Militaire was founded for cadets at Fontainebleau in January 1803, before being transferred to Saint-Cyr in 1808, and by the end of the Empire had trained some 4,000 officers.

The criteria which Napoleon applied in his choice of officers for the Grand Army has for long been a controversial subject among historians. How far, for instance, did he actually follow 'meritocratic' principles, or the strict rule of 'careers open to talents', in his military appointments and promotions? How far, on the other hand, did he allow his professional selection to be influenced by more obviously social considerations? These questions have a significant bearing on his whole concept of leadership, of 'honour', and even of 'notability' in a wider social sense. The system he had inherited from the Revolution represented an often uneasy mixture of the rapid advancement of precocious talent, helped by timely patronage, to which his own earlier military career was the most spectacular testimony, and the more routine criterion of seniority of service. We may discount the elective principle altogether, since it had virtually disappeared before Brumaire, and there was no prospect of its revival after the coup.

In fact, Napoleon quickly established a monopoly over the promotion of all his superior officers – generals and *corps* leaders most notably – and went some way to doing so over the lesser ranks as well. In 1805, while he allowed the commanding colonels to propose two-thirds of the nominees to company-grade rank, subject of course to his own approval, he kept the selection of the remaining third entirely to himself. And here, as in his civil appointments, rapid leap-frogging up the ranks was certainly not normal. There were some conspicuous exceptions among the divisional generals and the very much more exclusive group of marshals (four with honorary status and fourteen on the active list) named on 19 May 1804 at the Empire's inauguration. Cases of favouritism within his own clan, or of nepotism on behalf of the families of certain ministers and senators for example, could also be cited. But otherwise, the established criteria which chiefly governed officer promotions were length of previous service in the army, the period of service in existing ranks, and evidence of bravery. As Jean-Paul Bertaud has shown in his sample analysis of 480 company-grade officers (captains, lieutenants, and sub-lieutenants) who served at some time between 1800 and 1814, Napoleon believed that military 'talent' was to be found predominantly 'among the higher ranks of society – those who, thanks to their birth or fortune, were fit to give or receive schooling'.[5]

Indeed, one might well ask to what extent such professional and social criteria themselves defined the essential ethic of martial valour propagated during the Empire, and how it differed from that of the Revolutionary Republic before it. This was one of the issues raised in a lively debate between John A. Lynn and Owen Connelly, which seems alas to have petered out after its first promising salvoes a few years ago.[6] Lynn, in his main article, argues that the motivation of the French armies underwent an important 'moral evolution' from the old regime to the wars of the Revolution, and then to those of the Empire. The Revolution had upheld the ideal of an 'Army of Virtue', especially during the years 1791–94, in which personal interests were subsumed and if necessary sacrificed in a higher patriotic cause. Some elements of that republican ethic continued during the subsequent years, in spite of growing distortions during the Directory. Under Napoleon, however, it was wholly eroded and superseded by the concept of an 'Army of Honour', a more obviously personalized heroic standard, which offered *associated* glory and personal rewards within his increasingly monarchical code of values. Connelly, in his critique, makes the obvious objection that we have no agreed or hard-and-fast definition of 'Virtue' with which to sanify the armies of the Revolution. So, too, 'Honour' (in the abstract sense of a martial ethic) was not necessarily incompatible with the various titular and pecuniary 'honours' by which Napoleon lavishly rewarded his faithful officers and satisfied their personal military ambitions. Many of his lesser officers and very many more of his rank and file fought and died virtuously for the former ethic, without any prospect of the latter rewards.

Now, we need not doubt that the ideologues of the Jacobin Republic had indeed propagated an abstract code of public 'Virtue', at once civic and martial, and had justified both political purges at home and military conquests abroad in terms of it. But the assumption that the Republican armies were motivated primarily by such moral and public-spirited principles seems questionable on several grounds. Stoic sacrifice in defence of the home citadel was one thing; massive predatory armies on the warpath in conquered territories was quite another. Their sheer size alone ensured that they could not be armies of liberation for many of the subject peoples in the strategic areas of Belgium and the Rhenish left bank. The evidence points to widespread despoliation, including a good many cases of blatant looting for personal gain, in those lands. As T.C.W. Blanning has nicely put it in his detailed study of the French conquest of the Rhineland, 'the Kantians had expected Socrates; what they got was more like Glaucon'.[7] The reality of 'virtuous' conquest – 'war on the châteaux, peace to the cottages', as earlier Girondin rhetoric naïvely declared – had turned out rather differently. It had been bluntly spelt out by the Directory in its instructions to Commissar Joubert in January 1796: 'the principle which contains everything there is to be said on the subject of the occupied territories is: *above all else the army must live*.[8]

It would perhaps be more appropriate to ask what the officers of the Republican and those of the Napoleonic armies had *in common*. First of all, they shared the natural instincts of careerism, and this theme of continuity across the Brumairean divide was as pronounced among the military as among the civil élites. Secondly, they had to face the chronic problem of military defaulters with little obvious sense of 'Virtue' or 'Honour' among their rank and file, as we shall see shortly. And thirdly, they had orders to apply a consistent policy of 'living off the land' in the annexed or occupied territories, on the pretext that the warriors of liberation might be justly 'nourished by the fruits of their victories'. Having inherited that policy, Napoleon systematized it on a much greater scale. In this respect, there seems little material difference between Commissar Joubert's orders of 1796 and those which Napoleon himself gave to his officers for the exploitation of resources in the subject states of the 'Grand Empire'. The exactions of François Roullet de la Bouillerie, the receiver-general of the Grand Army, who was also appointed treasurer-general of the *Domaine extraordinaire* after its creation early in 1810, were typical of the way in which revenues and provisions were siphoned off for Napoleon's use beyond the Imperial frontiers.

As for the rank and file, it would be difficult to establish any overriding moral motivation among the vast mass of the conscripts. The National Convention's decree of the *amalgame* of 21 February 1793 had united the regulars and the volunteers into a single uniform army of the line. The emergency *levée en masse* of 23 August 1793 had raised armies totalling some 800,000 at their height early in 1794, and at that time they were drawn largely from the territory of 'old France'; but such numbers could not be maintained indefinitely. The basis of Napoleon's military recruitment in fact owed much more to the Jourdan–Delbrel Law of 5 September 1798, which had established conscription as a regular means of making up shortfalls on volunteering. Under its terms, during times of national emergency all Frenchmen were potentially liable to military service for an unlimited period. At other times, volunteers aged between eighteen and thirty were to be enlisted for an initial period of four years, which was then renewable for a further two. All other Frenchmen who had reached the age of twenty became eligible for conscription until the age of twenty-five, and for this purpose were to be divided into five 'classes'. While Napoleon changed several of the technical details of this law during the years from Brumaire to 1811, when the military regulations of the Empire were more comprehensively codified, he kept its basic provisions. These included both the *de facto* exemptions granted to certain categories of married men and to widowed or divorced breadwinners with dependent children, whose immunity was formally legalized in September 1808, and the practices of 'substitution' and 'replacement' allowed to others who could afford the going price, which itself increased appreciably over the period.

It was entirely characteristic of Napoleon's authoritarian system that the technical mechanisms for raising and voting the annual quotas were brought increasingly under centralized controls. At first, the mayors and their municipal councils played their part alongside the superior departmental authorities, but by all accounts not very effectively. Before long, Napoleon had turned yet again to his prefects to remedy the situation, and after the law of 6 August 1802 they were assisted by the recruitment councils then created. The canton now became the larger unit used for raising the contingents. The recruitment councils, which consisted of the prefect, the military commander of the department, and a recruiting officer, had charge over the drawing of lots and the mobilization of the ensuing draft. Their very composition ensured a decisive shift from what Isser Woloch calls 'localism' to a more 'routinized, bureaucratic conscription'.[9] On 24 September 1805 the formal power of voting the annual contingent and fixing its departmental quotas was transferred from the legislative body to the senate.

The result, according to the best recent estimates, was that the draft raised an annual average of some 73,000 recruits between 1800 and 1810, and that as from 1805 the standing army usually numbered between 500,000 and 600,000, on paper at least.[10] Such figures, moreover, included the quotas raised in the non-French departments under direct annexation, which varied over the whole period from a quarter to a third of the total, compared with the corresponding one-third to two-fifths drawn from 'old France'. Auxiliaries from the subject and allied states of Germany, Italy, Holland (itself directly annexed in 1810, as we have seen), and Poland collectively accounted for most of the rest. The Rhenish Confederation, for example, had undertaken to provide 63,000 troops in the event of war, of which the Bavarian share alone was 30,000. After 1807 the duchy of Warsaw also raised significant contingents, keeping alive the earlier tradition of the Polish legions serving in the French Republican armies. Their particular contribution is best remembered for the heroic exploits of Prince Joseph Poniatowski, whom Napoleon appointed as a marshal of France (the only foreigner so honoured) two days before his death in the battle of Leipzig on 18 October 1813. In this way the whole burden of mobilizing manpower for the Napoleonic armies was spread over a much wider arc than had been the case during the 1790s. Of the Grand Army raised for the Russian campaign in 1812, whose numbers barely exceeded 611,000, the strictly French contingents probably made up a third. Only in the last desperate campaigns of 1813–14, when the levies extended to many unseasoned recruits, naval ratings, 'Guards of Honour', and National Guardsmen, did the total muster rise to a million.[11]

Like all other European armies of its time, the Grand Army suffered from a chronic problem of desertion and draft evasion, which is itself an interesting comment on the heroic ethic under the Eagle standards. Georges Lefebvre's view that the number of military defaulters became serious really only as from 1812 has not stood up to more recent research, and must now certainly be discounted.[12] In an exploratory article published thirty years ago, Eric A. Arnold, Jr, showed on the contrary that the twin problems of desertion and draft evasion were already causing major concern during the period from December 1804 to July 1806, even when Napoleon's popularity was riding high on the strength of his famous victories at Ulm and Austerlitz. As the minister Fouché himself noted in his police bulletins of the time, the number of defaulters in the eight departments most affected (the Ariège, Haute-Garonne, Basses-Pyrénées, Haute-Vienne, Ardèche, Gironde, Landes, and Deux-Sèvres) amounted to roughly half their combined quota for the year 1806.[13]

More recent research has shed new light on the nature of this problem, on its regional variations and chronological fluctuations, and on how the army sought to deal with it. Isser Woloch, for instance, in the article cited earlier, remarks that 'conscription overshadowed every problem of administration in Napoleonic France' and highlights it as 'the battleground, the ultimate contest of wills between individuals and local communities on the one hand and a distant impersonal state on the other'.[14] As such, it was a 'battleground' which originated – often literally – in the home, and which seriously troubled many areas *within* the Imperial frontiers, as eligible young men sought exemption from military service, while others who were called up either refused to report for duty or deserted from the ranks. For those who were able to take advantage of the regulations governing 'substitution' and 'replacement', however reluctantly conceded by the military authorities at different times, especially by the definitive law on 'replacement' of 26 August 1806, the cost was mainly financial. In the national levies which followed between 1806 and 1810, the proportion of 'replacements', excluding the apparently less controversial 'substitutions', was 4.5 per cent (some 25,000 conscripts out of a total of 556,000), a much lower figure than in 1800. And 'replacement' itself, as Woloch also shows, was by no means confined to professional trainees or well-to-do *notables*.[15] But for those actually called up, desertion or draft evasion incurred much harsher penalties, such as summary fines on the families concerned, the billeting of troops in their homes, and the exposure of the culprits themselves to physical punishment by the mobile columns of soldiers sent out to hunt and arrest them.

Some general features of desertion and draft evasion seem now to be well established. The problem, as Alan Forrest for instance has shown in a detailed work covering both the Revolutionary and Napoleonic years, was most acute in the infantry units, could be troublesome in those of the artillery, but was comparatively slight in the more élite cavalry regiments.[16] It was often influenced by short-term factors like the harvest season, when young peasants had a particular wish to be with their families. Draft evasion was more likely to occur in mountainous, forested, or marshy areas which provided some natural cover for the *réfractaires* or *insoumis*, as such defaulters were variously branded by the authorities. Here, they would often have the advantage of local knowledge, as well as refuge and succour from their communities, whose solidarity in this as in other adversities was often tenaciously defiant. Similarly, as Forrest again observes, the wider regional variations of both draft evasion and desertion followed a fairly consistent pattern in France. Their incidence was highest in the western provinces (scene of the old *Chouannerie*), in those of the Massif Central, in the departments of the north close to the Belgian frontier, and in the south-west generally, especially Aquitaine. 'In stark contrast, the plains of the East and the Paris region were models of obedience and patriotic devotion.'[17]

The great irony, as Woloch and Forrest agree, is that the Napoleonic state eventually won its long battle to enforce conscription in the years immediately preceding its final collapse. Where earlier punitive methods or more conciliatory gestures like amnesties had proved insufficient, the rigours of the mobile columns then began to have a very marked effect on draft evasion. Indeed, whereas desertion continued to worry the military authorities, and actually increased in 1810–11, draft evasion was drastically reduced around that time, and had in fact already been declining for several years.[18] This itself helps to explain how Napoleon's massive levies in the closing years of the Empire proved more effective, in quantitative terms, than most of the earlier ones. Woloch describes the year 1811 as 'the *annus mirabilis* of conscription' and speaks of 'three bumper crops of conscripts in a row', that is for the years 1811, 1812, and 1813, which offset the continuing plague of desertions.[19] But then catastrophe followed. The emergency call for 300,000 men in November 1813 ultimately met with a different response, and as military defeats in the battle of France took their toll, the whole system of conscription steadily fell apart.[20]

If one takes a global view of military recruitment and of desertion and draft evasion under Napoleon, some approximate statistical conclusions at least now seem permissible. According to Arnold, a figure of 2.6 million men is a reasonable estimate of the total number officially drafted for the French armies during the wars of the Consulate and Empire.[21] This, in Gunther Rothenberg's estimation, represented less than 7 per cent of the total population of 'old France', a figure further reduced if the high number of defaulters is also taken into account.[22] As for the latter, it is of course impossible to state exactly what the total number of deserters and draft evaders over the whole period amounted to. Yet Arnold, again, suggests that the cumulative figure may have reached half a million men between 1800 and 1815, which would have been equivalent to almost a fifth of the total numbers officially mobilized during those years.[23] This would seem broadly in line with a contemporary estimate by Hargenvilliers, who managed a special section of the ministry of war during the years 1798–1814. In 1808 he reckoned that the total number of deserters from the successive drafts between the Year VII (in effect the inception of the Jourdan–Delbrel Law) and 1806, and who had still not been captured, was upwards of 250,000.[24] Finally, if the burden of official conscription is measured specifically as a percentage of the eligible male population itself, some available estimates are hugely discrepant. At the lower end, for example, Lefebvre's earlier evidence suggests that not much more than two-fifths (41 per cent) of the eligible total were actually called up, even under the big levies of 1812 and 1813.[25] Forrest, by contrast, in his much fuller and more recent account, claims that 'by 1812 nearly 80 percent of young Frenchmen of conscription age were being trawled into the military'.[26]

'A man like me has little regard for the deaths of a million men,' Napoleon is claimed to have said in a letter to Metternich of 1813.[27] In expressing this chilling testament, he could surely not have known how close the brutal truth came to matching his casual arithmetic. While estimates of the total war losses suffered by the French armies have varied considerably, a consensus now seems to have formed behind the detailed research and statistical conclusions of Jacques Houdaille. According to his revised estimates, the 89 departments which remained French at the final peace settlement of 1815 lost a combined total of about 1.4 million men in the land armies alone during the whole course of the wars from 1792 to 1814, something under 500,000 in the Revolutionary wars, and around 916,000 in those of the Empire.[28] These figures include the men killed in action, the much higher numbers who later died of their wounds or from illness, exhaustion, or exposure to the cold, and all prisoners of war not later accounted for. No one has ever been able to establish how many others were permanently invalided. The Russian campaign of 1812 was of course notoriously lethal. Earlier estimates of well over 400,000 casualties have since been revised, and Jean Tulard puts the total losses then suffered by the French and their allies through death, imprisonment by the enemy, and desertion at around 380,000.[29] Cumulative French losses in the Peninsular War of 1807–13, 'the Spanish ulcer' as Napoleon once called it, may have totalled 300,000.[30]

It is fair to conclude that while human losses even on such

a scale may not have reduced the literal *quantity* of troops Napoleon could draft in his expanded Empire, they had a devastating effect on the *quality* of his levies for the campaigns of 1813–14. All these stark facts, the dark side of the coin of glory, need to be remembered when his heroic military achievements are finally judged. As an instrument of conquest, the Grand Army was conspicuous not least for its sacrificial ethic. It is another great irony that this itself was to add an evocative pathos to the appeal of the Napoleonic legend after 1815.

. . . .

THE CONTINENTAL BLOCKADE

From one angle, Napoleon's intensification of the economic war on Britain can be seen as a pragmatic extension of his strengthened military position in northern Europe, whose aims were specific to their immediate context late in 1806. Yet from another, it seems more like the climacteric of a much longer Anglo-French maritime conflict. That too was part of Napoleon's inheritance from the Revolution, and it limited his options from the moment hostilities were resumed after the Peace of Amiens (March 1802–May 1803). The territorial expansion of France during the Revolutionary wars had been propelled essentially by a continental dynamic, but the same process also disguised a progressive loss of her power at sea. The difficulties of sustaining far-flung naval operations had been apparent to Napoleon from the start of his rule, when his Egyptian campaign had foundered under the counter-attack of the British navy. The irony is that his spectacular military victories of 1805–7 coincided with a steady reduction of French naval strength, especially after the decisive British victory at Trafalgar on 21 October 1805, against which Decrès, his long-serving minister of the marine (1801–14), had no effective answer.

During the years immediately preceding the Revolution, colonial re-exports had made up nearly a third of the total exports of France, and a fifth to a quarter of her industrial production had then been exported to the Antilles and the Spanish colonies. She had lost many of these valuable colonial markets and sources of supply since the start of the maritime wars in 1793, and this had exacerbated the earlier disruption caused to her overseas trade by the slave revolt of 1791 on Santo Domingo, much her most important sugar island. France's slave trade itself, a lucrative branch during most of the eighteenth century, had also been adversely affected, not least because of persistent naval interceptions by the British. The direct impact on Atlantic ports like Bordeaux and Nantes, once so prosperous, had been serious. To add to the dislocation, many traditional industries and services in the dependent hinterlands of the maritime ports, such as shipbuilding, the manufacture of sailcloth and rope, sugar refining, and tobacco processing, had spread the creeping depression further inland. In all, the long-term effects of naval eclipse had taken a heavy toll on the commercial and industrial sectors of the French economy by the end of the Revolutionary wars.[31]

By the terms of the Treaty of Amiens France recovered her colonies, but the peace was too short-lived to have much commercial effect. After its rupture, the country's colonial losses again multiplied, its trans-Atlantic trade was exposed to the stranglehold of the British naval blockades, and its Mediterranean traffic, most notably that of Marseilles with the Levant, was slowly slipping into its time of troubles. After the abandonment of his project for a descent on England in 1805, a year of disaster for the French fleet, Napoleon saw the harsh reality of his position. He had to concentrate on continental conquest and, for the time being at least, allow the British their apparent mastery at sea. A year later, however, having defeated the Austrians and Russians at Ulm and Austerlitz, and the Prussians at Jena and Auerstädt, he formulated a different policy based on an idea which was not in fact original. Since he could not strike at Britain directly on the seas, and was thus evidently powerless to resist her expansion into global markets, he might yet bring her down by the indirect means of blockade from the Continent. The aim, as he confidently boasted, was 'to conquer the sea by mastery of the land'.

Napoleon's own economic ideas were naïve, and have sometimes been described as a crude form of 'neo-mercantilism'. He seems to have formed an early idea that Britain's commercial wealth was fundamentally fragile, and that the 'nation of shopkeepers' could be quarantined from the European mainland and left to stew in their own juice. He did not understand the mechanisms of international markets, banking, or credit finance, and he evidently thought that Britain's paper pound would go the way of the *assignats*. As for his own subjects, he knew that home manufacturers would welcome protection against foreign competition, and was usually willing to oblige them. It seemed to him a natural extension of clannish interests to, as it were, the 'national' family. But he was much less sympathetic to merchants who wanted to trade freely across frontiers, denouncing them more than once as a selfish breed 'without honour or fatherland'.

Above all, Napoleon believed that French economic life could be regulated by central controls, like any other branch of his administration, and that manufacturers and merchants could be made to obey his orders. He made this abundantly clear in his treatment of the advisory chambers of commerce which were established in twenty-two towns, following the Consular *arrêté* of 24 December 1802, and of the consultative chambers for manufacture, arts and crafts similarly decreed on 12 April and 29 July 1803. He was responsive to the notion of the French 'industrial soldier' fighting British competitors, and as Metternich observed in January 1808, he thought of the French corsairs as 'military merchants' whose vessels were 'nobler shops than those of peaceable citizens'.[32] Or again, as one of his ministers, Chaptal, later described Napoleon's attitude to French trade, 'he claimed to be able to manoeuvre it like a batallion and from it demanded a submission every bit as passive'.[33] In effect, the logic of his industrial and commercial reasoning was military, not economic.

It therefore fell to others to formulate the more refined economic rationale of Napoleon's project for a 'Continental Blockade' or 'Continental System', as it has been variously called. In fact, that process had been under way at least since 1805, and among those who seem to have had a particular influence on it was one of Napoleon's economic advisers, Montgaillard, to whom the first use of the terms '*système continental*' and '*blocus continental*' are usually attributed. The policy, thus conceived, reasserted all the prohibitions enacted against British trade under the Directory, and indeed under the late Consulate and early Empire, but now extended them over all the lands which had been and were still to be subjected to Napoleonic rule. The nub of the argument was that if Britain could not literally be boxed in by sea, she must be shut out by land from all areas over which the French had a continental hegemony. If she were denied traditional outlets for her manufactured goods and colonial re-exports on the European mainland, her industries and foreign trade would soon suffer from excess. And if at the same time she was forced to pay for her essential imports from Europe in specie, the drain on her bullion reserves would undermine her currency, reduce her capacity to finance foreign coalitions against France, cause social unrest, and eventually force her to sue for peace. In other words, what Napoleon and his advisers were now formulating was not a blockade, in the normal sense, but really a *self*-blockade or a *boycott* of British trade.

The official proclamation of the Continental Blockade came with the Berlin decree of 21 November 1806. It declared that the British Isles were in a state of blockade and forbade all communications with them. All seizure of British ships and goods was sanctioned as lawful prize, and all British subjects found in areas controlled by French troops or their allies would be treated as prisoners of war. Besides his conquest of Prussia, which completed a vital military prerequisite for the application of this policy in northern Europe, Napoleon also claimed to have a legitimate pretext for his action. The British order in council of 16 May 1806 had declared a naval blockade along the French coast, and Napoleon made much of this perceived outrage in the first part of his Berlin decree. The British response was predictable. New orders in council of January and November 1807 toughened and extended the terms of the naval blockade, and at the same time obliged neutral ships to call at a British port, have their cargoes inspected, pay duties, and apply for special licences to trade with enemy ports. Napoleon, by his Milan decrees of 23 November and 17 December that same year, in turn extended the terms of the Berlin decree to all neutral ships complying with such orders, which was in effect to assimilate them to British shipping.

From the winter of 1806–7 onwards, then, the whole process of Napoleon's empire-building assumed a new economic significance. It goes without saying that the Continental Blockade was officially proclaimed at different times in all the departments which had been directly annexed to the Empire by January 1811. Acceptance of its terms became a necessary function of Napoleon's treatment of all the subject states as well. The Blockade was thus formally extended to Italy, Switzerland, the Rhenish Confederation, and Holland during the course of 1807, then to the Iberian peninsula in 1808 and to the 'Illyrian Provinces of the Empire' late in 1809. When he was in a position to do so, Napoleon also put pressure on his allied states – Russia at

Tilsit in 1807, and Austria after its acceptance of his marriage alliance early in 1810 – to enforce his decrees against British trade in the same way. Another of his allies, Frederick VI of Denmark, who had given up hope of preserving the precarious neutrality of his kingdom and finally opted for the French side in September 1807, suffered an immediate and violent retribution, when the British fleet bombarded Copenhagen that same month. Some earlier writers have even argued that at least two of Napoleon's own military campaigns, the invasions of Spain in 1808 and of Russia in 1812, were themselves largely inspired by the economic motive of forcing reluctant peoples to apply his Blockade more rigorously.

So far, then, Napoleon's Continental Blockade could be considered as an aggressive policy whose aim was to destroy the economic power of his most elusive enemy. If its military emphasis also seems predominant here, this aspect was visibly reinforced by his stationing of Imperial troops with surveillance duties alongside the customs officials, the notoriously unpopular *douaniers*, in a number of major ports, more especially along the North Sea coast. And yet, the whole project of the Blockade was never confined to such destructive aims alone. However fancifully, Napoleon and his economic advisers were also set on the more constructive aim of harnessing the markets of the Continental mainland for Imperial industry and trade. Their optimistic assumption was that the elimination of British competition would encourage home manufacturers and merchants to fill the vacuum, if necessary by preferential trade deals with the subject and allied states. They envisaged a whole network of economic dependencies which could be geared to the interests of the Empire, and which would compensate in some way for the resources it had lost at sea. In an earlier and more detailed work on the subject, I have likened this aim to a 'French Continental market design' and argued that it was an integral part of Napoleon's Blockade policy, particularly in the inland areas. However, since the French design fell far short of a genuine free trade zone across the whole of Napoleonic Europe, and never in fact allowed commercial reciprocity to the subject and allied states, I have similarly likened it to an 'Uncommon Market', which ultimately failed precisely because it was too one-sided.[34] Napoleon's 'principle', as he put it in a letter to Eugène de Beauharnais of 23 August 1810, was 'France first' (*la France avant tout*).[35]

105

As the implementation of the Continental Blockade was extended and met widespread resistance, in the Empire as well as foreign states, so its terms were significantly modified. When the merchants of the Bordelais complained of glutted stocks of wine and spirits, Napoleon allowed them special 'licences' for trade with Britain, a major client of long standing, from a relatively early stage of the Blockade. Realizing the fiscal value of such concessions, he extended them to other commodities and then regularized the system of 'licences' by his Saint-Cloud decree of 3 July 1810. When the harvest in Britain proved deficient that year, he was again prepared to allow generous 'licences' for grain shipments to the enemy from surplus stocks in the west country of France. The whole purpose of the Blockade, he then argued, was to strike at Britain's *exports*, and to encourage her to import in exchange for bullion. Whether his reasoning was disingenuous, or simply mistaken, the evidence suggests that British agents did not actually pay for the French grain shipments exclusively in specie.

Moreover, by the Trianon tariffs of 5 August and 17 September 1810, Napoleon further increased the range of colonial goods (treated formerly as contraband) whose import into the Empire he now declared permissible, but at the same time subjected them to exorbitant duties. His fiscal motives again seem only too apparent. By contrast, he took a much tougher stand against British manufactured goods. The Fontainebleau decree of 18 October 1810 strengthened the whole apparatus of customs surveillance along the North Sea and Baltic coasts, especially at the traditional British inlet of Hamburg on the river Elbe, where a special commission was set up to confiscate the offending goods. For the next two years the seizures multiplied, provoking angry protests from the native merchants, and this episode is often referred to as the 'customs terror'.

In assessing the effects of the Blockade on Britain, in the French Empire, and on the Continent more generally, we should then take its dual purpose and its rather ambivalent implementation into account. In its more aggressive guise as a 'war-machine', it also revealed the limitations of Napoleon's land-locked power. It manifestly did not destroy Britain's industrial and commercial economy or force her to sue for peace. It certainly had some impact on her exports during the first half of 1808 and again from the autumn of 1810 to the summer of 1812, when comparatively tight customs surveillance on the

Continent was further complicated by a rupture in Anglo-American relations, which denied her valuable outlets across the Atlantic just when they were most needed. The pressure was most acute in 1810–11, when crisis overtook the British economy, although for reasons which were not always directly linked with the Blockade. But for most of the period 1806–13 during which the Blockade was officially in force, British manufacturers and merchants either succeeded in smuggling their goods into Continental Europe, using a whole relay of bases to evade the *douaniers,* or else managed to find alternative markets outside Europe, again chiefly in the Americas.

As a result, Britain's ability to finance foreign coalitions against France was not noticeably reduced. Indeed, out of a total of nearly £66 million paid to her various allies between 1793 and 1815, almost half was spent during the last five years of the period, that is mainly *after* the Blockade was supposed to have taken its toll on such resources. In addition, it cost her nearly £80 million, much of it in specie, to support Wellington's army in the Peninsula and elsewhere during the years 1808–16.[36] In spite of recurrent upsets, her financial structures were fundamentally strong enough to meet the burden of that prolonged conflict. By the end of the Napoleonic wars, Britain's superiority over France as a commercial and industrial power, as a technological innovator, and as an international banker to the wider world was greater than it had been in 1793, and it was long to remain so.[37]

Ironically, Napoleon's 'war-machine' probably had a more destructive effect on Imperial resources in the long term. Insofar as he was lured into Spain and Russia in order to enforce the Blockade more rigorously, it contributed to a draining process which saddled his treasury with growing deficits and ultimately weakened his ability to defend the Empire from military collapse. Furthermore, the Blockade prompted contraband and fraudulent traffic wherever it was officially in force, not least along the inland frontiers of the Empire. Apart from their moral implications, which many observers at the time regarded as a serious indictment of the system itself, such practices had a damaging effect even on legitimate trade, and customs duties which might otherwise have accrued to the State were lost. As a general rule, whenever Napoleon was on campaign and needed his troops, customs surveillance lapsed and smuggling was rife. This was especially evident during the

Wagram campaign of 1809, when the Dutch were perhaps the principal offenders, a fact which King Louis did not try to hide – 'well then, try to stop the skin from sweating' – and which undoubtedly influenced Napoleon's decision to depose him and annex Holland directly to the Empire in 1810. The problem of smuggling became more or less ubiquitous during the campaigns of 1813. After desertion from or draft evasion in the army, it could be seen as the next most common and destructive form of resistance to Napoleonic rule throughout the Blockade.

All the assumptions Napoleon had made about the efficacy of his regulatory system were thus proved wanting by the hard facts of economic survival and human fallibility. Cases of corruption among the Imperial customs officials, who often complained of inadequate salaries, were numerous and notorious, and some at least involved prominent military officers as well. In the absence of reliable sources, no one has ever been able to estimate the full extent of such shady deals in the 'black economy' generated by the Blockade; but equally, no one has ever doubted that it must have been colossal. Even when the 'customs terror' of 1810–12 in northern Europe imposed much harsher penalties on smugglers, the physical destruction of confiscated goods was often indiscriminate. In his desperate need for money after the disaster in Russia, Napoleon's issue of trade 'licences' became so prolific that the Blockade had in effect been undermined from within even before the Allied advances in Germany and Spain ensured its total collapse during 1813.

As for the French Continental market design, it had little of course to offer the shipping of the maritime ports. The Atlantic seaboard and the Mediterranean coast of France appear to have kept some vital commercial functions going during the first year or more of the Blockade, partly through the coasting trade, but mainly through the life-line of neutral (chiefly American) shipping. The British orders in council and Napoleon's own Milan decrees made this much more hazardous, however, and as a general rule the maritime ports suffered their worst troubles in the years 1808–14.[38] The plight of the dependent industries and services in their hinterlands deepened, although Marseilles at least found some compensation as a commercial nexus in the Rhône corridor and in the manufacture of artificial soda, which enjoyed official support and increasingly fed the local soapworks as from 1809–10. One major victim of the loss of maritime markets was the French linen industry, an archaic branch which continued to decline almost everywhere.

Elsewhere, and in other economic sectors, however, the effects of the Blockade could be agreeably different, as the former sea-borne traffic was diverted towards routes and markets on the European mainland. Paris held its own as a manufacturing centre for fashion ware and luxury goods, made some impressive progress in the production of cottons, and remained much the most important capital market of the Empire.[39] The silk industries of the Lyonnais maintained a reasonable output too, thanks to lavish Court patronage and a particularly valuable export trade to Russia, until Tsar Alexander I decided at the end of 1810 to abandon the Blockade and impose punitive measures against French goods instead. The Belgian industries, textiles and metallurgy alike, generally benefited from access to the large Imperial home market, and on a lesser scale so did those of the annexed Rhenish departments. My own research on Alsace, an eastern frontier province which lay at the hub of the inland entrepôt routes to Switzerland, Germany, and parts farther afield, confirms that it was a major beneficiary of the Blockade's continental thrust. The legitimate Rhine trade of Strasbourg (Bas-Rhin) increased markedly after 1806, doubling and at peak periods possibly even quadrupling its pre-Blockade volume. Some contemporaries claimed that the city then handled as much as a third of the Empire's foreign trade. Similarly, the cotton industries of Mulhouse (Haut-Rhin), particularly printed calicoes, were among the most successful in all France. There were some notable improvements in mechanization, especially in spinning ('mule-jennies'), and these were equally evident in the progress of the cotton industries of the Seine-Inférieure, Eure, and Nord departments. Their effect on the chemical industry, chiefly in the manufacture of artificial dyes and bleaching materials, was also favourable.

All the above might be seen as advances within the 'private' sectors of the Imperial economy. To them one should add the benefits which also accrued in the 'public' sectors, that is in all the industries and services geared for military contracting: armaments, clothing (woollen uniforms more especially), transports, field supplies, and food provisioning most of all. In some areas, including the garrison towns, such military markets actually held the key to economic buoyancy, notwithstanding several upsets due to over-speculation and the army's notorious habit of paying producers late. By contrast, the sailcloth industry generally languished, a victim of the Empire's naval eclipse.

The regional and sectoral variations of the Blockade's kicks and kindnesses are then clear. What of the chronological fluctuations? There is no doubt that the years of relative peace on the Continent between July 1807 and the late summer of 1810, Spain and the Wagram campaign apart, were also the most productive for the cotton enterprises, the Empire's most dynamic industrial sector, which gained most from the official exclusion of competing foreign goods. It was during this period, too, that the French market design made its most significant penetration into Germany, which in turn gave access to the transcontinental trade routes to the Baltic and eastern Europe. While the town fairs of Frankfurt am Main and Leipzig had passed their heyday somewhat earlier, they remained important international markets for a whole range of goods, and Imperial exporters were certainly among the major beneficiaries in the favourable years. The Italian peninsula, which Napoleon was always inclined to think of as an Imperial 'game preserve' (*chasse gardée*), offered not only raw silk for the Lyonnais but concentrated urban markets in the north for French manufactured goods. In fact, the Imperial decrees of 10 June 1806 and 10 October 1810 turned the Kingdom of Italy into something like an official 'reserved market' for French textiles and several other goods. They may have helped Imperial exporters, but they also severed traditional trade links between the kingdom and other countries, such as Switzerland, and at the same time obstructed old commercial exchanges within Italy itself.

It seems equally clear, however, that the favourable cycle was seriously disturbed by the economic crisis of 1810–11, which first hit the larger banking and merchant houses of the Empire, and then spread depression in the manufacturing sectors as well. Although not the direct cause of the crisis, the Blockade policy certainly exacerbated its impact. The main cause of the trouble in France was the knock-on effects of the banking crises in Britain, the Hanse towns, Holland, and Switzerland, which rather suddenly caught up with those who, perhaps anticipating the swingeing duties introduced by the Trianon tariffs, had over-speculated in colonial consumer goods and industrial raw materials during the earlier months of 1810. As the banking and merchant houses called in their existing loans and refused to give new credit, merchants and manufacturers found it increasingly difficult to trade normally. Their real problem during the following winter lay in commercial and industrial glut, in oversupply rather than dearth of goods. Production targets had to be cut, and industrial unemployment rose appreciably. That was the context into which the 'customs terror' was now also injected. The cumulative impact of all those factors ruined many enterprises which lacked adequate capital reserves to ride out the crisis, and prefectoral reports of the time often speak of a 'cascade of bankruptcies'.

What followed the crisis was slow and difficult recovery in the latter half of 1811 and during 1812, but the most productive phase of the French Continental market design had passed. Indeed, the internal contradiction which had characterized Napoleon's economic policy from the time of the Berlin decree, if not earlier, was never more exposed than in the two or three closing years of the Empire. The principle of 'France first' presupposed a growing or at least stable purchasing power among the client states beyond the Imperial frontiers, for how else were they to afford the appreciably higher prices of French goods? But the creeping depression which most of those states experienced as from 1812, most notably in Germany, actually made them poorer rather than richer customers. The depression was most pronounced in agriculture, which was all the more serious for being much the largest economic sector. The French Empire at its height was a huge grain trade zone and usually also a self-sufficient one. It did not need to import foreign surpluses because it was more than likely to have surpluses of its own. As many of the subject states thus found themselves unable to sell grain at a reasonable profit, and since the Blockade at the same time officially prohibited its disposal through British shipping, the purchasing power of their domestic populations gradually fell. And that, in turn, inevitably meant a lower demand for French goods.

For all those reasons, internal and external, the ultimate failure of the French Continental market design is not in doubt. The generally good figures for French exports to Germany and Italy in the years 1806–12, and even to Spain before the Peninsular War, came nowhere near to filling the vacuum left by cumulative maritime losses. The official values of the total foreign trade of France during the last years of the old regime (1787–89) were not again to be attained until about 1826.[40]

Napoleon cannot be blamed directly for those maritime losses, which to a large extent preceded his rule, and which his impotent navy could not recover. He may even be given credit for trying to remedy the damage through his Blockade policy, and for presiding over some significant advances in certain inland regions and in certain economic sectors, like cottons. But the fundamental flaw in his economic policy was its ruthless one-sidedness. The notion of a wider European common market, or *Zollverein*, offended all his basic instincts. If he had offered the subject and allied states genuine reciprocity of trade in the huge Imperial market, in other words if he had given them a real incentive to cut their ties with Britain, who knows how differently it might all have ended?

. . . .

TEMPORAL POWER VERSUS SPIRITUAL AUTHORITY

The extension of Napoleon's temporal power through military conquest, political subjugation, and the pursuit of economic dominance should be clear from the foregoing sections. Yet even before its erosion and eventual collapse, there were clear signs that he was losing another and rather more subtle battle in his dealings with Pope Pius VII. All the hopes which the two men may have had of a lasting reconciliation between Church and State at the time of the Concordat of 1801 and the Imperial coronation of 1804 were painfully dashed in later years. If the 'Grand Empire' was constructed in spite of their worsening rupture, its eventual fall was at least partly due to Napoleon's brutal treatment and alienation of the pope, as the exiled emperor was himself to lament on St Helena. This conflict between temporal power and spiritual authority had so many dramatic turns during the years 1806–14 that it has been likened to some of the celebrated confrontations of medieval times – of the Emperor Henry IV against Gregory VII, or of King Henry II against Thomas Becket. While Napoleon could never conceive of any penitential visit to 'Canossa', even to save his throne, he could not seriously contemplate any murder in the cathedral either. The result was a prolonged psychological deadlock, especially once the pope had excommunicated the emperor and then himself been forced to endure nearly five years of exile from Rome. But still, it was Pius who in the end emerged victorious, his spiritual authority strengthened,

112

notwithstanding his abject humiliation during the preceding years.

It is tempting to recount the conflict in primarily personal terms,[41] but there were also underlying structural reasons for it, some going well back into the old regime, and these need to be clarified first. They stemmed, fundamentally, from Napoleon's own conception of how the Church–State relationship established by the Concordat and the Organic Articles ought to work. Jean Godel, in a brilliantly perceptive digest of his own more detailed research on the concordatory church in the diocese of Grenoble (Isère), identifies three main 'tensions' within that relationship, and explains the paradox of how Napoleon unwittingly undermined his own Church policy.[42] Before the schism of the Revolutionary years, public disputes involving the French Church had usually been between the ultramontane party (who supported the absolute authority of the pope in matters of faith and discipline) and the Jansenists (who by contrast stood up for the old 'Gallican Liberties', and who often had the backing of the *parlements*). It had often been difficult in fact to separate purely canonical issues, such as theological doctrine or the pope's right of investiture, from those which had an obvious extension into temporal affairs, such as papal annates from France or the influence of the Jesuits over education, canon law, and censorship.

Napoleon believed he could harness something useful from both those traditions, selectively it must be said, and on a new basis subject to his own secular authority. On the one hand, if he clearly favoured a reassertion of some gallican precepts, which could be justified as a patriotic defence against papal interference, he was hostile to their earlier association with presbyterian principles as favoured by some Jansenist reformers. Thus, on the other, he strongly upheld the rights of bishops over all the lower clergy, which matched his concept of proper hierarchical authority, but at the same time he was determined to curb any resurgence of old ultramontane loyalties. On a number of occasions he pointedly reminded Pius VII that there were things which should be rendered unto Caesar, and indeed that such obedience to the temporal power was a divine injunction. Pius, for his part, having already accepted the loss of the Church lands in France, sought compensation in a clearer recognition of his canonical authority over the French Church. And so, if the old conflict between episcopalism and presbyterianism

113

was decisively settled in favour of the bishops, that between ultra-montanism and gallicanism soon revived and was to trouble the concordatory church throughout this period. The third of Godel's 'tensions' concerned the different perceptions which the government and the French laity had of the status of the clergy. In short, the Catholic faithful simply refused to regard their priests as mere passive servants of the State. When put to the test in such communities, Napoleon's authoritarian methods could not ride roughshod over a popular religiosity going back many centuries.

It is clear, then, that Napoleon's Church policy was unlikely to proceed smoothly in strict accordance with his own aims. What is more, he had plainly not anticipated some of its more paradoxical effects. For a start, the Concordat, almost by def-inition, could hardly be presented as an agreement between Napoleon and himself. By involving Pius VII as an official party to its original terms, he had ensured from the start that it could not work effectively without the pope's continued approval, and this became increasingly difficult to secure as the heavy-handed logic of the Organic Articles became more pronounced. So, too, Napoleon's insistence on absolute loyalty from all ranks of the clergy presupposed that his temporal power would always be enough to bring the pope to heel. But when Pius refused to be bullied into submission, he inevitably engendered an-other crisis of conscience among the French clergy, which was ultimately resolved in favour of his own spiritual authority. When Napoleon's temporal power itself began to falter in the closing years of the Empire, where else was all that clerical loyalty, all the lessons in subservience and obedience he had tried so hard to drum into the bishops and lower clergy alike, to go – if not to Rome?

If we turn next to the *specific* issues which divided Napoleon and Pius VII during the years following the Imperial corona-tion, it is soon apparent that they were not confined to the working of the Concordat in France alone. Since they involved Napoleon's wider Imperial ambition on the Continent at large, they also necessarily affected the pope's spiritual authority over all European Catholics, and not least his own temporal rights in Italy. While those issues were interrelated and do not fall neatly into chronological patterns, four in particular seem most prominent: the extension of Napoleon's secularizing measures south of the Alps, most notably in the Kingdom of Italy; his military occupation and eventual annexation of the Papal States, which also had a bearing on the application of his Continental Blockade in the Italian peninsula; the quarrel over his divorce of Josephine, which in due course was also to imply a temporary rupture between Pius and the Habsburg emperor; and finally his failed attempt to browbeat the French bishops into defying the pope over disputed investitures.

Among his reasons for travelling to Paris for Napoleon's coronation, Pius VII had hoped that the emperor would mark the occasion by restoring the Legations of Bologna, Ferrara, and Ravenna to Rome. He was to be disappointed, for only a few months later Napoleon declared those lands an integral part of his new Kingdom of Italy. If his reorganization of Church–State relations in the former Republic of Italy had caused Pius serious concern, his more elaborate overhaul of that whole structure in May and June 1805, when he was in Milan to be crowned as King of Italy, was even more alarming to the pope, who had not been consulted on the matter at all. The prospect of a systematic introduction of the French Civil Code, with its provisions for divorce without resort to clerical courts, clearly offended Catholic doctrine on the sanctity of marriage. In the same way, plans to reduce and control the role of the clergy in primary and secondary education in the kingdom, which struck at another traditional Catholic stronghold, seemed no less provocative.

Worse was to follow shortly and, from the pope's point of view, much nearer home. Pius had shown no inclination to support Napoleon's project for an invasion of England from his camp at Boulogne during 1805, nor to drive out British ships from his ports, more especially from Ancona on the Adriatic. During his campaign against Austria that year, Napoleon ordered the seizure of the papal port in October, so as to pre-empt an Austro-British junction higher up the Adriatic coast. The pope's angry reaction and demand that Ancona be restored to him forthwith met with an even fiercer answer from Napoleon, who was now flushed by his decisive victories over the Austrians and Russians at Ulm and Austerlitz. As he wrote to his uncle, Cardinal Fesch, then still his ambassador to Rome, in an accompanying letter of January 1806: 'For the pope's purposes I am Charlemagne. . . . I expect the pope to accommodate his conduct to my requirements. If he behaves well, I shall make no outward changes; if not, I shall reduce him to the status of bishop of Rome.'[43]

In the event, Pius was powerless to stop Napoleon from incorporating the whole of Venetia into his Kingdom of Italy after the Treaty of Pressburg with Austria at the end of 1805, and then from installing his brother Joseph in the newly formed kingdom of Naples in the following March. Ironically, Ancona had actually been a very useful base for this latter operation. With Napoleon now determined to keep it, what hope might Pius have of recovering the more distant Legations? As a mark of his displeasure, the emperor recalled Fesch from Rome in May 1806, appointing the layman Charles Alquier, a former regicide in the National Convention, in his stead. In the following month, the pope reluctantly accepted the resignation of Consalvi, but not before his outgoing secretary of state had assisted him in writing a crucial letter to Napoleon. In it, he explained why his position as Supreme Pontiff to Catholics everywhere, whose wellbeing obliged him to be neutral to all conflicting Powers, would not allow him to turn out foreign nationals from his own lands, or close his ports to their shipping, or support Napoleon's aggressive plans for a new dependent confederation of all Italian states. In short, he would never allow Rome to join any such confederation.

Yet if this was a powerful statement of his spiritual authority, Pius had no physical force with which to resist Napoleon's expanding designs in the peninsula. During the rest of 1806 the other papal ports were occupied by French troops, who also expelled enemy nationals from Rome. Cardinal Maury in effect deserted the pope and was inveigled from his see of Montefiascone into taking up a post at the emperor's side in Paris. When Francis II of Habsburg renounced his title of Holy Roman Emperor in August, Napoleon, the new Charlemagne, no longer had even a symbolical rival south of the Alps. The French bishops, the papal legate Caprara, and Spina (who had once represented the papacy in the negotiations for the Concordat) were now all urging Pius to accept the logic of his position and come to some agreement with Napoleon. But his continuing refusal to do so was announced shortly afterwards, and it was, indeed *could* only be, couched in spiritual terms: 'We are in God's hands; who knows whether the persecution with which His Majesty menaces Us has not been decided by the decrees of Heaven in order to bring about the revival of faith and to reawaken religion in the hearts of Christians?'[44] The result was a progressive rupture in the pope's relations with Napoleon, whose territorial consequences – military occupation (1808) and then formal annexation (1809) of all the remaining Papal States by France – have been noted in the first sub-section of this chapter. During the course of that rupture, and being unable to prevent it, the more pliant Caprara was recalled from Paris in 1808.

Pius VII had one great weapon left: the canonical authority to excommunicate Napoleon. It was a fateful decision from which he had flinched for well over two years, and whose likely effect in Catholic Europe had also persuaded the emperor to delay his formal annexation of the Papal States for much the same time. With their annexation on 17 May 1809, however, Pius had no further need for restraint, and the bull of excommunication was signed and published on the following 11 June. Napoleon, who was then engaged in his Wagram campaign, immediately sent orders (through Murat, king of Naples) for the 'shutting up' of the pope and the arrest of Cardinal Pacca, his secretary of state, who had taken refuge with him in the Quirinal Palace. In the general confusion which ensued, and in a brazen manner which certainly exceeded any specific orders from a superior officer, the young General Radet now carried out his plan to abduct Pius.

The pope's forcible removal from Rome involved a frantic journey in the oppressive heat of July 1809 which not only caused him acute discomfort but also briefly affected his health. He was then sixty-six. As he was transported north, one of Napoleon's sisters, Elisa, grand duchess of Tuscany, was unwilling to allow Pius (whom she now described as 'a very embarrassing present') to stay in Florence. Having been separated from Pacca, his companion for the first stage of the journey, he was moved on to Alessandria under a different escort. There, his presence proved equally embarrassing to Prince Borghese, Pauline Bonaparte's husband and Napoleon's governor general of the departments beyond the Alps. And so the route continued to Grenoble, at which point Napoleon, again victorious after the battle of Wagram earlier that month, was at last able to send his own instructions. At first angered by the abduction, which he declared was in breach of his earlier express orders to Murat, he then commanded the pope's removal from French soil to Savona, near Genoa. Pacca, meanwhile, was imprisoned in the mountain fortress of the Fenestrelle in Savoy.

So began the first exile of Pius VII, which was to last for very nearly three years. At Savona, he was held in the bishop's palace under the close surveillance of General Berthier, Lagorse (the colonel of police), and Chabrol (prefect of the department of Montenotte). Having dispersed the papal curia in Rome and removed the papal archives and secretariat to Paris, Napoleon tried on several occasions to entice the pope there as well, but always received a resolute refusal. Among the issues which attracted major public attention during the closing months of 1809 was Napoleon's divorce. Josephine had been unable to give him the one thing he most needed to secure his dynasty: an heir. For reasons of state, and with sincere personal regrets, he felt obliged to look elsewhere if he was to·perpetuate his line and secure the Imperial succession. The pope's co-operation in granting a divorce would have been enormously helpful to him, but of course it was not forthcoming.

Napoleon and Josephine had first married under the civil law of the Revolutionary Republic in 1796, and that fact was one of the anomalies not specifically confronted at the time of the Concordat. To resolve it, Pius had persuaded them to remarry according to Catholic rites on 1 December 1804, the day before the Imperial coronation. The ceremony had been conducted in secret by Cardinal Fesch, in fact, but he was now claiming that it was invalid, since Napoleon at the time had considered it no more than a symbolical religious formality to please Josephine, and since there had been no other witnesses in any case. The pope altogether rejected such a cynical story; and when Napoleon announced his firm intention to divorce Josephine at the end of November 1809, he knew that he would have to do so without papal blessing. The procedure by which the dissolution of the Imperial marriage was then formally announced on the following 16 December was, yet again, a *senatus-consultum*, and on 14 January 1810 a Church court in Paris (the *Officialité*) confirmed the annulment. Relations between the emperor and the pope were further soured by the affair of the thirteen 'black cardinals'. The latter, having absented themselves from the religious ceremony at which Napoleon and Marie-Louise of Austria were married in Paris on 2 April 1810, were soon afterwards driven out of an Imperial reception at the Tuileries, stripped of their red robes, and then imprisoned. Reacting to their public humiliation, Pius declared that he regarded them as his only true representatives in France.

The impasse persisted for the rest of that year. It was all the more galling to Napoleon since a number of French dioceses had by then fallen vacant, and the pope was of course unwilling to invest any of his new nominees. At first, Napoleon tried to get round the difficulty by proposing that French cathedral chapters might elect his nominees as 'vicars capitular', who although not having the spiritual authority of bishops might yet take effective charge of official episcopal business. It thus appeared that Pius, who found this wholly inadmissible, was to be ignored, and indeed his regime at Savona was now considerably toughened, as his communications with the outside world were steadily cut. Then, in June 1811, Napoleon summoned a national council of French and Italian bishops in Paris to approve another of his plans, that in the event of continued papal refusal, the investiture of new bishops might be conducted by French metropolitans instead. Pius, weakened by a nervous illness, had momentarily seemed to go along with the principle of this proposal in May that year, but had then immediately changed his mind and made his opposition to it plainly known. As a result, the bishops attending the council rejected Napoleon's claim of papal approval, which ill fitted his simultaneous denunciation of the pope's 'indifference to the true interests of religion', and proceeded to swear an oath of 'true obedience to the supreme Roman Pontiff, successor of Saint Peter, prince of the Apostles and Vicar of Jesus Christ'.[45]

In view of its refusal to resolve the investiture question without the pope's prior written consent, Napoleon promptly dissolved the council and even imprisoned some of the dissident bishops as a punishment. Later that year, however, Pius *was* prepared to make an important concession. Having received another and still grander deputation of bishops and 'red' cardinals from the emperor, which arrived in Savona in September, he issued a brief addressed to 'the Bishops of the Empire'. In it, he now accepted the proposal that metropolitans might invest new bishops if the pope had not himself done so six months after their nomination. Napoleon's reaction, conveyed through his minister of cults, was to order the deputation to reject the papal brief out of hand, since Pius was still unwilling to recognize the validity of the council of Paris, and had also remained studiously silent on the status of bishoprics in the Papal States. The emperor evidently believed that the pope was 'ripe' for further, more substantial concessions, and that he could afford to wait and meanwhile ignore his captive in Savona. He was proved disastrously wrong. The vital chance of a compromise had been lost, and the deadlock intensified. In his frustration, Napoleon even made a vain call for the pope's resignation, to make way for someone 'with a stronger head'. In June 1812 Pius was removed to Fontainebleau on the orders of Napoleon, who feared that a British landing off Savona might lead to the kidnapping of his prisoner, while he was himself engaged on the Russian campaign. It was another rushed and excruciating journey, which made the pope so ill that those attending him feared for his life.

The exile of Pius VII at Fontainebleau brought him into more immediate contact with Napoleon, and their personal meeting over six days in January 1813 is well known. No detailed record of it has survived, however, and one cannot say what exactly was then agreed between them. Yet certain points, which emerged only afterwards, do seem clear enough. A confidential document, this time actually signed by Pius under pressure from the emperor, *was* produced on 25 January and news of it, but not its specific terms, published in the *Moniteur* two days later. It is usually referred to as 'the Concordat of Fontainebleau'. Napoleon, in his elation, ordered the release of the 'black cardinals', of the French bishops detained after the council of 1811, and of Cardinal Pacca himself. Pius, for his part, certainly appears to have agreed, as he had in Savona in 1811, that metropolitans might invest new bishops after a delay of six months, if the pope had not done so. But he had never agreed to the establishment of a papacy in Paris or in Avignon, and he had also persuaded Napoleon to give up some other impossible demands and extracted from him significant concessions concerning papal sovereignty in Rome itself.

As things turned out, the new concordat soon became a dead letter. Consalvi (one of the 'black cardinals') and Pacca, after their release, were among those – trusted confidants – who immediately made their way to Fontainebleau. At first, they found Pius dispirited and full of remorse at having signed the concordat. It was not difficult for them to persuade him that he had acted under duress, in a physical condition weakened by long illness, and without his preferred counsellors at hand to advise him. They reinforced his own view that Napoleon had broken the confidentiality of the agreement, such as it was, by announcing its conclusion in an official journal and presenting it to the senate for ratification. In any case, they convinced him, his signature on the document was not irrevocable. And so soon afterwards, having recovered his morale, Pius wrote Napoleon a letter in which he complained that he had been deceived, and formally announced his full retraction. The emperor was too preoccupied with military matters to execute his reported oral threat of guillotining the counsellors who now formed the pope's entourage at Fontainebleau. Confronted yet again by what he saw as the most obstinate and incomprehensible intransigence, he chose simply to ignore the letter of retraction and pretend that the new concordat still prevailed.

It was a vain sham which lasted for almost a year, and Napoleon's worsening military position during the winter of 1813–14 in due course exposed it as such. Outraged by Murat's treacherous deal with the Allies, which promised him territorial gains in the Papal States, Napoleon eventually decided to bring the pope back into play, as a last resort. In January 1814 he wrote to tell Pius that he was intending to restore the Papal States to him, and so to cut Murat's conspiracy short. The pope was unmoved, refusing to enter into a treaty he knew the Allies would not recognize, and Napoleon was left to vent his frustration in more characteristic fashion. That same month he gave orders for Pius to be removed from Fontainebleau – not to Rome, as had been rumoured, but to Savona once more. All the cardinals who had been attending him were again taken into custody.

The pope's journey south proved triumphal, as crowds gathered everywhere to hail him, and this time his captivity in Savona was to be brief. In March 1814, as Paris was on the point of surrendering to the Allies, Napoleon sent orders for him to be taken further down into Italy. By the time he reached Parma, the presence of Austrian troops guaranteed his freedom. On 24 May, after nearly five years of exile, he returned to Rome amidst scenes of popular exultation, his spiritual authority vindicated. His temporal rights, limited though they had been, would also be regained soon enough. Consalvi, now back in office as his secretary of state, was already discussing terms with the Allies for the restitution of all the Papal States to their traditional ruler. The final territorial settlement at the Vienna Congress completed the restoration of Pius VII – even in the long-disputed Legations of Bologna, Ferrara, and Ravenna.

NOTES AND REFERENCES

1.   Stuart Woolf, *Napoleon's Integration of Europe*, London, 1991, p. 11.
2.   Helmut Berding, 'Le Royaume de Westphalie, État-Modèle', *Francia*, vol. 10, 1982, pp. 345–58.
3.   Clive H. Church, *Revolution and Red Tape: The French Ministerial Bureaucracy 1770–1850*, Oxford, 1981, pp. 270, 374.
4.   François de Dainville and Jean Tulard, *Atlas administratif de l'Empire Français d'après l'atlas rédigé par ordre du Duc de Feltre en 1812*, Geneva and Paris, 1973.
5.   Jean-Paul Bertaud, 'Napoleon's Officers', *Past & Present*, no. 112, Aug. 1986, p. 94.
6.   John A. Lynn, 'Toward an Army of Honor: The Moral Evolution of the French Army, 1789–1815', *French Historical Studies*, vol. 16, Spring 1989, pp. 152–73; and see also Owen Connelly's critique of this article and Lynn's response, ibid., pp. 174–82.
7.   T.C.W. Blanning, *The French Revolution in Germany: Occupation and Resistance in the Rhineland 1792–1802*, Oxford, 1983, p. 263.
8.   Quoted in ibid., p. 59.
9.   Isser Woloch, 'Napoleonic Conscription: State Power and Civil Society', *Past & Present*, no. 111, May 1986, pp. 106–7.
10. Owen Connelly, 'Army, French', in Owen Connelly, ed., *Historical Dictionary of Napoleonic France, 1799–1815*, Westport, Conn., 1985, p. 23.
11. Ibid.
12. Georges Lefebvre, *Napoléon*, 5th revised and expanded edn, Paris, 1965, pp. 200–1.
13. Eric A. Arnold, Jr, 'Some Observations on the French Opposition to Napoleonic Conscription, 1804–1806', *French Historical Studies*, vol. 4, Fall 1966, pp. 452–62.
14. Woloch, 'Napoleonic Conscription', p. 101.
15. Ibid., pp. 116–17.
16. Alan Forrest, *Conscripts and Deserters: The Army and French Society during the Revolution and Empire*, New York and Oxford, 1989, pp. 169–70.
17. Ibid., p. 71.
18. Woloch, 'Napoleonic Conscription', pp. 122–3.
19. Ibid., pp. 123, 124.
20. Ibid., pp. 126–7.
21. Eric A. Arnold, Jr, 'Conscription', in Connelly, ed., *Historical Dictionary*, p. 126.
22. Gunther E. Rothenberg, *The Art of Warfare in the Age of Napoleon*, London, 1977, pp. 134–5.

23. Arnold, 'Conscription', p. 127.
24. Forrest, *Conscripts and Deserters*, p. 70.
25. Lefebvre, *Napoléon*, p. 200.
26. Forrest, *Conscripts and Deserters*, p. 169.
27. Quoted in ibid., p. 19.
28. Jacques Houdaille, 'Le problème des pertes de guerre', *Annales historiques de la Révolution française* , vol. 42, 1970, pp. 46–61; and esp. (for his revised estimates) 'Pertes de l'armée de terre sous le premier Empire, d'après les registres matricules', *Population*, vol. 27, 1972, pp. 27–50.
29. Jean Tulard, *Napoleon: The Myth of the Saviour*, Eng. edn, London, 1984, p. 304.
30. Owen Connelly, 'Peninsular War', in Connelly, ed., *Historical Dictionary*, p. 387.
31. François Crouzet, 'Les conséquences économiques de la Révolution: A propos d'un inédit de Sir Francis d'Ivernois', *Annales historiques de la Révolution française*, vol. 34, 1962, pp. 182–217, 336–62; and 'Wars, Blockade, and Economic Change in Europe, 1792–1815', *Journal of Economic History*, vol. 24, 1964, pp. 567–88.
32. Quoted in Marcel Dunan, *Napoléon et l'Allemagne. Le Système continental et les débuts du royaume de Bavière, 1806–1810*, Paris, 1942, p. 311.
33. J.-A.-C. Chaptal, *Mes Souvenirs sur Napoléon*, Paris, 1893, p. 275.
34. Geoffrey Ellis, *Napoleon's Continental Blockade: The Case of Alsace*, Oxford, 1981, esp. ch. 3, 'The French Continental Market Design'; and see also Ellis, *The Napoleonic Empire*, Basingstoke and London, 1991, ch. 6, 'The Imperial Economy'.
35. Napoleon I, *Correspondance de Napoléon Ier publiée par ordre de l'empereur Napoléon III*, 32 vols, Paris, 1858–69, vol. 21, p. 70.
36. John M. Sherwig, *Guineas and Gunpowder: British Foreign Aid in the Wars with France 1793–1815*, Cambridge, Mass., 1969, pp. 345, 355, 365–8.
37. François Crouzet, *De la supériorité de l'Angleterre sur la France. L'Économique et l'Imaginaire XVIIe–XXe siècles*, Paris, 1985.
38. Paul Butel, 'Crise et mutation de l'activité économique à Bordeaux sous le Consulat et l'Empire', *Revue d'Histoire moderne et contemporaine*, vol. 17, 1970, pp. 540–58.
39. Louis Bergeron, *Banquiers, négociants et manufacturiers parisiens du Directoire à l'Empire*, Paris, 1978.
40. Ellis, *Napoleon's Continental Blockade*, pp. 285–9.
41. The personal aspects of that conflict have been admirably recounted in E.E.Y. Hales, *Napoleon and the Pope: The Story of Napoleon and Pius VII*, London, 1962, to which I am much indebted for many of the details of this sub-section.

42. Jean Godel, 'L'Église selon Napoléon', *Revue d'Histoire moderne et contemporaine*, vol. 17, 1970, pp. 837–45; and see also his *La reconstruction concordataire dans le diocèse de Grenoble après la Révolution (1802–1809)*, Grenoble, 1968.

43. Quoted in Hales, *Napoleon and the Pope*, p. 94.

44. Quoted in ibid., p. 98.

45. Quoted in ibid., pp. 159–60.

Chapter 5

THE SOCIAL ACCRETIONS OF POWER:
THE IMPERIAL *NOTABLES,* NOBILITY, AND 'SPOILS SYSTEM'

The central argument of this chapter is that Napoleon progressively pursued what might be called a 'social policy', and that it was intimately linked with his dynastic designs and wider Imperial 'spoils system'. The 'Grand Empire' was to be an essential element of its realization, at once the showpiece of his grandeur abroad and the lubricant of his system of social honours at home. This whole process was gradual and pragmatic rather than preconceived, and its significance cannot be fully understood unless the essential background to Brumaire is taken into account.

Five aspects of the subject are discussed here, and although my approach is again more topical than narrative, it is set out in a broadly chronological sequence. First, we need to consider what the Revolutionary land settlement had implied for the development of French society during the 1790s. That, secondly, has an important bearing on the nature of the official lists of *notables* which began to appear from quite early in the Consulate and later evolved into a much more elaborate system of social honours. Thirdly, within that wider social group, whose very existence Napoleon regarded as a vindication of his policy of *'ralliement'* or 'amalgamation', a more exclusive élite can be clearly identified: the Imperial nobility itself. The material endowment of the latter, in turn, owed much to the 'spoils system' he imposed on the subject states of the 'Grand Empire' during and after his conquests of 1805–7. What part the old nobility played in the public life of his Empire, whether as active functionaries or as more honorific figureheads of social 'amalgamation', forms the last sub-section of the present discussion.

125

. . . .

THE REVOLUTIONARY LAND SETTLEMENT

One factor which perhaps more than any other influenced the course of French social history from the Revolution to the Empire was the sale by successive political regimes of lands confiscated from the Church and the émigrés. Although it was a gradual process conducted over at least a decade, rather than a sudden convulsive shock within the land market, it was evident everywhere, from the largest cities down to the smallest villages. It was a central element of the financial policy of successive Revolutionary assemblies, and it was of course organically linked with the mass of paper money (*assignats*) in circulation until the early months of 1797. It was to have an enduring effect on the nature of French society, not only during the Napoleonic period, but throughout the nineteenth century and indeed up to the present day. Marcel Marion did not hesitate to describe it as a 'land revolution' (*cette révolution foncière*) in his 'classic' pioneering study of the question early this century. He was equally clear that those who bought the national lands (*acquéreurs des biens nationaux*) collectively formed the largest category of beneficiaries from the Revolution, who took full advantage of the generally favourable terms of sale, and conversely that the State seriously undermined its own finances by disposing of valuable assets at far less than their nominal value.[1]

The process started early with the nationalization of all Church property and the royal domains, the so-called 'lands of first origin', on 2 November 1789. Their sale began during the course of the following year, and it is now widely accepted that most of their richest prizes (urban tenements, fertile agrarian land, and major vineyards) were bought up within two to three years. Attention therefore turned to the lands of the French émigrés, and in 1792 these were first sequestrated (9 February) and then confiscated outright (27 July) by the State. They became known as the 'lands of second origin', although their widespread sale appears to have begun only towards the end of 1793, when their stock was increased by additional confiscations from political suspects and condemned persons. The best recent estimates by Florin Aftalion suggest that the combined capital value of both those categories of confiscated property amounted

126

to some 4,000 million livres, assessed in the pre-inflationary currency of 1790, or roughly equivalent to a fifth of the total capital value of all French land at that time. By 1797, however, the public treasury had received payments of perhaps no more than 1,000 million francs in *real* terms, and there had also been innumerable frauds.[2]

The social origins of those who chiefly benefited from the land sales are now well established. Any suggestion that the sales marked the democratization of French landownership can be ruled out at once. As a general rule, the main beneficiaries were men who had already established their position as town and/or country proprietors of some substance. Most were better-off peasants, who individually tended to buy on a relatively small scale, often converting the usufruct of holdings they had actually been working for many years into full legal title, and of course the wealthy bourgeoisie, the largest and most conspicuous individual buyers almost everywhere. In the latter group at least, which itself included professional administrators and men of the legal profession alongside contractors, merchants, and manufacturers ready to swim with the tide and serve the Revolutionary governments, the main purpose of such acquisitions was by no means always economic. In many cases, their primary concern was to enhance their social status, often through the purchase of prestigious town houses (private *hôtels*) or country estates. They were anxious to safeguard their earlier material gains under Napoleon's regime, and in return were willing to be counted among his '*ralliés*', for official purposes at any rate.

Others again, like those of the mercantile oligarchy of the western seaboard, whose former prosperity was grievously affected by French colonial losses and the British naval blockades during the maritime wars, tried to save what they could of their 'liquid' capital by investing in land. But even such transactions, which have sometimes been described as a form of 'fugitive capitalism', could not arrest the slow decline of many of the older commercial houses concerned. Numerous individual illustrations of such survival or decline can be found at Bordeaux and Nantes, which had been the most prosperous ports of the Atlantic coastline during the eighteenth century.[3] In striking contrast, the Revolutionary land sales created a bonanza market for a newer breed of entrepreneurs, speculators, and government contractors alike, risen parvenus who were eager to improve their social standing by astute investment in national lands. Their type is well represented by the likes of Père Grandet, du Bousquier, Malin, Sauviat, Descoings, Bontems, and Rigou, among several others, all fictional characters in the novels of Balzac's *Comédie humaine* during the July Monarchy. The real, historical characters who inspired them had ingratiated themselves into the social élites of post-Revolutionary France, and indeed been recognized as such in the official lists of *notables*, long since.[4]

The crucial point, as already explained in chapter 3, is that Napoleon not only accepted the Revolutionary land sales but granted their new owners full legal title. In the Concordat of 1801 Pius VII formally recognized the loss of all alienated Church property in the enlarged French Republic, once and for all, and neither pressed for nor received any financial compensation. The new legal title of all alienated émigré property was similarly guaranteed by the Civil Code of 1804. In this respect, the terms of the Code were actually only a detailed reaffirmation of measures passed some years before. It is true, of course, that Napoleon had made gestures of goodwill to the returning émigrés early in the Consulate in an attempt to win their political support. By an *arrêté* of 20 October 1800, for instance, he had lifted the sequestration on the unsold property of émigrés whose names had been eliminated from the proscribed list. A *senatus-consultum* of 26 April 1802 had confirmed this concession, while specifically excluding woodlands and forests already declared inalienable on grounds of national defence by the law of 23 December 1795, as well as buildings which had passed into public use. More to the point, however, a Consular *arrêté* of 18 July 1800 had unequivocally laid down that all earlier land sales legally contracted at the expense of émigrés were to be considered as irrevocable, even if their names no longer appeared on the proscribed list. From the start of the Consulate, while it suited Napoleon's purpose to restore some unsold émigré lands to their former owners, and in other cases to allow them the first option of repurchase when their alienated property reappeared on the market, the legal position was quite clear. All émigré lands actually alienated by due contract were irrecoverable, unless their new owners were willing to sell.

. . . . . .

THE *NOTABLES*

The concept of social 'notability' under the old regime had been inseparable from the legal status of hereditary nobility. Indeed, such terms as '*les notables*' or '*les grands*' had usually denoted the more prominent aristocratic families of ancient lineage, those who were seen as the main exemplars of high social distinction. Most of the lesser nobility and the more recently ennobled commoners (*anoblis*) had been exempt from the staple direct tax (the *taille*), an immunity which was itself the most common mark of 'privilege', but they had not enjoyed the same social pre-eminence as the *haute noblesse*.[5] The 'Assembly of Notables' which Louis XVI had summoned to Versailles in February 1787 in an attempt to secure a fundamental tax reform offers a revealing sample of the sort of people who were then thought to matter most in high politics. The composition of the 144 *notables* then assembled was as follows: 7 princes of the blood, 14 prelates, 36 great nobles, 12 councillors of state, 37 magistrates of the sovereign courts (Robe nobility), the civil magistrate of the Châtelet de Paris, 12 deputies from the *pays d'états*, and 25 municipal heads of cities. The latter, in theory, were meant to represent the third estate, but all were themselves venal office-holders (*officiers*) with privileged status.[6]

For what now seem more principled and public-spirited motives than was once thought, that assembly had been unwilling to approve the Crown's specific proposals to tax the privileged orders on a more regular basis, and such reforms had of course come only with the Revolution. The legal distinctions between the old social orders, that is between official *privilégiés* and commoners (the great mass of what had been the third estate), had been outlawed in principle as early as the Declaration of the Rights of Man and of the Citizen on 26 August 1789. On 19 June 1790 the Constituent Assembly had abolished nobility, as such, along with all its titles and outward trappings. These reforms, first achieved under the constitutional monarchy, had then been assimilated as part of the stock-in-trade of republican rhetoric, for instance in the constitutions of both 1793 and 1795. Under those constitutions, in short, the whole concept of 'notability' had become a sort of political anathema, and all terms denoting it had disappeared from the official language of 'citizenship' propagated during the Revolutionary Republic.

The reappearance of the concept of 'notability' in the public life of the Consulate no doubt testifies to Napoleon's hierarchical view of French society, but it may also obliquely reflect the superficiality of egalitarian rhetoric during the Revolutionary decade. On the other hand, 'notability' had lost the highly exclusive meaning it had had under the old regime, and its nuances changed again as Napoleon increasingly imposed his will on the official forms of his regime. The earliest lists of the Consulate, those drawn up in accordance with the Ventôse law of the Year IX (4 March 1801), in fact referred to 'notabilities' in all the departments of the French Republic. These lists reveal a predominantly official element, made up mainly of men employed in local administration and the legal services, and they were unmistakably republican in character. Their very composition was to a certain extent preordained, since some of the incumbent personnel not only appeared on the lists *ex officio* but could also use such influence to job in many others of their own sort. They included local officials of the Directory who had adjusted their careers to the new political circumstances after Brumaire. The next most numerous group were generally described as 'landowners' (*propriétaires*), including many who had gained in social prominence through the purchase of national lands, most notably among the professional bourgeoisie. The military component varied from department to department, but on the whole it was not particularly significant. More surprising perhaps was the comparatively thin representation of magnates from trade and industry. The old nobility formed only a very small percentage, and the clergy virtually none at all.

In any event, these early lists gave no more than a provisional definition of 'notability' under the Consulate, since a major change was introduced by the *senatus-consultum* of 4 August 1802. This measure, which inaugurated the life consulate, also created the departmental electoral colleges and laid down that their members *had* to be chosen from among the 600 highest taxpayers (*plus imposés*) of each department. In this way 'notability' acquired a more obviously plutocratic meaning, and '*notables*' henceforth superseded '*notabilités*' in the official nomenclature of the later Consulate and in that of the Empire. Now, the criterion used for establishing the highest taxpayers was their liability to the main land tax (*la foncière*). The proprietary element, thus defined, therefore gained in proportional importance, while the wealthy men of finance, trade, and industry remained relatively under-represented, except insofar as they were themselves landed proprietors paying the *foncière*.

There is, then, no doubt that Napoleon regarded landownership as the key hallmark of 'notability' in the Imperial departments, and that the vast majority of his subjects similarly associated social pre-eminence with the status of '*propriétaire*'. *Rentiers*, those able to live off independent means by playing the stock market, enjoyed some social standing too, but again chiefly in cases where they had invested some of their 'liquid' assets in land. Indeed, this is an even more dominant theme in the lists of the sixty to eighty 'most distinguished' persons (*personnes les plus marquantes*) of each department, which Napoleon ordered to be drawn up in the closing years of the Empire.[7] Intended to identify the most prominent *notables* of all, the *crème de la crème* as it were, these lists were a testament to large-scale landownership and its associated social influence, which is why the old nobility had a much higher proportional representation in them than in the earlier ones.

In the Empire at large, the total number of greater or lesser *notables*, that is all those whose names appeared on the departmental and arrondissement electoral colleges, along with State officials and the members of the various advisory public bodies, has settled on the convenient round figure of 100,000 at the height of the Empire. Their professional status is not known in a good many cases, but in a major computerized analysis of those who can be so identified, Louis Bergeron and Guy Chaussinand-Nogaret have gone a long way to establishing the relative importance of the various constituent groups. Using a sample of 66,735 members of both the departmental and the arrondissement electoral colleges over the whole Empire in 1810, these authors found that the largest categories were made up of *propriétaires* (24.55 per cent), of those involved in the lower levels of local administration (18.12 per cent), and of functionaries in civil administration (15.76 per cent). The respective percentages (in parentheses) of the other groups of *notables* here included were as follows: liberal professions (14.37), trade and handicrafts (10.79), working landowners (*propriétaires exploitants*) (8.23), military officers (surprisingly only 2.35), clergymen (1.23), and all others (4.60).[8] After their similar analysis of the levels of income enjoyed by these different professional groups, Bergeron and Chaussinand-Nogaret feel able to conclude that 'the landed proprietor was the social and also the economic model of the *notable*'.[9]

One might then ask how much income an individual would have needed in order to be recognized as an official *notable*. According to Jean Tulard, the lowest requirement for membership of the departmental electoral colleges was 3,000 francs of annual landed income, on average, which would have corresponded to roughly 60,000 francs of capital – admittedly only a crude measure.[10] A higher figure would no doubt have applied in the richer departments, but equally the base would have been even lower in other poorer ones. Most of the members were of course obscure provincial men, far removed from the grandeur of the Imperial entourage, and therefore perhaps rather banal representatives of the concept of 'notability'. Yet collectively they formed the wider social élite of the Empire, the most numerous witnesses to Napoleon's 'politics of amalgamation'. In his own phrase, they were the 'blocks of stone' (*masses de granit*) which formed the common leaven of his official social hierarchy. As such, the vast majority of them had no prospect of receiving his higher social honours, let alone his material endowments which accompanied them, and we need now to consider the much more exclusive group of subjects who did enjoy such favours.

. . . .

THE IMPERIAL NOBILITY

It is a textbook platitude that Napoleon reintroduced social distinctions on a formal basis as a function of his Imperial ambition. In fact, the origins of his system of honours preceded the proclamation of the Empire. 'Arms of honour' for distinguished service appeared as early as Brumaire and the second Italian campaign of 1800. These were consistent with article 87 of the Constitution of the Year VIII, which had stipulated that 'national awards will be made to warriors who have rendered extraordinary service in fighting for the Republic'.[11] Something rather grander and more institutional was clearly intended by Napoleon's creation of the Legion of Honour on 19 May 1802, although its rewards were later so lavishly bestowed that its original exclusiveness was heavily diluted. The

first awards which were actually accompanied by land endowments were the senatoriates (*sénatoreries*), as defined in January
1803. Only thirty-six of the senators were in due course granted
such an honour, whose area corresponded to that of an assize
court, and which also brought their beneficiaries a stately home
and an annual income of 25,000 francs, on top of their regular
senatorial stipends, in recognition of their official jurisdiction
there. The wherewithal came from unsold properties held in
the national domain, and Louis Bergeron has likened the
status of these favoured senators to that 'of a kind of superpre-
fect or regional prefect'.[12] As Tulard has shown, however, the
actual benefits of the senatoriates often fell well short of their
nominal value.[13]

After 18 May 1804, however, the scale and value of Napoleon's honours certainly increased, and this has sometimes been
referred to (not very elegantly) as his 'rehierarchization' of
French society. The proclamation of the Empire was accompanied by the appointment of its ten 'grand dignitaries' and of the
ten 'grand civil officers' of the Imperial household. The 'grand
dignitaries' and four of the eighteen marshals named on 19
May 1804 with honorary status (Kellermann, Lefebvre, Pérignon,
and Sérurier) immediately became members of the senate *ex
officio*. So in due course did the princes of the Empire, the
first of whom received their titles in 1806. On 30 March 1806
the twenty-two 'ducal grand-fiefs of the Empire' were created
from conquered lands in Italy: twelve from the recent Venetian
accessions to the Kingdom of Italy itself, six in the new kingdom
of Naples, and the rest at Massa-Carrara, Parma, and Piacenza.
These Napoleon awarded mainly to his top military commanders, notably the marshals, and to certain ministers. By another
decree of 30 March 1806 he granted the principality of Guastalla
to his sister Pauline, a title she shared with her husband, Prince
Borghese.[14]

But Napoleon's system of honours really came into its own
with the decrees of 1 March 1808, which created the titles of
count, baron, and chevalier of the Empire and laid down the
criteria for elevation into the new Imperial nobility. The title
of count, for instance, was declared suitable for ministers, senators, councillors of state for life, presidents of the legislative
body, and archbishops. That of baron was considered appropriate for the presidents and other prominent members of the
departmental electoral colleges, presidents and attorneys-general

of the high courts of law, bishops, and mayors of large cities. The title of chevalier of the Empire was earmarked for officers of the Legion of Honour but was actually bestowed much more widely. In theory, the recipients of all the Imperial titles first had to show evidence of a qualifying income, grade for grade, which was fixed at 200,000 francs a year for dukes, 30,000 for counts, 15,000 for barons, and 3,000 for chevaliers; but in practice such requirements seem to have been leniently interpreted.

Of course, Napoleon had full discretion to award any of the above titles to other *notables* who fell outside those official categories and who had 'distinguished themselves by services to the State'. He used that prerogative lavishly to reward his prefects and more particularly his top military commanders. Most of the marshals and several of the leading generals had already received the title of duke, as we have seen, while a few more favoured marshals and two of the civil 'grand dignitaries' enjoyed the rank of prince: Bernadotte (appointed prince of Ponte Corvo in 1806), Berthier (of Neuchâtel in 1806 and of Wagram in 1809), Talleyrand (of Benevento in 1806), Cambacérès (of Parma in 1808), Davout (of Eckmühl in 1809), Masséna (of Essling in 1810), and Ney (of the Moskwa in 1813). Many other officers were distributed over the lesser ranks of the counts, barons, and chevaliers of the Empire. Such rewards for military service strengthened the martial flavour which had already become typical at the ceremonial functions of the Empire. By his decree of 13 July 1804 Napoleon had stipulated that, at official State ceremonies, marshals would process ahead of senators and itinerant councillors of state; lieutenants-general before presidents of the appeal courts, archbishops, prefects, and presidents of the assize courts; brigadiers-general before bishops, sub-prefects, and presidents of tribunals; and subaltern officers before other civil officials. As Jean-Paul Bertaud has commented, 'the cortège thus formed remained the convention throughout the nineteenth century. By placing officers at the head of this "imperial procession", Napoleon clearly indicated that they were the leading corps in the state.'[15]

In an earlier work I have listed sixty-four names, including members of the Bonaparte family and those related to it by marriage, under the heading 'Chief Appointments and Honours bestowed by Napoleon' up to 1815. If the titles of the satellite kingdoms and subject states are included here, then forty-six of the honours listed bore foreign place names, of which a fair number were associated with the scenes of famous battles.[16] While the Imperial titles did not bestow tax or legal exemptions, most of them were accompanied by quite lavish land-gifts (*dotations*), and the aim was plainly to set their recipients (*donataires*) apart as the illustrious standard-bearers of Empire. At the top of the hierarchy, some of the land-gifts were made convertible into hereditary estates (*majorats*) by male primogeniture, the 'ducal grand-fiefs' being among the most prominent. Here again, the award of such a high honour was subject to evidence of an additional hereditary income either from landed property or from Bank shares and/or State bonds (*rentes sur l'état*). The qualifying figure for dukes was 20,000 francs, for counts 10,000 francs, and for barons 5,000 francs, while the chevaliers were not eligible for hereditary titles of this kind. In many cases the income attached to Napoleon's *dotations* was actually fixed high enough to allow the *donataires* concerned to qualify for a *majorat* at one of those levels. It seems, however, that these hereditary titles were confined to some 200 heads of family, a figure consisting of 37 counts, 131 barons, and of course the princes and dukes of the Empire.[17] And again, most of the beneficiaries can be identified as marshals, favoured generals, ministers, councillors of state, and senators.

The most careful estimate of the total number of Imperial titles bestowed before Napoleon's second abdication on 22 June 1815 is that of Jean Tulard, who puts the figure at 3,364. It is made up as follows: 34 princes and dukes, 459 counts, 1,552 barons, and 1,319 chevaliers of the Empire.[18] The latter, incidentally, should be distinguished from the chevaliers of the Legion of Honour, whose numbers had swollen to 34,361 out of a total membership of 38,163 by the time of Napoleon's first abdication in April 1814, the other 3,802 being officers of the Legion. At this point it was not much more than a decorative institution for the reward of faithful soldiers, who made up more than 90 per cent of its eventual complement.[19] Compared with other honours, its own might be described as 'long on titles but short on cash'. Tulard omitted from his list of Imperial nobles all members of Napoleon's family and those related to it by marriage, and he also acknowledged that archival omissions or dubious cases had been a problem in its compilation. In view of this, the actual total was probably nearer 3,600. If one takes it as reliable and counts all the men, women, and children concerned, then the number of Imperial nobles and their families was probably around one-seventh of its old royal counterpart before 1789,[20] which would give an approximate total of 28,000.

Such comparatively small numbers should have made the Imperial nobility more socially exclusive, in theory, but this was hardly the case. A social analysis of Tulard's list reveals that 58 per cent were of bourgeois origin, 22.5 per cent of the old nobility, while the remaining 19.5 per cent (invariably made up by the army) came from the popular classes.[21] Expressed in professional terms, the same list testifies to the preponderance of military men, who accounted for 59 per cent, compared with 22 per cent who were higher State officials (ministers, councillors of state, prefects, bishops, inspectors, judges), 17 per cent who were *notables* of other sorts (senators, members of the departmental electoral colleges, and mayors), and 1.5 per cent grouped under the heading of 'talents' (doctors, academics, members of the Institute, archivists, painters, architects, sculptors, composers, and the like).[22] The remaining 0.5 per cent consisted of commercial and industrial magnates, a surprisingly low proportion, which seems altogether out of line with their real economic importance and with the regular administrative or advisory services many gave Napoleon, both in Paris and in the major provincial towns. In any event, the fusion of all such social and professional groups defined the essentially *post*-Revolutionary character of the Imperial nobility.

. . . .

THE 'GRAND EMPIRE' IN NAPOLEON'S 'SPOILS SYSTEM'

If we now return to the pragmatic interpretation of Napoleon's 'social policy', the Revolutionary land settlement is again the essential background factor. Its very finality implied, in effect, that he did not have a large enough stock of disposable State lands within the extended national frontiers of France with which to endow his own family and his official élites on the scale he desired. He had to look beyond them for the wherewithal to make such endowments real. His evolving system of social honours was thus an inverse function of his relatively restricted territorial assets during the Consulate, and of the much more lavish 'spoils' of conquest which came his way in the later years. The social accretions of Empire did not appear all at once, like a crop of mushrooms overnight; they came in staggered phases, which were themselves determined by the chronology of war. The dates at which the various Imperial titles were created and the associated land-gifts then bestowed alone suggest that the conquests of 1805–7 marked the crucial point of departure. It was then that the 'spoils' of war began to multiply, providing income in the subject states which had not been disposable before, and this set a pattern for later conquests and further endowments.

In the process of forging the 'Grand Empire', Napoleon came to see it as much more than an area of dynastic placement for his family, of military vassalage and of would-be economic dependency. It was also to serve his wider social designs. The mechanism of his 'spoils system' was crude but clear: briefly put, the old feudal princes in the subject states were to be dispossessed of a substantial part – in some places as much as a half or more – of the revenues deriving from their domain lands, and this was to be turned over to his own benefit, or to that of his satellite rulers. In a letter of 4 January 1808 to his brother Jerome, who had pointed out the legal complications of such dispossessions in the kingdom of Westphalia, he issued the following barely concealed rebuke:

> I am greatly wearied by distinctions which I find ridiculous between the allodial domains [estates held in absolute ownership] and those which are not. My intention has been to reserve for myself a clear half of the Domains; now, I mean by domains, the allodial lands, the dependent lands (*apanages*), in short *the lands of the Princes*, under whatever title as may be the case, without which you would be giving me nothing and my army would be without reward.[23]

In pursuing his 'politics of grandeur', Napoleon increasingly used those foreign domains as the lubricant of his land-gifts in France, by which his favoured élites were to be endowed. For this purpose, the subject states of Germany, Italy, and Poland – in that order – provided much the largest share of the resources. According to an official document kept in the Archives Nationales in Paris, whose implications have been analysed in detail by Helmut Berding in a valuable monograph, the conquered Westphalian and Hanoverian lands were easily the most important here. Taken together, they alone accounted for a third of the total number of *dotations* (1,334 out of 4,042) and for well over half the annual income (10.5 out of 18.2 million francs) which had accumulated by January 1810, when the *Domaine extraordinaire* was also established to funnel through the revenues set aside for Napoleon's own use.[24]

At the same date, the Italian land-gifts, although more numerous, produced comparatively modest revenues, which themselves had accumulated since Napoleon's victories over the Austrians in 1805 and his expulsion of the Neapolitan Bourbons in 1806. The *Monte Napoleone*, a sinking fund set up in Milan in 1805 for the original purpose of liquidating the public debt of the Kingdom of Italy, accounted for 1,844 *dotations* together worth 1.5 million francs, while the proceeds from Parma (450,000 francs) and from the kingdom of Naples (240,000 francs) were smaller still. The 27 *dotations* granted in the duchy of Warsaw then produced a combined income of nearly 930,000 francs. These awards had been earmarked as early as June 1807, even before the duchy's official creation, and were drawn from the nationalized royal domain lands in Poland. In the event, their value had been substantially boosted by the 'spoils' of the Treaties of Tilsit (July 1807) and of Schönbrunn (October 1809).[25] They were enjoyed exclusively by certain favoured marshals (Davout, Lannes, and Lefebvre most notably) and a number of Napoleon's generals, and all in due course acquired the status of French *majorats*, as Monika Senkowska-Gluck has shown.[26]

Let us remember, too, that all of the above revenues were raised *in addition to* the various exactions carried out by the Grand Army, whether in money or kind, in the subject states. Taken together, such levies seriously disrupted Jerome's budgets in the kingdom of Westphalia, especially when the richest Hanoverian lands were directly annexed to the Empire in December 1810. Their effect on the public finances of the duchy of Warsaw was no less incapacitating. The original 27 *dotations* alone deprived its treasury of roughly a fifth of its potential revenue from the nationalized domain, and the problem worsened as from 1809, when Austrian territorial cessions (Galicia more especially) by the Treaty of Schönbrunn enabled Napoleon to increase the value of his endowments in the duchy. The additional cost of maintaining more than 80,000 troops within its borders further exacerbated its budgetary deficits.

Another document in the Archives Nationales, covering the

period from 30 March 1806 to 24 June 1813, shows that the *dotations* varied enormously in value.[27] In fact, it lists the principal beneficiaries alone in eleven grades. At the top, a total of 10 *donataires*, who included Napoleon's sisters Pauline and Elisa along with some of his most favoured military commanders or civil officials (Berthier, Davout, Masséna, Ney, Caulaincourt, Soult, and Bessières), theoretically enjoyed individual *dotations* ranging from 1.5 million down to 401,000 francs, with a combined value of over 8.6 million. The next most favoured group had 8 *donataires* whose individual *dotations* ranged from 400,000 down to 201,000 francs, with a combined value of more than 2.8 million. At the bottom end of the scale, however, 248 *donataires* enjoyed *dotations* of no more than 5,000 to 10,000 francs each, with a combined value of just under 2 million. All other *donataires*, not here listed, but plainly the vast majority, received even smaller awards. In their case, the *dotations* obviously cannot have included any land-gifts or titles, as such, but only a share of the income deriving from Napoleon's confiscations abroad.

It would, then, be more accurate to describe most of the *dotations* not as *lands*, in the sense of entitled property, but as *rents* or *money* made over to the beneficiaries through French agents specially charged with their collection. It is equally clear from the figures cited above that the Imperial nobility were not the only recipients of such awards. By 1814, according to official inventories drawn up for Napoleon, a total of nearly 6,000 *donataires* had been given *dotations* worth around 30 million francs a year – officially at least.[28] This last cautionary note must be stressed, since the actual benefits appear often to have fallen far short of their nominal values, as numerous complaints by the *donataires* themselves confirmed at the time.[29] In any case, the whole system collapsed with the retreat of the French armies under the offensive of the Allied Coalition in 1813–14. By the time of Napoleon's first abdication, all of his *dotations* had been effectively annulled. The army had always held the key to his 'spoils system' and his 'politics of grandeur'; in the end, they all foundered together.

This is not the place for a detailed examination of the wider social effects of Napoleon's policies in the subject states of Germany, Italy, and Poland, on which my earlier textbook offers at least a twelve-page statement.[30] The most important general conclusions must suffice here. Evidence published on those countries during the last thirty years or so seems to confirm that the Napoleonic interlude there was too short to have a fundamental impact on their basic agrarian structures. Their old feudal aristocracies not only proved resistant to official social reforms imposed from France but were also adept at working within their terms to defend and often even enhance their own position. In her important research on the application of the *Code Napoléon* in the various states of the Rhenish Confederation as from the summer of 1807, for example, Elisabeth Fehrenbach has shown that it was widely evaded or else distorted by the old feudal lords. Seigneurial dues and the other servile obligations of the peasantry may have been outlawed in principle, but in practice they persisted in most places, notwithstanding the relief many gained from the effective abolition of arbitrary labour services in the grand duchy of Berg in 1811.[31] In general, Napoleon's vision of a uniform legal code to supersede the older and more fragmentary feudal procedures remained largely unfulfilled. If his reforms really had taken root in the subject states of Germany, and one might well add of Italy and Poland as well, it would have been much more difficult for the Allied statesmen assembled at the Vienna Congress in 1814–15 to restore so much of the old social order in those countries.

Now, there is no doubt that the Civil Code spelt the final and definitive legal extinction of surviving feudal practices, in all their forms, in France itself. As a general rule, one may say that the French social reforms, first decreed by the Revolutionary governments and then codified and extended by Napoleon, had some long-term impact on the directly annexed departments as well. This was especially the case in those lands which, like Belgium, the Rhenish left bank, and Piedmont-Liguria, lay closest to France and were also exposed longest to its rule. But, further afield, and in territories brought under Napoleonic subjugation relatively late, official policies aimed at 'defeudalization', 'rationalization', and 'modernization' had had a much less profound impact by 1815. In many states east of the Rhine and south of the Alps, lasting social reform was to come only with the revolutions of 1848–49, and even then not everywhere by any means. Beyond the formal frontiers of the Empire, Napoleon had loosened but not broken the old agrarian bonds. He may have advanced the course of 'Progress', as several German and more particularly Italian writers of the later nineteenth century were to claim, but he had not himself destroyed the feudal order. His military humiliation of proud peoples may have been an important spur to a national awakening among them, but such a reaction was still motivated more by their old dynastic and clerical loyalties than by any clear vision of the unified and secular nation-state ahead.

The central paradox of Napoleon's hegemony in the subject states is that his 'spoils system' and the relentless exactions of the Grand Army actually undermined his declared aim of legal and social reform. The constitutions of those states may well have *read* as models of enlightened government, and they may have set beacons for the future. At the time, however, they were never systematically implemented in the vast hinterlands of the 'Grand Empire'. There, the principle of legal equality enshrined in the *Code Napoléon* was hardly well served by the creation of favoured groups of *donataires*, who constituted not so much a 'state within a state' as a large band of privileged absentees. Bluntly put, what Napoleon chiefly wanted from the subject states was soldiers, provisions, and money. All became increasingly necessary to him as his military ambitions and 'spoils system' became more grandiose at the height of the Empire. To get them, he was often prepared to ignore or simply override the official letter of his Code. As a realist, he found that it was usually more productive to come to some practical arrangement with the old aristocracies, the dominant class in most of conquered Germany, Italy, and Poland. In short, to siphon off his 'spoils' there, he made his compromise with the feudal system. There were of course huge regional variations in the impact of his rule; but in the long term its social effects were conservative rather than radical. In this respect, he had more in common with the enlightened despots before him, with the warrior-kings of the older European dynasties, than with the later architects of the modern state.

. . . .

THE FATE OF THE OLD NOBILITY

One of the most intriguing questions of this period is where the old nobility, or '*ci-devants*' as they were often still called, stood in relation to the newer breed of Imperial *notables*, and how far they were themselves assimilated into Napoleon's system of government and social honours. There are no definite answers here, because the evidence of the secondary sources available for the years of the Consulate and Empire is still rather restricted, not least in English works. To fill in the missing details, we need many more regional and particular studies of the sort Robert Forster has devoted, some years ago now, to the nobility of Toulouse during the eighteenth century and to the Burgundian house of Saulx-Tavanes over the period from 1700 to 1830.[32] In his more general survey published around the same time, Forster offers additional evidence to confirm the reasonable supposition that the old nobility were not in any real sense the 'winners' of the Revolution.[33]

According to this latter source, at the end of the old regime the former second estate had owned about a quarter of the land of France directly, with seigneurial claims over much more, and many had enjoyed the social status still associated with the rights of seigneurial justice.[34] As a result of the legislation and events of the Revolution, however, most noble families had suffered a diminution of their wealth and status, to a greater or lesser extent. All who had once enjoyed seigneurial dues had had to accept the outright loss of such income, notwithstanding the large regional variations in its proportional importance, following the abolition of those dues in stages between 4 August 1789 and 17 July 1793. Most of the émigrés among them had also suffered significant losses through the confiscation of their principal capital asset, landed property, even if many had indeed been able to recover much of it or at least salvage something from the wreck through the good offices of agents acting on their behalf during the 1790s. What, then, did the overall damage amount to? Citing his 'hypothetical provincial nobleman' as an average case, Forster estimates that he would perhaps have lost only one-fifth of his land but as much as one-third of his income, while most of the Parisian nobility had probably been hit even harder.[35] Furthermore, all rights of seigneurial justice had been abolished, which in the long term was bound to have a leavening effect on the social standing of the old nobility in the eyes of former tenants and, perhaps too, on their own perception of themselves. In all, 'whoever won the Revolution, the noble landlord lost'.[36]

Now, while that general conclusion seems unexceptionable, what matters here is the *relative* scale of the damage, which can to some extent be measured statistically in a wider social context. Although estimates of the total number of the nobility before the Revolution have varied considerably over the past two hundred years, the more recent consensus among scholars favours the lower ones. If all the men, women, and children of the former second estate are counted, those of the more established Sword and Robe nobility alike, as well as the various categories of *anoblis*, then the figure is probably around 200,000.[37] Donald Greer's pioneering work over sixty years ago established that at least 1,158 of them had perished as political victims of the Revolution, 878 from Sword and 280 from Robe families. Even if allowances are made for the inevitable omissions, such incidence of death through political causes is likely to have been well under 1 per cent of their order, although it represented 8.25 per cent of the *total* number of deaths among all classes attributable to the Terror and the civil war in France.[38]

According to a later study by Greer, moreover, at least 16,431 nobles emigrated at different times during the Revolution, a figure which he reckons at 16.75 per cent of the total number of émigrés.[39] The same figure would amount to 8.22 per cent of the total number of nobles cited earlier. Forster estimates that almost 10,000 noble families (and their property) were thus directly affected by the emigration, that is about one noble family in four.[40] The figures cited in a more recent short statement on the subject by Vincent Beach seem partly at variance here. On the one hand, he states that of some 97,000 émigrés who can be identified by social class (out of an overall total of over 150,000 during the whole Revolutionary era), nobles made up 17 per cent, which would put their own absolute figure at 16,490 persons – almost identical to Greer's estimate. On the other, he claims that it represented only about 5 per cent of their order, which in turn would imply that the total number of nobles was nearly 330,000 – a figure well in excess of Forster's estimate, and also much too high?[41] Yet however such discrepancies are reconciled, one point at least is clear: the great majority of the old second estate, perhaps two-thirds to three-quarters of noble families, had *not* been directly affected by emigration during the 1790s. And so, whatever their other losses may have been, they had presumably not suffered from the punitive land confiscations, as such.

In fact, such evidence as we have for the Napoleonic period plainly suggests that the old nobility were then still the largest *individual* landowners in France, including Paris. Their further recovery of property under Napoleon, which included the repurchase of alienated lands as well as the restitution of sequestrated lands (most typically forests) which had remained within the national domain, has already been noted. Many nobles continued to matter in their localities precisely *because of* the social status which was still associated with such landed wealth. It is then all the more significant that most of them appear to have eschewed a prominent role in the political life of the Consulate and Empire. For some, such active collaboration may have seemed beneath their dignity and principles. For those among them who had returned to France from the long privations of exile, there were more immediate and more private priorities to attend to – families to regather, confiscated estates to recover, and delapidated buildings to repair. In many cases, one imagines, Napoleon's amnesties of 1800 and 1802 offered the first real opportunity for family life after the years of dispersal across Europe. Even those who are assumed to have 'rallied' to him did so with varying degrees of commitment and enthusiasm.

Indeed, it is difficult to know by which criteria we can best measure the extent to which the old nobility 'rallied' to Napoleon. All of the 750 to 760 who accepted titles of the Imperial nobility may certainly be said to have done so in a formal sense. Yet the most active '*ralliés*' among them are probably more accurately identified as those who at different times accepted ministerial, prefectoral, mayoral, or diplomatic appointments, or who became members of the council of state, of the senate, and of the legislative chambers. Again, it would seem fair to include others who were active in provincial assemblies, perhaps as members of the departmental councils or as presidents of the electoral colleges, and the scions of old Robe families who received official posts in Napoleon's judicial system. Finally, all former nobles who served in his armies should certainly also be counted. But what are we to make of many others whose collaboration with the regime was more honorific and occasional? The mere appearance of the old nobility on the official lists of *notables* is perhaps the most deceptive criterion of all. As prominent landowners they were more than likely to feature among the *plus imposés* in most departments, even if their role in public life was limited or wholly passive.

Chronological distinctions may help to clarify such difficulties. In the earliest years, while the émigrés were still returning to France, and when the future of the Napoleonic regime was far from certain, the old nobility were relatively insignificant among the active '*ralliés*', at any rate if one looks beyond the armies and the immediate entourage of the central government. In France as a whole, to take even the most official index, Tulard found that they made up less than 3 per cent of the *notabilités* named on the first lists of 1801.[42] Their proportion was admittedly higher in the much more typical lists of *notables* who formed the departmental electoral colleges in the years following 4 August 1802, although usually it did not exceed 10 to 15 per cent.[43] Only in the later and more exclusive lists of the *personnes les plus marquantes*, mainly as from 1810, did their representation rise to about one-fifth. Some earlier writers have explained this apparently significant increase as an effect of Napoleon's deliberate attempt, after his Austrian marriage and the birth of an heir, to give his regime a more 'aristocratic' flavour by offering the old nobility official appointments and other honours. It may also be true that more of them *were* then willing to be associated with an emperor who had after all seemed fit enough for marriage with the ancient house of Habsburg. But again, the appearance of more noble names on the official lists was not necessarily clear proof of their active participation in the government of the Empire.

Such caveats should be borne in mind as individual cases or larger professional samples are now examined by way of illustration. It is clear, for a start, that some former nobles were prepared to accept ministerial office or membership of the other central organs of state under Napoleon. The most prominent were Talleyrand, minister of foreign affairs (1799–1807); Champagny, minister of the interior (1804–7) and then of foreign affairs (1807–11); Montalivet, minister of the interior (1809–14); and Caulaincourt, minister of foreign affairs (1813–14, 1815). Others again hailed from the former Robe nobility, like Cambacérès (second consul, and briefly minister of justice at the start and end of the period), Roederer (a councillor of state), and Molé (minister of justice in 1813–14). Berthier, Napoleon's long-serving chief of staff and for some time minister of war (1799–1800, 1800–6), on whom he heaped a number of the highest honours, was the son of an *anobli* who had gained royal favour towards the end of the old regime. Similar cases can be found in the senate, whose membership had risen to over 140 by 1814 through Napoleon's lavish promotion of favourites, far exceeding the 80 originally envisaged. The tribunate was perhaps too short-lived and troublesome a chamber to be a representative sample in the present context, but the legislative body at least offers an interesting social physiognomy. Of slightly over 700 men who served as legislators at some time between 1800 and 1814, it seems that very few of those whose origins are known came from the old nobility. Available samples suggest a percentage in single figures, rising perhaps to 10 per cent in the years 1811–13.[44]

All these might be thought of as examples of former nobles who accepted a functional 'political' role under Napoleon in a public sense. Three of those named above were also included among the ten 'grand dignitaries' of the Empire: Talleyrand (vice-grand elector), Berthier (vice-constable), and Cambacérès (arch-chancellor). Two others, Champagny (intendant-general of the crown) and Caulaincourt (grand master of the horse) featured among the 'grand civil officers' of the Imperial household, and the inevitable Berthier also joined their company here as master of the hunt. As a group, the 'grand civil officers' had a rather more honorific status within the Imperial entourage, and perhaps for this reason included an even more impressive sampling of former nobles, such as Ségur (grand master of ceremonies), Montesquiou-Fezensac (grand chamberlain), Rémusat (first chamberlain), and de Luçay (first prefect of the palace). The empress Josephine's household included de Rohan (first almoner) and the likes of Mesdames de Rémusat, de Luçay, de Lauriston and de Talhouët. Indeed, at different times and in all sorts of capacities, a veritable galaxy of old noble names appeared in the service of the Imperial households: d'Aubusson de la Feuillade, Bouillé, Choiseul-Praslin, Croy, d'Haussonville, La Rochefoucauld, Mercy-Argenteau, Montmorency, Rochechouart-Mortemart, and Turenne, for example.[45] Nearly all of those named here, and a good many others besides, also received Imperial titles, in some cases complete with lucrative *majorats.*

If one again looks beyond the immediate entourage of the Imperial government and Court, the old nobility provided a no less significant catchment class for the high departmental administration. One particularly important and revealing professional sample is the prefectoral corps, because it formed the backbone of Napoleon's executive government in provincial France. Thanks to Edward Whitcomb's detailed analysis, we have a good idea of the social status of the 281 men who served in the corps at one time or another during the Consulate and Empire. By the time of Napoleon's first abdication in April 1814,

53 of his incumbent prefects (43 per cent of the total) were of the old nobility, and they then also held a disproportionate number of the more important prefectures. While this was certainly their highest percentage over the entire period, Whitcomb also found that their fastest *rate* of appointment had actually come during the years 1800–7, when their proportion increased from 23 to 37 per cent. Since prefects of bourgeois origin were always in the majority, although falling proportionally from 77 to 57 per cent between 1800 and 1814, the higher representation of old nobles towards the end of the Empire was not due to any deliberate policy of direct replacement. It is explained much more by Napoleon's preference for '*ci-devants*' in appointments to the newly formed departments of 1810–11, especially in Germany, and in his filling of vacancies which occurred around the same time.[46] Whitcomb's companion study of Napoleon's diplomatic service, a sample of rather more than 200 persons, reaches broadly similar conclusions. His evidence here is that the proportion of old nobles in the ministerial and secretarial echelons of the service rose appreciably in the years after 1809.[47]

As for the old nobility who served in Napoleon's armies, as a good many had also done in those of the Revolutionary period, we have sufficient evidence to assess their proportional importance at three levels. At the highest rank of the marshalate, former nobles were quite well represented. Of the original eighteen marshals appointed on 19 May 1804, five (of whom three admittedly had honorary status) could claim some sort of noble background dating from the old regime. Berthier's father had been ennobled in 1763; Davout came from an old noble family of Burgundy; Kellermann, of the Alsatian nobility, had gained hereditary status in 1788; while the family origins of Pérignon and Sérurier lay in the lesser nobility. Three of the eight marshals added later during the Empire fell into the same social category: Marmont (appointed in 1809) was of minor noble stock, Poniatowski (in 1813) was a Polish prince, and Grouchy (in 1815) came from an old family of the Sword nobility.[48]

Officers who attained the rank of general provide a second and much more numerous sample. The invaluable pioneering work of Georges Six published nearly fifty years ago established that at least 305 of the generals who served under Napoleon at some stage during the years of the Empire were of the old nobility. Of these, 174 had been appointed to that rank before

1789 and had then also served in the French armies during the 1790s, while the other 131 had gained such commissions sometime during the Revolution itself. If most of them were descended from military families of relatively modest status (*écuyers*), at least 90 others came from titled families of the old regime. Six's evidence also suggests that their *proportional* incidence may eventually have declined somewhat under Napoleon, from a high-point of 30 per cent of all generals during the later Directory to 20 per cent by the end of the Empire. But, even so, they remained throughout a significantly larger group within his high command than the generals who came from what could be considered as 'working-class' backgrounds.[49]

Finally, Jean-Paul Bertaud's selective analysis of the much more numerous officers of company-grade rank reveals a social composition which is significantly different from that of the higher ranks. His sample of 480 captains, lieutenants, and sub-lieutenants serving in 1814 represents only about 2 per cent of more than 20,000 who held those ranks under Napoleon, but it remains a useful index, not least because most of the officers concerned had done long service. Of the 137 appointed before 1800, none were of the old nobility; while of the other 343 appointed during or after that year, only 4.9 per cent could claim such origin.[50] Most of these latter, one imagines, would have come from former *écuyer* families. In fact, what the findings of Six and Bertaud indirectly confirm is that the great majority of Napoleon's officers below the rank of marshal were of various bourgeois stock, even allowing for a sizeable proportion (around 30 per cent) at company-grade rank who were the sons of landowners or working farmers (*cultivateurs*).

Analyses of such professional samples may strike some readers as rather anonymous exercises, devoid of personal colour, and this chapter will therefore conclude with two contrasting *individual* reactions to the Napoleonic regime. The first is the case of the marquis de Lafayette. Hero of the American War and a major participant in the French Revolution during its early years, when he staunchly defended the principles of individual liberty under a constitutional monarchy, he had fled to Belgium on its overthrow in August 1792. After his capture there, he had been held a prisoner for five years, most of the time in Austrian custody at Olmütz, before being released under the terms of the Treaty of Campo Formio in 1797. Returning to France in 1800 soon after Napoleon's *coup d'état*, he would certainly have been an influential '*rallié*', a role for which the first consul was evidently very eager to groom him, and in May 1800 his name was removed from the list of proscribed émigrés.

Yet while their early personal relations remained cordial, Lafayette made his disapproval of the new regime clear enough, by politely declining offers of an appointment as ambassador to the United States, a seat in the senate, and membership of the Legion of Honour. In March 1802 he applied for retirement from the army, but the decisive break came later that year when he openly opposed Napoleon's life consulate. He spent the remaining years of the Consulate and Empire mostly on his estate, the Château de La Grange in the Seine-et-Marne, unwilling to become involved in politics, a 'castaway' (*naufragé*) as he then ironically described himself. He re-emerged briefly as an elected member of the chamber of representatives during the Hundred Days, was prominent in calling for Napoleon's abdication after Waterloo, but then again retired into private life. Not a very exciting story, perhaps, but surely one of firm principles. Who can say how many thousands of other nobles, more especially of other émigrés, are represented by Lafayette's conspicuous absence from the Napoleonic scene? Although we lack precise evidence, Tulard nevertheless estimates that close on 80 per cent of the old nobility, who are sometimes referred to as 'the émigrés of the interior', chose not to join the ranks of the '*ralliés*'.[51] If that was indeed the case, the efficacy of Napoleon's 'politics of amalgamation' would appear in a somewhat different light. We should need to be even more wary of easy generalizations about the social 'fusion' of all classes under his regime.

The other case concerns the fortunes of the La Tour du Pin family. It offers a story of aristocratic survival and realism of a different kind, and it shows what could be achieved by the adjustments of a personal career to changing political realities. The comte de Gouvernet hailed from an ancient family of the Sword nobility of the Dauphiné. After doing service in the royal army before the Revolution, he had been sent for a time as French minister to The Hague in 1791. Twice later during the Revolution he had been driven into exile with his family, first in America and then in England, while succeeding to the title of comte de La Tour du Pin de Gouvernet (officially extinct under the decree of 19 June 1790) on the execution of his father, the former minister of war (1789–90), in 1794. Returning to France after the fall of the Directory, he retired for several years to his family château of Le Bouilh, near Bordeaux, before serving Napoleon as prefect in Brussels (department of the Dyle) from 1808 to the end of 1812, and then more briefly as prefect in Amiens (department of the Somme). There, he was in post to welcome Louis XVIII as the king journeyed from Boulogne to Paris for the First Restoration in 1814. His immediate reward was a posting as minister to The Hague, along with a place among the French plenipotentiaries to the Vienna Congress, and his creation as a peer of France in 1815. In 1820 he received the title of marquis de La Tour du Pin and was also appointed as French ambassador to Turin, where he remained until his retirement in 1830.

And so, in the space of more than forty years, our subject had served the old Bourbon monarchy as a soldier, the Revolution briefly as a diplomat, Napoleon as a top administrator, and the Bourbons again as a diplomat of high status. He had also known the pain of family executions, the hazards of emigration, and the loss of the family's seigneurial dues, though not (it seems) the outright confiscation of its lands. At his side throughout that long career was his more redoubtable wife, born Henriette-Lucie Dillon, a legendary beauty, and once a member of Marie-Antoinette's household. Her memoirs, written between 1820 and her death in 1853 but published only much later, are a fascinating testimony to the spirit of resilience of her order in riding over the various political upheavals which so often determined its fate.[52] She and the marquis were to survive all but one of their six children.

The last word may fittingly be left to the marquise herself, as it offers an intriguing insight into Napoleon's attitude towards the old nobility who were willing to serve him, and of their attitude towards him. Early in 1813, when news came that her husband had been dismissed from the prefecture in Brussels, she took it upon herself to request a personal meeting with the emperor in his receiving room at Trianon. This is her account of the audience:

> The door opened, the footman signed to me to enter, and closed both halves of the door behind me. I was in the presence of Napoleon. He came forward to meet me, saying quite amiably, 'Madame, I fear you are very displeased with me.'

150

I bowed in assent, and the conversation began. I have lost the account I wrote of this long audience, which lasted fifty-nine minutes by the clock, and now, after so many years, I cannot remember all the details. The sum of it was that the Emperor tried to prove to me that he had been compelled to act as he had done. I then briefly described to him the general attitude of Brussels society, the esteem which my husband, unlike all his predecessors, had succeeded in acquiring . . .

Then, as he walked to and fro in that great salon, with me trying to keep pace beside him, he spoke these amazing words: 'I was wrong. But what can be done about it?' It was, perhaps, the only time in his life that he made such an admission, and it was I who was privileged to hear it.

I replied that it lay in his power to set matters right, and, passing a hand across his brow, he said: 'Yes, there is a report on the Prefectures. The Minister of the Interior is coming this evening.' He went on to name four or five Departments and added: 'There is Amiens. Would that suit you?'

'Perfectly, Sir,' I replied without hesitation.

'In that case, it is settled. You may go and tell Montalivet.' And, with that charming smile which has so often been spoken of, he added: 'And now, am I forgiven?' I replied politely that I also needed forgiveness for having been so outspoken. 'Oh, you were quite right to be so,' was the answer. I curtsied, and he walked to the door to open it for me himself.[53]

. . . .

NOTES AND REFERENCES

1. Marcel Marion, *La vente des biens nationaux pendant la Révolution*, Paris, 1908.
2. Florin Aftalion, *The French Revolution: An Economic Interpretation*, Eng. edn, Cambridge, 1990, pp. 186–7.
3. See, e.g., the individual cases cited in Paul Butel, 'Crise et mutation de l'activité économique à Bordeaux sous le Consulat et l'Empire', *Revue d'Histoire moderne et contemporaine*, vol. 17, 1970, p. 557; and in Geoffrey Ellis, 'Rhine and Loire: Napoleonic Elites and Social Order', in Gwynne Lewis and Colin Lucas, eds, *Beyond the Terror: Essays in French Regional and Social History, 1794–1815*, Cambridge, 1983, pp. 255–6.
4. This interplay between history and literature in Balzac's novels is nicely analysed in Ronnie Butler, *Balzac and the French Revolution*, Beckenham, 1983, esp. pp. 19–31.
5. Marcel Reinhard, 'Élite et noblesse dans la seconde moitié du

XVIIIe siècle', *Revue d'Histoire moderne et contemporaine*, vol. 3, 1956, pp. 5–37.

6. Jean Égret, *The French Prerevolution 1787–1788*, Eng. edn, Chicago and London, 1977, p. 6.

7. The departmental series of *Grands notables du Premier Empire* has been published since 1978 under the auspices of the Centre National de la Recherche Scientifique, École des Hautes Études en Sciences Sociales (Centre de Recherches Historiques), and under the general direction of Louis Bergeron and Guy Chaussinand-Nogaret.

8. Louis Bergeron and Guy Chaussinand-Nogaret, *Les «masses de granit»*. *Cent mille notables du Premier Empire*, Paris, 1979, p. 43.

9. Ibid., p. 62.

10. Jean Tulard, 'Problèmes sociaux de la France impériale', *Revue d'Histoire moderne et contemporaine*, vol. 17, 1970, pp. 651, 663.

11. Text as cited in Eric A. Arnold, Jr, ed. and trans, *A Documentary Survey of Napoleonic France*, Lanham, Md, 1994, p. 33.

12. Louis Bergeron, *France under Napoleon*, Eng. edn, Princeton, 1981, p. 64.

13. Jean Tulard, *Napoléon et la noblesse d'Empire: Avec la liste complète des membres de la noblesse impériale (1808–1815)*, Paris, 1979, pp. 27–32.

14. Monika Senkowska-Gluck, 'Les donataires de Napoléon', *Revue d'Histoire moderne et contemporaine*, vol. 17, 1970, pp. 680–1.

15. Jean-Paul Bertaud, 'Napoleon's Officers', *Past & Present*, no. 112, Aug. 1986, p. 97.

16. Geoffrey Ellis, *The Napoleonic Empire*, Basingstoke and London, 1991, pp. 115–17.

17. Bergeron, *France under Napoleon*, p. 69.

18. Tulard, *Noblesse d'Empire*.

19. Ibid., pp. 48–9.

20. Bergeron, *France under Napoleon*, p. 69.

21. Tulard, 'Problèmes sociaux', p. 656; *Noblesse d'Empire*, p. 97.

22. Tulard, 'Problèmes sociaux', p. 655; *Noblesse d'Empire*, p. 94.

23. Quoted (in French) in Helmut Berding, *Napoleonische Herrschafts- und Gesellschaftspolitik im Königreich Westfalen 1807–1813*, Göttingen, 1973, p. 120 n. 7.

24. 'État général des biens existant dans les Pays conquis, des Revenus qui restent disponibles et des donations accordées par Sa Majesté, Réversibles à la Couronne' (January 1810): Archives Nationales, AF IV 1040, reproduced in Berding, *Königreich Westfalen*, p. 148.

25. Ibid.

26. Monika Senkowska, 'Les majorats français dans le duché de Varsovie (1807–1813)', *Annales historiques de la Révolution française*, vol. 36, 1964, pp. 373–86.

27. 'Tableau indicatif du nombre des Donataires et de la quotité des Dotations de premières classes accordées par Sa Majesté Impériale depuis le 30 mars 1806 jusque et y compris le 24 juin 1813': Archives Nationales, AF IV 311, reproduced in Berding, *Königreich Westfalen*, p. 150.
28. Berding, *Königreich Westfalen*, pp. 65–6.
29. Jean Tulard, 'Les composants d'une fortune: Le cas de la noblesse d'Empire', *Revue historique*, vol. 253, 1975, pp. 122–7; and *Noblesse d'Empire*, pp. 111–17.
30. Ellis, *The Napoleonic Empire*, pp. 82–93.
31. Of Elisabeth Fehrenbach's major writings on this subject, see esp. *Traditionale Gesellschaft und revolutionäres Recht. Die Einführung des Code Napoléon in den Rheinbundstaaten*, Göttingen, 1974.
32. Robert Forster, *The Nobility of Toulouse in the Eighteenth Century: A Social and Economic Study*, Baltimore, 1960; and *The House of Saulx-Tavanes: Versailles and Burgundy 1700–1830*, Baltimore and London, 1971.
33. Robert Forster, 'The Survival of the Nobility during the French Revolution', *Past & Present*, no. 37, July 1967, pp. 71–86.
34. Ibid., p. 71.
35. Ibid., p. 82.
36. Ibid., p. 86.
37. Ibid., p. 74.
38. Donald Greer, *The Incidence of the Terror during the French Revolution: A Statistical Interpretation*, Cambridge, Mass., 1935, Table VI, pp. 161–3.
39. Donald Greer, *The Incidence of the Emigration during the French Revolution*, Cambridge, Mass., 1951, Table I, pp. 109–12.
40. Forster, 'The Survival of the Nobility', p. 75.
41. V.W. Beach, '*Émigrés*', in Samuel F. Scott and Barry Rothaus, eds, *Historical Dictionary of the French Revolution, 1789–1799*, 2 vols, Westport, Conn., 1985, vol. 1, p. 353.
42. Tulard, *Noblesse d'Empire*, p. 26 n. 8.
43. Ibid.
44. Thomas Beck, 'Legislators', in Owen Connelly, ed., *Historical Dictionary of Napoleonic France, 1799–1815*, Westport, Conn., 1985, pp. 299–300; and Irene Collins, *Napoleon and his Parliaments 1800–1815*, London, 1979, pp. 140–2.
45. Tulard, *Noblesse d'Empire*, pp. 102–4, 153.
46. Edward A. Whitcomb, 'Napoleon's Prefects', *American Historical Review*, vol. 79, 1974, p. 1094.
47. Edward A. Whitcomb, *Napoleon's Diplomatic Service*, Durham, NC, 1979.
48. Louis Chardigny, *Les maréchaux de Napoléon*, Paris, 1977, p. 42 n. 1.

49. Georges Six, *Les généraux de la Révolution et de l'Empire*, n.d. [1947], pp. 28–9.
50. Bertaud, 'Napoleon's Officers', pp. 103–4.
51. Tulard, *Noblesse d'Empire*, p. 104.
52. *Memoirs of Madame de La Tour du Pin*, ed. and trans by Felice Harcourt, introd. by Margaret Crosland, Eng. edn, London, 1985.
53. Ibid., pp. 402–3.

Chapter 6

REPRESENTATIONS OF POWER, FOR AND AGAINST:
PUBLIC OPINION, EDUCATION, AND THE ARTS

The Consulate and Empire have sometimes been portrayed as a dismal time for the expression of public opinion and cultural creativity, much of which was driven into covert corners or even into exile. The judgement is understandable, given the steady intrusion of the political regime through censorship of the press and theatre, in its educational policy, and by its public manipulation of the arts. All were used in some way as functions of its official propaganda. Yet in other respects the verdict seems too harsh; for in spite of the heavy hand of State intervention in all those spheres, they were never asphyxiated. There were other, indeed more subtle, ways in which public opinion and artistic vitality could be expressed. By the end of the period, their achievements were rich and enduring. Conquering warriors, whether one is for or against them, usually provoke comment, and contemporary 'value judgements' on Napoleon were certainly no exception.

In cultural terms, the Revolutionary and Napoleonic era mark the cross-roads of the European Enlightenment and Romanticism, and some critics have even seen in it the early antecedents of later Realism. If 'official' art had a central theme, it might be described as monumentalism in the service of Imperial grandeur, while 'unofficial' literature and art expressed the same transition from older Neo-classical forms to newer Romantic ones. The propaganda of the regime was usually aimed at boosting public morale, whose fluctuations were often unpredictable, and at presenting Napoleon to the people in the best possible light. Its educational policy served its utilitarian perception of the practical needs of the State. Its critics, of course,

155

denounced such policies as manipulative and sycophantic, and resented the assault on their intellectual and artistic freedom.

We thus find an interesting tension between the 'official' and 'unofficial' culture of that time, between State-sponsored celebrations and private creativity, and the exponents of both often drew on and developed the same artistic inheritance. The social and intellectual élitism of Napoleon's liberal critics was the more self-conscious for their alienation from his regime. This chapter is an attempt to penetrate those conflicting mentalities from both the public and private points of view. The subject is treated not as a cultural specimen abstracted from its social milieu, but in the context in which the educators, propagandists, censors, artists, and writers had dealings with the State or in other ways reflected the *mentalités* of their time.

. . . .

THE PERSONALIZATION OF POWER: THE VISUAL ARTS

The common source of the various representations of Imperial grandeur was Napoleon's determination to concentrate all its outward manifestations on himself. What emerged at the height of the Empire was the official celebration of an essentially *personalized* heroic ethic, a 'self-image' which could then be projected before the eyes and into the hearts of all subjects. It seems fitting, then, to begin with an account of Napoleon's own concept of power. That it was intimately associated with military glory, and that it also became less convincing once his ability to deliver spectacular victories declined in the later years, seems clear. Less familiar perhaps is the comprehensive range, civil as well as military, his public display of grandeur assumed in the ascendant years.

Heraldry and symbolism are a case in point, and they nicely testify to the changing 'self-image' of Napoleon's evolving ambition. The passage from republican Consulate to hereditary Empire was followed, only a few weeks after 18 May 1804, by the announcement that a new armorial bearing had been adopted by the State. In place of the red Phrygian cap surmounting the Roman lictor's axe and fasces, symbols of the Revolutionary Republic, the eagle now appeared. It was Napoleon's own choice from a number of alternatives presented to him by the Imperial Council, and it was of course a deliberate attempt to match the symbolism of his regime with that of

156

Charlemagne. The task of designing the new emblem was entrusted to J.-B. Isabey, and the outcome was the familiar image of the eagle with wings outstretched. The military and naval equivalent, soon adopted as a battle-standard, was the eagle of the Roman legions. Beneath this mounted emblem the Republican tricolour was indeed attached as well, although its very position suggested its now subsidiary status.[1] The eagle thus came to symbolize the 'Grand Empire' and the Grand Army alike. Napoleon himself was often simply called 'the Eagle'; his troops fought 'under the Eagles' (*sous les Aigles*); and in due course the King of Rome was affectionately nicknamed 'Eaglet' (*l'Aiglon*).

Napoleon's presumptive inheritance of the old Frankish imperial tradition was demonstrated in other ways, sometimes with questionable historical accuracy. One instance was his use of the golden bee as a badge on his own coronation mantle, on the ceremonial dress of princes and grand dignitaries of the Empire, on that of other Imperial nobles, and in place of the fleur-de-lys on the coat of arms of the city of Paris. The dubitable attribution, as June K. Burton has suggested, may have reflected Napoleon's belief that the golden bee had been the badge of Childeric, father of Clovis, early Merovingian predecessors of the Carolingians.[2] The personalization of power through symbols was more explicit still in the use of distinctive initials, notably the capital N surrounded by laurel leaves on Napoleon's coronation cape, on the throne at Fontainebleau, on the exteriors of the Imperial palaces, and on a number of public buildings. The initial J, also fashioned in Romano-Empire style, similarly served the decorative pretensions of the empress Josephine.

The concentration of public emblems on Napoleon himself reflects in other examples of the Empire style, such as the official coinage, engraving, painting, interior decoration, architecture, sculpture, and the like. It has been claimed that he instructed the Monnaie de Paris to issue more medals in the course of his reign than had been struck during the preceding century.[3] He intervened personally at the Institute to supervise the commission charged with the preparation of the *Histoire métallique de Napoléon le Grand*, another project conceived in grandiose Neo-classical style. The Revolutionary Republic had adopted Liberty as its symbol of state, in a form familiar to us in its feminine allegory, an early antecedent of 'Marianne'. After

157

1802 this republican emblem changed, as all official coins were struck with Napoleon's manly profile, though in a guise still reminiscent of a Roman ascetic. As from 1807, flushed with military victory, territorial and dynastic aggrandizement, he wanted coins more obviously imperial in style. The emperor's head wreathed in laurels now symbolized the return of glory under a new Caesar. So, too, the Legion of Honour and the titles of the Imperial nobility were given elaborate decorative insignia, grade for grade.[4] What all these emblems of Imperial status had in common was Napoleon's keen sense of an heroic past, and of his own achievement in recapturing its glories for France. Neo-classical and Carolingian motifs, sometimes interworked with others brought back from Egypt, suited his purpose well. They were sufficiently distant in the collective memory of his subjects to allow their technical exponents a good deal of artistic licence.

The opportunities in the visual arts were particularly attractive. Indeed, it seems clear that painters, architects, sculptors, and interior decorators were much less able than the literary community to work independently of the State. Their raw materials were generally dearer and their art more dependent on patronage. Private patronage had suffered from the emigration and financial straits of many noble families during the Revolution, while the disappearance of the royal court had eliminated one of the traditional exemplars of taste. Not only had the Revolutionary state itself become the foremost patron of the visual arts during the 1790s, regulating commissions through its purse-strings, but it had often determined the very space required for their public display. It had come to have a major influence on taste even before the advent of Napoleon. His own impact, however, was on an altogether grander scale, in the private as well as public spheres. Nietta Aprà's appraisal of the Empire style nicely illustrates its many decorative flourishes in furniture, tapestry, the ceramic arts, precious metalware, and glasswork.[5] The Imperial palaces were lavishly adorned through official patronage, and they served as sumptuous models for aspiring *notables* to emulate on a smaller scale in the decoration of their own houses. As Aprà comments, 'it was the Emperor himself who took up the task of dictating a style suggesting both greatness and severity, . . . the ostentation and pompousness of the Empire style proper'.[6]

French painting of the later eighteenth century is usually

characterized as Neo-classical in style, often rather austere, and as a reaction against the sensualism of 'decadent' art and its more frivolous rococo embellishments. With the Revolution, political themes had become more pronounced, for instance in the celebration of public events that marked many of the republican festivals, where symbolical appeal was important. The Stoic ethic of civic virtue, even of 'moral art', favoured such didactic display, but had generally been used to enhance the public enactment of Revolutionary principles rather than the personal grandeur of political leaders. The emphasis under Napoleon was quite different. The Neo-classical and Romantic styles were eminently adjustable to the personal glorification of the first consul and emperor. His celebrated 'Roman' head, his great battles, the Imperial coronation, courtly pageants, the lingering fascination of exotic motifs and remembered scenes in Egypt – all in some way inspired the artists. 'Napoleon's interest in art was not aesthetic . . . but social', Burton has commented, but 'he did appreciate immensity and equated big with beautiful'.[7]

The long career of Jacques-Louis David (1748–1825) brilliantly links the old regime with the Revolution and with the Napoleonic Empire as a formative period in the development of French art. A fascinating account first published in 1855 by one of his most faithful pupils, Étienne-Jean Delécluze, gives us a unique insight into the work of the master and his celebrated school.[8] It is an admiring and often touching appraisal, yet an honest and critical one too, and it certainly testifies to David's often stormy relations with other artists and with the Imperial authorities alike. His passage to becoming the officially designated 'first painter to the Emperor' in 1804, then an officer of the Legion of Honour and a chevalier of the Empire in 1808, was indeed a troubled one, involving major shifts of ideological allegiance. Anita Brookner's modern study of the painter suggests that his political views had probably remained relatively innocent and unformed in the pre-Revolutionary years, notwithstanding the tendency of some critics to see his more acclaimed works of that time as an anticipation of his later republican convictions.[9] Such early paintings as *The Death of Seneca*, *The Oath of the Horatii* (a Neo-classical masterpiece first exhibited in Rome in 1785), *The Death of Socrates*, and *Brutus receiving the Bodies of his Sons* certainly suggest a Stoic perception of civic virtue expressed through high-minded moral actions.

159

But their terrible power lay much more in David's sublimation of his own inner torments, which drew here on time-honoured tragedies from the classical past, than in any premonition of the impending Revolution in France.

What cannot be doubted is that the Revolution, when it *did* come, was a major influence in politicizing David's artistic vision and public career. It gave him the chance to merge his private grievances against the old Royal Academy of Painting, the dead weight of a tyrannical establishment, as he saw it, in the public cause of its destruction. In the course of this increasingly frenetic campaign he broke with his own master, J.-M. Vien, and eventually achieved his aim. The National Convention decreed the suppression of the Academy on 8 August 1793, and then that of all the other Academies six days later. At the same time, the didactic and in due course overtly republican thrust of David's paintings was closely related to major Revolutionary events up to 1794. Most notable were *The Oath of the Jeu de Paume* (finished as a drawing but never as a canvas) and his emotionally charged, almost religious representations of the assassinated republican martyrs of 1793: *Lepelletier* (a canvas destroyed many years later by the victim's daughter, a staunch royalist, who had bought it from David's heirs), *Marat,* and *Bara.*

The public reception of these three latter works was influenced to a large extent by a major shift of political alignments in the National Convention during the summer of 1793, as the Girondins were expelled and the Montagnards established themselves as the new governing group. David, who had been elected as a deputy to the Convention, threw himself so passionately behind their cause in the years 1792–94 that some of his colleagues then considered him 'delirious' (*en délire*), as Delécluze observed. His feverish activities were evident in the committees of public instruction and of general security, on both of which he served at different times, but undoubtedly had their greatest public impact at the various Revolutionary festivals, in whose organization he played the leading role. David became, in effect, the pageant-master of the Jacobin Republic, erecting huge painted symbolical displays of cardboard, plaster, and silver foil (none of which survived as such), perhaps most memorably at the Festival of the Supreme Being on 8 June 1794.

After the elimination of the Montagnard leaders in late July

1794, David was extremely fortunate to survive the Thermidorian reaction which followed. He was indeed imprisoned twice, but was finally set free in late October 1795. The whole experience certainly had a dampening effect on his political ardour and a melancholic one on his art. Brookner speaks appropriately enough of 'David's quietness of performance in the years 1795–99'.[10] No doubt chastened by his earlier traumas, he was wary of new political alliances. As he once put it in a memorable remark of that time, he would no longer attach himself to men, only to principles. Although he began work on a portrait of Napoleon (never to be finished) after the latter's triumphant return to Paris in December 1797, he had declined the earlier invitation to accompany the Army of Italy and paint the campaigns there. He also declined another invitation by Napoleon to join the Egyptian expedition in 1798, preferring to concentrate on his painting. The result was *The Intervention of the Sabine Women*, first conceived of during his imprisonment, and completed in 1799. It was a work of much more mature reflection than anything he had painted during his feverish Revolutionary avatars, and it showed that his instincts were sensitively attuned to the changing political mood in France. Its meaning is unmistakable: in the presence of young children, the unarmed women intervene, as if with healing power, to stop conflict among the male warriors. It may be seen as a heartfelt plea for national reconciliation, and perhaps at the same time as a personal expression of the painter's wish to make peace with his enemies and regain a wider public acceptance.

After Napoleon's victory in the Marengo campaign of 1800, which reinforced his *coup d'état* after some initial uncertainties, David's public career was drawn into a new course, with what real sincerity on his part it is difficult to say. His heroic paintings under the Consulate and Empire could be seen as works done to order, in obedience to his commissioning master, whose public celebrations were of course their central subject. Yet, all the while, David was working on his own private 'commission', *Leonidas at Thermopylae*, which was eventually finished in 1814 after fourteen years of interrupted effort. It is well known that Napoleon disliked the painting intensely, chiefly because its representation of impending military defeat prompted an unwelcome superstition about his own eventual fate. For other reasons, too, including not least the rising cost of David's commissions, the two men had by then become increasingly estranged.

Those were developments of the later Empire, however, and the fact remains that for most of the Napoleonic period David was its foremost painter laureate. In that sense, his pictorial contribution to 'the myth of the saviour' and 'the cult of the hero' was colossal. His *Napoleon crossing the Saint-Bernard* (1801), painted without sittings or any other real co-operation from his subject, was executed very much according to Napoleon's wishes. Heroic display altogether eclipsed any semblance of historical accuracy. The first consul had actually crossed the Saint-Bernard on a mule in fine weather, not on a fiery white horse in a windstorm. The impression was all that mattered to him, which is why the work has sometimes been seen as a less than successful mixture of Romantic energy and statuesque inertia, as too formal and idealized by half. The names carved on the stones beneath the horse's feet were self-consciously evocative: Hannibal – of the Carthaginian challenge to Rome; Charlemagne – of the mighty Frankish Empire; and Bonaparte – of the incumbent republican hero, soon to be a new Caesar.

And David it was, fittingly enough, who received the supreme accolade of painting this same passage from Republic to Empire for all posterity. His principal Imperial commissions were the *Coronation* (or *Sacre de Joséphine*) and *The Distribution of the Eagle Standards*, whose copious reproductions in textbooks over the years have probably established them as the visual representations of Napoleonic grandeur most familiar to readers. The *Coronation* (eventually finished towards the end of 1807, by which time David had already painted his celebrated portrait of *Pius VII* in 1805) impresses by its sheer scale, for it is an enormous canvas. It had been thought prudent not to tempt public disapproval by focusing on the moment in the ceremony in Notre-Dame on 2 December 1804 when Napoleon took the crown from the pope's hands and placed it on his own head. Instead, the painter's brief was to portray the subsequent act by which Napoleon crowned his empress. David's preparation of the details here was as methodical as ever, as a number of surviving sketches testify, but again there was a licence for unhistorical adornment. '*Madame Mère*', who had not approved of the ceremony, was then in Rome and did not attend it; neither did Cardinal Caprara. Yet both are conspicuously present in the painting. For Napoleon, the key requirement was the sumptuous display of universal adulation. On seeing the work for the first time in January 1808, he at once admired its realism, and said to the painter: 'good, very good, David. You have understood my thoughts, you have made me a French knight.'[11]

The Distribution of the Eagle Standards made a still greater trajectory across staggered time. The event depicted had taken place on 5 December 1804, three days after the Imperial coronation, when Napoleon and Josephine, their household retinue, and sundry military detachments had processed past prominent landmarks of the capital to the École Militaire. Its façade had been transformed into an enormous covered gallery, approached by steps leading up from the Champ de Mars, all lavishly decorated with military trophies and Imperial regalia, including the imposing eagles, set out on top of columns against the sky. In this dramatic atmosphere Napoleon had demanded and duly received an oath of allegiance from his marshals, generals, and other military representatives then present. David's painting of the event was not finished until 1810, by which time Napoleon had divorced Josephine (who had to be painted out of the canvas), and the painter's unpopularity had noticeably increased.

Critics have seen the *Eagle Standards* variously as a mainly decorative work devoid of artistic profundity, or as a Romantic *tour de force* which (for David) evoked powerful memories of past oaths long since renounced, or even as a representation of the social orders now merged in common loyalty to their new protector who had guaranteed their gains from the Revolution. This latter interpretation seems far-fetched, and might actually be more aptly applied to David's portraits of civilian worthies of the Empire. Perhaps the most notable here was that of *Comte Français de Nantes*, a former republican who had risen to be a count of the Empire and a councillor of state. A prefect and fiscal official to boot, Français typified the social ascent of the new class of Imperial *notables* only too well. David has captured his obvious self-satisfaction looking down at us, quite literally, from his elevated position in the portrait itself, where he poses magnificently clad in his official robes.

Whatever David's intentions in these works of the later Empire may have been, his star was already falling. The Imperial court, now complete with a new empress, had distanced itself from him, partly in reaction to his notoriously difficult character, but mainly because his demands for higher fees and greater honours were considered increasingly importunate. In 1812 he nevertheless finished a portrait of *Napoleon in his Study*, under-taken significantly on a private commission, which by all accounts was not displeasing to the emperor. Napoleon, preoccupied no doubt with preparations for his Russian campaign, was known to be suffering from persistent insomnia around that time. The full-length portrait shows him standing in official dress, and now visibly plumper all over, right hand tucked into his waist-coat in his most classic pose, apparently eager to work for his subjects even during the dark hours of the early morning, per-haps on the document bearing the word 'CODE' which lies on the desk behind him. The whole impression given is one of an indefatigable civil ruler, pictured in an intimate civil setting, which may now seem a rather incongruous and even fragile image in that year of unprecedented military disaster for him.

David's eclipse during the late Empire is also explained by the increasingly independent and innovatory work of his own pupils – Gros, Girodet, Guérin, Gérard, Ingres, and the mini-aturist Isabey, among others. Of these, Antoine-Jean Gros (1771–1835) was the most notable rival, not least because he too painted on Imperial commissions and left some of the most memorable depictions of Napoleon of the entire period, in a style sometimes characterized as Romantic classicism. He had been introduced to Napoleon and joined his service during the first Italian campaign, when he painted a number of its scenes, while David was refusing to commit himself to the new military star. Gros had then also served on the commission charged with selecting the works of art which were to be trans-ferred from Italy to Paris. His own *Napoleon crossing the Bridge at Arcola* (1796), painted in the atmosphere of the campaign itself, and so much admired by the hero, is often preferred to David's *Napoleon crossing the Saint-Bernard*, which was finished a few years later. Whereas David, even by his own admission, never excelled at 'action'-painting, this early work by Gros cer-tainly showed his talent for capturing physical movement on a canvas.

Later, having established himself as a Napoleonic propa-gandist, Gros turned his skills to other aspects of the emerging cult of the hero. In *Napoleon visiting the Plague Hospital at Jaffa* (1804), an eerie representation of a scene from the Egyptian campaign, his master is portrayed as a compassionate com-mander sharing the sufferings of his stricken soldiers and, it seems implied, dispensing miraculous cures by touch, just like

St Louis and the crusader kings of old. If the painter's own convictions in the matter are not beyond doubt, the impression given by the work itself was in stark contrast to the shocking stories Napoleon's enemies had put around, not least in Britain, that he had later ordered the poisoning of the plague victims in order to hasten the French retreat. The image of a compassionate Napoleon, who understood and shared the hardships of his troops, is also foremost in *The Battle of Eylau,* which Gros finished in 1807. The historical battle of February that year, fought in a snowstorm, had actually ended in a sort of stalemate, and with heavy losses on both the French and Russian sides, but is here transformed into a famous victory.

After the fall of Napoleon, it became even clearer that the future lay not with the marooned 'first painter' but with his former pupils. David, very much a *persona non grata* in the eyes of the twice-restored Bourbons, went into exile in Brussels in January 1816, where he devoted his remaining years to his art, returning to the Neo-classical forms which had marked his début. Gros, quickly adjusting his career to the new regime, was allowed to continue work on a commission he had received in 1812 to decorate the dome of the Pantheon. By the time he finished the work in 1824, all images of Napoleon and the King of Rome had been eliminated from its compositions, and the painter was promptly rewarded for his efforts with a baronetcy from Charles X. During the Restoration he also worked on other royal commissions, before changing popular tastes eventually left him isolated in his turn. Exposed to public ridicule at the Salon of 1835, he responded tragically by taking his own life.

One other figure who had a major influence on Imperial art, Dominique-Vivant Denon (1747–1825), also merits particular attention. Appointed as Napoleon's director-general of museums towards the end of 1802, he had a somewhat different role to play. The Louvre, where he was mainly based, had been opened as a museum on 10 August 1793, and was officially renamed the Musée Napoléon in July 1803. Denon made his personal contribution to Empire style mainly through engravings, often inspired by his own heroic experiences in Egypt, but he is perhaps best known for his untiring public work as a great collector. Whether by the crude method of looting, or by more subtle diplomatic persuasion, he redoubled his efforts to bring works of art to Paris from the conquered lands. During his office he built up fine collections of paintings, coins, porcelain, and tapestries, some of which were to be repossessed by the Allies and returned to their former owners, chiefly after the Hundred Days. Among those of the dispossessed peoples who had had the courage earlier to speak out in protest against such artistic plunder was Antonio Canova, the distinguished Italian sculptor. This did not, however, prevent him from accepting some notable commissions (for busts more particularly) from Napoleon, from members of his family, and from other Imperial dignitaries. One of his most famous works is *Venus Reclining* (1807), his nude statue of Pauline Borghese (Bonaparte).

In spite of his great admiration for Canova, Napoleon was never able to persuade the sculptor, too much an Italian patriot at heart, to commit himself firmly to the Imperial cause. There is no doubt that architecture and sculpture were major manifestations of Napoleon's monumental vision of Empire, but in patronizing them he relied very largely on the services of Frenchmen. The latter at least were willing to work to the terms of his commissions, which might almost be likened to a form of cultural '*dirigisme*', especially in Paris itself. The Conseil des Bâtiments Civils, which assisted the ministry of the interior, supervised the whole range of civic architecture. The appointment of Louis Bruyère as director of public works in the capital in 1811 strengthened such central controls. The restoration and redecoration of the Imperial palaces was entrusted to Pierre Fontaine (who in 1813 officially became the 'first architect to the Emperor') and Charles Percier, the two most influential exponents of the Empire style, whose partnership was to last thirty-five years. Besides their decorative commissions at Malmaison, Saint-Cloud, Versailles, the Tuileries, Compiègne, Fontainebleau, and the Élysée, they at different times undertook major work on a number of civic buildings and monuments, most notably the Louvre, the Arc de Triomphe du Carrousel, and the Temple de la Gloire (the Madeleine).[12]

Napoleon's own understanding of architecture and sculpture was vainglorious but inexpert. As he wrote in a Note of 14 May 1806 on arches:

It is essential that all the designs should conform to the same general description. One of the first two must be a Marengo arch, and the other an arch of Austerlitz. I shall have another erected somewhere in Paris, to be the arch of Peace, and a fourth to be the

166

arch of Religion. With these four arches I am confident that I can finance French sculpture for 20 years. . . . Generally speaking, no opportunity should be missed to humiliate the Russians and the English.[13]

This grandiose vision was not without its practical sequel, for apart from those earmarked for the Imperial palaces, the main commissions to architects and sculptors were indeed concentrated in the years 1806–12. Significantly, too, they were to be funded in large part by indemnities extracted from conquered enemies.

The building programme thus began in the lustre cast by Napoleon's spectacular military victories of 1805–7. It included commemorative monuments, public buildings, fountains, gardens, squares, streets, and even some purely functional amenities, like the *quais* and bridges of the Seine, and the markets or *halles* of the capital.[14] Perhaps the monument best known nowadays is the Arc de Triomphe de l'Étoile, whose erection on the heights of the Champs-Élysées was decreed in 1806 in a commission to Jean Chalgrin and Arnaud Raymond, but which was not officially inaugurated until 1836, under the July Monarchy. Other commissions sponsored such familiar landmarks as the column on the Place Vendôme and the Paris Bourse. On the birth of an heir to the Imperial throne in 1811, the Palais du Roi de Rome was commissioned, but military reverses after 1812 cut short work on its construction. Napoleon's aim, announced quite early during the Consulate, was to make Paris 'not only the most beautiful city that ever existed, but the most beautiful city that could exist'.[15] (His nephew, Napoleon III, was to sponsor a similar programme to rebuild the city half a century later, entrusting the project to Baron Haussmann.)

In all, Napoleon's contribution to the visual arts can be measured more by its scale, by the manifestations of 'big is beautiful', than by the originality of style and methods. As Claude Bergeron has reminded us, most of his architects and sculptors were men trained in the eighteenth century, who under the Empire were given the opportunity to erect colossal buildings and colonnades they had often thought of earlier but been unable to execute for lack of patronage.[16] According to the same author, the teaching of architecture under Napoleon also drew on eighteenth-century forms and was influenced by the precepts of painting, both of which had been concentrated in the

Louvre after the abolition of the old Academies in 1793. This also reflected in the preponderance of artistic disciplines in the Fourth Class (Fine Arts) of the Institute and at the École des Beaux-Arts. The more progressive teaching of architecture, which placed its emphasis on solidity, functional convenience, and economy rather than on decorative flourishes, came later in the nineteenth century. Originating in the work of J.-L.-N. Durand at the École Polytechnique, founded in 1795, this trend gained a foothold in the École des Beaux-Arts when one of his pupils, J.-B. Rondelet, became a professor there in 1806.[17]

Finally, it was not only by commissions but also through his system of social honours that Napoleon sought to reward his most successful servants in the visual arts. According to one authority, at least 28 artists (excluding foreigners) had been awarded the Legion of Honour by the end of the Empire: one at the rank of commander, one other at that of officer, and 26 at the rank of chevalier. Besides David, the officer here referred to, the chevaliers included four of his pupils – Gérard, Guérin, Gros, and Girodet. Furthermore, if one interprets the term 'artist' in a wide sense, eight men were granted the higher honour of elevation into the Imperial nobility between 1808 and 1811. The title of chevalier of the Empire was bestowed on David, Visconti, Vivant Denon, Regnault, and the sculptor Houdon; that of baron on Forbin and Turpin de Crissé; and that of count on Vien, who was also appointed a senator.[18] On the other hand, Napoleon was less lavish in granting such honours to artists than Louis XV and Louis XVI had been before the Revolution, and very much less generous than Louis XVIII and Charles X were to prove during the Bourbon Restoration.

．．．．．．．．．．．．．．．．．．．．

THE PRESS, CENSORSHIP, AND STATE PROPAGANDA

From the earliest days of the regime, press censorship and other restrictions on the expression of dissident opinion were introduced. The regulation of the press began in earnest when a Consular *arrêté* of 17 January 1800 reduced the number of daily newspapers in Paris from 73 to 13, and it was increasingly tightened through the press bureau of the ministry of police during the next eleven years.[19] The climax came in 1810–11, when a major reorganization was imposed on both the Parisian and the local provincial press.[20] After these new draconian decrees, only four journals still had licences to publish in Paris: the *Gazette de France*, the *Journal des Débats*, the *Journal de Paris*, and the *Moniteur*. All were mouthpieces of the government, and the single journals then allowed in each department were to be obedient echoes of those central organs. The latter, most notably the *Moniteur*, were now little more than instruments of propaganda, carefully watched and manipulated by the relevant ministers. As from 1811, moreover, all political articles submitted for publication in the *Moniteur* first had to be edited by the minister secretary of state, Maret, who exercised official control over their insertion or rejection.

State propaganda had two main functions. To the negative aim of stifling opposition was added the more positive one of rousing morale among the 'citizen-soldiers' and civilian subjects of the emperor by an orchestrated celebration of his military victories and Imperial grandeur. French defeats, when they were reported at all, were invariably put down to inferiority of numbers.[21] Here, one may recall Madame de Staël's later remark that Napoleon tried 'to monopolize celebrity for himself'. In doing so, he used two new devices, the bulletin and the order of the day, as mediums through which to appeal to his subjects. And indeed, there is no denying the wider public impact of communications like the *Bulletins de la Grande Armée*. These began to appear in the *Moniteur* from the time of Napoleon's 1805 campaign, as well as being disseminated in the provinces by prefects, mayors, and (with much less success) the clergy, and their serial numbers then became a regular feature of his subsequent campaigns. Their exaggerated accounts of his glorious military achievements undoubtedly struck a chord among many readers – *male* readers, one imagines, most of all – and they were to live on in the legend well after 1815. They sometimes invoked a powerful nostalgia in later literary works as well, most memorably perhaps in the attraction they held for Julien Sorel, the central character of Stendhal's *Le Rouge et le Noir* (1830).

In this way, Napoleon had himself been actively instrumental in writing his own history. Although his propaganda was aimed less at his troops than at the French people as a whole, its popular effect is difficult to measure in statistical terms. One contemporary estimate (by Roederer) put the number of newspaper readers in Paris and the provincial departments at some 300,000, the capital itself accounting for a third, and predominantly rural areas for only one-sixth of them.[22] If that global

figure is even approximately reliable, it would have represented
no more than 1 per cent of the total population of France
under the Empire. On the other hand, some at least of Napoleon's legendary exploits found their way into a more obviously popular culture. The verses of the patriotic *chansonnier*
P.-J. Béranger, for instance, nearly always invoked an heroic
picture of Napoleon. Although Béranger was to enjoy a much
wider fame in later years, he first attracted significant public
attention towards the end of the Empire.

Whatever its limitations, official propaganda became an
important function of an Empire almost constantly at war,
having to draw each year on its uneducated masses for military
and fiscal levies. The regime expected, and was insistent on
receiving, regular reports from the prefects on the 'frame of
mind' (*état moral*) of the people. It also used techniques, most
of them exceedingly crude, to denigrate the enemy, and more
especially Britain. Napoleon even laid claim to divine sanction
for his military actions – '*Gott strafe England*', as it were! –
through a State-controlled religious journal. This was the *Journal des Curés*, which in 1806 supplanted all other remaining
religious journals, until it was itself incorporated in the new
Journal de Paris in 1811. Napoleon also sought to impose a
similar monopoly over national festivals. Under the Consulate,
these were confined to 14 July (the storming of the Bastille,
1789) and 21 September (the abolition of the Bourbon monarchy and establishment of the Republic, 1792); but after the
proclamation of the Empire they were gradually phased out
and replaced by other festival days, whose tone became increasingly military. As the traditional Feast of the Assumption
happened to coincide with Napoleon's birthday on 15 August,
it was officially celebrated in the unlikely guise of 'Saint Napoleon's Day' as from 1806. Other Imperial festivals were rather
more predictable: 14 October (the battle of Jena), 9 November
(the coup of 18 Brumaire), and 2 December (the anniversary
of both the Imperial coronation and the battle of Austerlitz,
the latter also being celebrated by a *Te Deum* in churches on
the first Sunday of that month).

It is hardly surprising that public theatres, which Napoleon
regarded as having a particularly subversive potential, were
obliged to work within the very strict limitations imposed by a
specially designated superintendent in Paris, Rémusat. A decree
of 29 July 1807 reduced the number of theatres in the capital

from 33 to 8 and more strictly regulated their productions. Tighter control of provincial theatres followed in due course. All plays perceived as challenging established authority were to be banned, as were those with an anti-religious bias.[23] At the same time, the Imperial government was willing to patronize major establishments which complied with its rules. Its lavish subsidies to the Théâtre Français (formerly the Comédie Française until 1803), the Odéon, the Opéra, and the Opéra Comique, most notably, were themselves stepped up from time to time.

It should, then, be clear that Napoleon regarded propaganda and censorship as vital instruments for projecting his image to the French people. By the classic ploys of *suppressio veri* and *suggestio falsi*, he sought to manipulate inarticulate public opinion in his own cause, while his ministers and other officials were expected to serve as acolytes at the same altar. As he once remarked, 'the truth is not half so important as what people think to be true'.[24] On the other hand, his system often worked deficiently, partly because of his reluctance to delegate authority, and partly also because some of his official censors worked independently of one another in different ministries. Besides Philippe Lagarde, who headed the press bureau of the ministry of police, and Maret at the secretariat of state, at least two other ministries (the interior and foreign affairs) had censorship bureaux. Of these latter, the Direction Générale de l'Imprimerie et de la Librairie, an agency of the ministry of the interior, eventually became the most important. Headed initially by Pommereul after its establishment in February 1810, and then by Portalis, it dealt with books, an area in which it soon came into conflict with prominent writers, as we shall see shortly. How far Napoleon was prepared to go in silencing his critics had already been brutally demonstrated in 1809, when the Nuremberg publisher Johann Palm was executed on his orders for printing the patriotic pamphlet *Germany in her Lowest Abasement*.

. . . .

EDUCATION AND THE HIGHER
INSTITUTIONS OF LEARNING

Education was another obvious area in which official propaganda could be disseminated as a major function of social regulation by the State. Despite Napoleon's tendency to view the education of the public as a utilitarian process, which could be run on martial lines according to the same principles of uniformity and of centralized and hierarchical authority evident in other branches of his civil rule, his achievements here were substantial, and some were to prove remarkably enduring. If his innovations had little significant impact on the general standards of popular literacy in his Empire, he certainly made a serious attempt to harness the talents among the existing social and professional élites, and to reorganize the career structures in which they might serve his regime.

Now, it has to be said that Napoleon and his chief educationalists were starting from a relatively low base. State provision for the education of the general public had made little real headway under the old regime. Church schools had then predominated almost everywhere at primary and secondary level, a fact which conversely reflects the minimal effect of the often elaborate theories of the secular Enlightenment on the practical difficulties of educating the popular classes.[25] The bolder initiatives devised by some prominent deputies during the French Revolution, for instance by Condorcet on behalf of the committee of public instruction of the Legislative Assembly, had not fulfilled their rhetorical promise. The so-called *écoles centrales*, most notably, the showpiece of a plan decreed by the National Convention in February 1795 to make a standardized form of State education more accessible at secondary level, had produced only mixed results under the Directory. So, too, had the project adopted in October that year to incorporate the State primary schools (which had been decreed earlier) with this same new model. Whether through lack of political will, or through inadequate funding and a chronic shortage of qualified lay teachers, or through the teaching of rather variable syllabuses which actually belied their name, the *écoles centrales* had had little impact on the general public by the time of Brumaire. As one authority on the subject has concluded, they had been only a 'qualified success' among particular republican groups with a prospective interest in public service.[26] The Church schools, meanwhile, had themselves been disrupted by the anticlerical bias of so much Revolutionary legislation and by the excesses of the 'dechristianization' campaign, although the extent of the damage has often been exaggerated.

And so, in default of a national educational system, Napoleon set out to build the foundations of one under the aegis of the lay State. He retained the principles of centralization and standardization, that is the basic conceptual model of the *écoles centrales*, which were now to be abolished altogether, but aimed to give it a much firmer institutional form. In this respect, the more authoritarian executive structures of his government were altogether better suited to his purpose. There was to be a strong emphasis on functional utility, not only in training the future military leaders of France, but also in civil education. The key innovation here was the fundamental law of 1 May 1802. It was in large part the brainchild of A.-F. Fourcroy, the distinguished scientist and a member of Napoleon's council of state, who had already established his reputation as an influential educational reformer since the time of the National Convention. It provided for the creation of a new hierarchy of primary schools, *lycées* and communal schools at secondary level, and colleges under a directory of public instruction, which was itself to be headed by a councillor of state in the ministry of the interior.

Indeed, as the director-general of public instruction, Fourcroy was given a personal role in the implementation of his plan. A *lycée* was to be set up in each court of appeal, and the instructors chosen by the first consul himself. In time, a total of 45 were in fact established, 4 of them in Paris, and from the start the regime exerted a direct influence over their admission of pupils. Of the 6,400 State scholarships tenable at these schools, over a third (2,400) were to be chosen by the government from among the sons of soldiers and officials, or from children born in the recently 'reunited' departments, while the remaining 4,000 were to be filled (in theory) by competition among pupils at the best secondary schools. Yet the effect, as is well known, was to favour better-off families almost entirely.[27] The administration of the *lycées* was dominated from top to bottom by officials nominated by Napoleon. Subservience and outward displays of loyalty to his government were axiomatic requirements in these new schools. Their regime was Spartan, their ethos decidedly military, which in the event did not appeal to most civilian families. Their core curriculum at first had two sections, one based on Latin and the other on mathematics; but in time a wider range of options was offered and a firmer emphasis given to the sort of religious instruction which the government considered acceptable.

Uniformity and obedience to the Napoleonic regime were

applied in primary and secondary schools in a number of other ways. The reinstatement of the *agrégation* as a qualification for the recruitment of teachers in 1808 is a case in point. So, too, the introduction of the baccalaureate examination in 1809 was aimed at a closer standardization of the curriculum in the *lycées*. Official regulation of the communal secondary schools and of private (most notably Church) schools also steadily increased. This process started early when, in October 1803, all private secondary schools were obliged to accept administrative councils whose members were vetted by the government, using the prefects as its most characteristic instrument of control. This policy reached a peak in 1811, when several tougher measures were issued in an attempt to curb the influence of the Church in private education. In practice, their bark was worse than their bite. The fact remains that clerical participation in teaching and educational administration revived during the Empire, in State as well as private schools, at least by comparison with the Revolutionary decade. One reason for this was entirely practical: there were, quite simply, not enough qualified lay teachers available.

The principle of centralized control was not surprisingly extended to the higher echelons of education in their turn. These, in due course, were given an elaborate form in the so-called 'Imperial University' – 'my University', as Napoleon was to call it in 1815. The latter was never in fact a university in the normal sense, more an agglomeration of teaching bodies intended to establish a State monopoly over public education beyond secondary level, an aim which had not been fully achieved by 1814. The idea of a 'University of France' was first enunciated in the law of 10 May 1806, and it too bore the unmistakable stamp of Fourcroy's influence. Four days earlier, in a report to the legislative body, he had clearly stated that 'education must impart the same knowledge and the same principles to all individuals living in the same society, so that they will make as it were one body, informed with one and the same understanding and working for the common good on the basis of uniformity of views and desires'.[28] The 'Imperial University' was actually implemented by the decree of 17 March 1808. Its structure was characteristically hierarchical, and from the start it enjoyed generous annual subsidies from the State. Louis de Fontanes, its first grand master, was chosen by Napoleon himself and given a wide-ranging jurisdiction, in the exercise of which he was assisted by a carefully selected council of thirty members, and by a chancellor, a treasurer, and inspectors general. From those commanding heights, authority was transmitted down through a whole hierarchy of officials in the twenty-seven provincial 'academies' and even in the local schools which collectively formed the 'Imperial University'.

Although Napoleon's initial intention had been to favour the appointment of lay teachers and administrators through-out his 'University', he certainly did not always get his way. Fontanes, the friend of Chateaubriand and in other respects also sympathetic to Catholic learning, was able to maintain a significant clerical influence over both appointments and the curriculum within the vast corporation under his charge. As a result, the 'Imperial University' was to become a sort of covert battle-ground in which progressives who favoured public in-struction based on the secular sciences were often in conflict with traditionalists who fought tenaciously to defend the older emphasis on the humanities and the position of the Church.[29] The uniformity of the lay system originally envisaged was to that extent undermined, while the fundamental loyalty to Napoleon of many who worked within it could not be wholly guaranteed. When the time came, Fontanes himself had no difficulty in adjusting his official career to the ways of the Bourbon Restoration.

As for the *savants* of the other higher institutions of learn-ing, many in practice also enjoyed a relative freedom to con-duct and communicate their research. The Museum of Natural History had been transformed from the old 'Jardin du Roi' in 1793. The Collège de France had replaced the former Royal College in 1795. In the same year the National Institute of Sciences and Arts had similarly subsumed the old French Acad-emy and other royal academies, abolished two years earlier. All continued to enjoy official encouragement under Napoleon; but they too were expected to enhance his prestige among the luminaries of the sciences and humanities, and were not immune from his wrath. When the 'Ideologues' in the Second Class (Moral and Political Sciences) of the Institute fell foul of him over the Concordat, as well as over the creation of special courts and the abolition of the *écoles centrales*, he dissolved that body in January 1803. The Institute was rearranged into four classes, which excluded some of his critics and silenced others who remained.[30] The new Second Class (French Language and

Literature) consisted of the 'Forty Immortals', who included several former Academicians, and on whom he bestowed great honours. In this sense he can be regarded as the architect of the Academy's refoundation.

Napoleon's admiration for and personal association with several distinguished scientists also produced its official rewards. The mathematician Laplace, for instance, one of the foremost spirits of the Society of Arcueil, and who was to have considerable influence in the Physical Science section of the Institute, served very briefly as minister of the interior at the start of the Consulate. He was appointed shortly afterwards to the senate, where he rose steadily in office, stature, and emoluments, as well as being elevated later to the Legion of Honour and receiving the title of count. Chaptal, one of his rather longer-serving and exemplary successors at the Interior and an early member of the council of state, had already earned a reputation as a theoretical and industrial chemist. He later served as a technical adviser to the government, notably on the council for trade and industry. He was appointed a senator on his retirement from ministerial office, and was later granted the title of comte de Chanteloup, after his own property, where many of his later experiments with sugar-beet production were conducted. Berthollet, another famous chemist of the time and doyen of the Society of Arcueil, had helped in the scientific preparations for and indeed shared the physical hazards of Napoleon's Egyptian campaign. He became in due course a senator, with a lucrative senatoriate to boot, an officer of the Legion of Honour, and a count of the Empire.

There are other examples of Napoleon's favours to the *savants* of the sciences and of their valuable services to him. The chemist Fourcroy, whose formative role in educational policy has already been noted, had been one of the founders of the École Polytechnique and of the École de Santé in Paris during the Revolution, and was also active in the Institute from its earliest days. Before his death in 1809, he too was made a count of the Empire. Monge, the mathematician and scientist, with a long and distinguished record at the École Polytechnique, had joined the Egyptian expedition and been honoured with the presidency of the Institute of Egypt. After Brumaire he helped to found the Society for the Encouragement of National Industry (1801). Napoleon appointed him to the senate (whose president he became in 1806), as a grand officer of the Legion of Honour, and in 1808 as comte de Péluse. Lagrange, finally, one of the leading mathematicians of the eighteenth century, was another who rose into the senate, before becoming a grand officer of the Legion of Honour and then a count of the Empire.

Such, then, were the most glittering prizes among the higher educational establishment and scientific élite of the time, where the theme of patronage and reflected glory at the top seems clear enough. In some cases, we can also detect the deliberate social advancement of men who had shared an old *camaraderie* with the future victor of Brumaire, whether in Egypt, or at the Institute, or in the *coup d'état* itself. Those who had been enthusiastic Brumaireans had a natural entrée into the favours of the regime.

As for the rest, many benefited in lesser ways from Napoleon's consistent interest in and willingness to encourage all useful technical training. This can be seen in his sponsorship of a Conservatory for Arts and Trades in Paris, of the smaller trade schools (*arts et métiers*) set up in some provincial towns, of the Society for the Encouragement of National Industry, and of prizes for the best mechanical inventions. In launching them, he was often able to draw on the expertise available in institutions which had first made their mark during the Revolution. And, here again, the most notable was the reconstituted École Polytechnique, which fed the special schools and through them the technical services of the State.[31] The special schools themselves were intended to be professional training grounds for both military and civil personnel. Besides the new École Spéciale Militaire created in 1803, special schools for law, medicine, natural history, physics, chemistry, geography, and several other disciplines were provided for in the ambitious law of 1 May 1802. The medical schools in particular already had a notable Revolutionary pedigree and continued to function without major change. But of the new foundations envisaged, only those in law were ever effectively implemented under the Empire; the others barely got beyond the project stage.[32] Félix Ponteil has described the special schools which were actually established as the 'appendices' of the *lycées*, since their entrants all had to meet the requirement of prior attendance at one of those secondary schools.[33]

In very sharp contrast, Napoleon's views on the education of females were blunt and condescending. What now briefly follows may well cause offence to readers who today regard the equality of the sexes as axiomatic. But, of course, we have to remember that we are dealing here with a mentality conditioned by earlier Corsican custom, and with the masculine assertiveness of a trained soldier whose domineering personality had been evident from the earliest days. Christopher Herold cites an abrupt exchange between Napoleon and Madame de Staël at a dinner party in Talleyrand's house in 1799. 'What woman, dead or alive, do you consider to be the greatest?' she then asked; 'The one who has had the most children', he replied.[34] Again, while residing at the château of Finkenstein, at a time when he was enjoying the intimate favours of Maria Walewska, Napoleon made the following assertion in a Note dated 15 May 1807:

> Religion is an all-important matter in a public school for girls. Whatever people may say, it is the mother's surest safeguard, and the husband's. What we ask of education is not that girls should think, but that they should believe. The weakness of women's brains, the instability of their ideas, the place they will fill in society, their need for perpetual resignation, and for an easy and generous type of charity – all this can only be met by religion, and by religion of a gentle and charitable kind.[35]

Or finally, in a conversation on St Helena in 1817, when he was no longer in any position to give effect to his word, he professed that 'women receive too much consideration in France. They should not be regarded as the equals of men; they are, in fact, mere machines to make children.'[36]

. . . . . .

LITERATURE

Such views obviously did not appeal to Madame de Staël, who was one of the most liberated as well as celebrated literary figures of her time. She had many encounters with Napoleon and his ministers, and records of some of them have fortunately been preserved. They testify to a steadily worsening relationship, which ended in her exile, first from Paris in 1802 and then from France altogether in 1803. Yet in the early years her attitude had been more adulatory, indeed naïvely so, for she apparently believed that this strong man of wonderful military exploits would also be the great liberator of France.

Las Cases recounts one episode in his *Mémorial de Sainte-Hélène* of 1823:

> Madame de Staël's *Delphine* was at this time [18–20 January 1816] a subject of conversation at our evening parties. The Emperor analyzed it: few things in it escaped his censure. The irregularity of mind and imagination which pervades it, excited his criticism: there were throughout, said he, the same faults which had formerly made him keep the author at a distance, notwithstanding the most pointed advances and the most unremitting flattery on her part. No sooner had victory immortalized the young General of the Army of Italy, than Madame de Staël, unacquainted with him, from the mere sympathy of glory, instantly professed for him sentiments of enthusiasm worthy of her own *Corinne*; she wrote him long and numerous epistles, full of wit, imagination, and metaphysical erudition: it was an error, she observed, arising only from human institutions, that could have united him with the meek, the tranquil Madame Bonaparte; it was a soul of fire like her's (Madame de Staël's) that nature had undoubtedly destined to be the companion of a hero like him.
>
> I refer to the Campaigns in Italy, to show that this forwardness on the part of Madame de Staël was not checked by the circumstance of meeting with no return. With a perseverance never to be disheartened, she succeeded, at a later period, in forming some degree of acquaintance, so far even as to be allowed to visit; and she used this privilege, said the Emperor, to a disagreeable extent. It is unquestionably true, as has been reported, that the General, wishing to make her sensible of it, one day caused her to be told, by way of excuse, that he was scarcely dressed; and that she replied promptly and earnestly, that it was unimportant, for that genius was of no sex.[37]

It is clear that *Delphine* (1802) and *Corinne* (1807) were to remain constant irritants to Napoleon. The former, a novel in which Madame de Staël poses the problem of the equality of the sexes, once prompted him to declare that 'I don't like masculine women any more than effeminate men. Everybody should play his own part in this world. What's the meaning of all this gypsying of the imagination? What remains of it? Nothing. All this is sentimental metaphysics, intellectual disorder.'[38] This particular outburst occurred around 1803. Much later, during a conversation on St Helena in 1816, the subject of *Corinne* elicited a similar dismissal: 'that family of Mme de Staël's certainly is a strange one. Her father [Necker], her mother [Suzanne

Curchod], and herself, all three kneeling before one another in perpetual adoration, smoking one another out with reciprocal incense for the edification and mystification of the public.'[39] And yet, as he said on another occasion that same year, 'I am certainly far from thinking or saying that she has a bad heart: the fact is, that she and I have waged a little war against each other, and that is all.'[40]

This rupture with the Napoleonic regime was to delay the publication in France of Madame de Staël's *De l'Allemagne* (1810), one of the greatest works of Romantic criticism of its time, of which 10,000 printed copies were summarily seized on the orders of Savary, then minister of police. Her interest in German aesthetics and religiosity was long-standing, and some commentators have explained this in terms of her Swiss and Protestant origins. As early as 1802, in the preface to *Delphine*, she had thought it necessary 'that a man of genius should one day enrich himself by the fecund originality of some German writers before the French will be persuaded that there are works in Germany in which the ideas are profound and the sentiments expressed with a new energy'.[41] Her own aim was to naturalize such 'sentiments' and 'energy' in France. All her discussions with German visitors to her Swiss retreat at Coppet, near Geneva, as well as her own visits to Germany (1804 and 1809) and to Vienna (1809), were poured into *De l'Allemagne* and refined in a most original way. French writers of the period were all too prone to regard German letters as distinctly inferior to their own, just as later historians until quite recently tended to see the *Aufklärung* as a servile imitation of the French *Lumières*. Yet here was Madame de Staël, taking her cue in part from the earlier work of another Germanophile, the émigré Charles de Villers, daring to argue that the French had much to learn from the aesthetic sensibility of their neighbours across the Rhine.

Madame de Staël's deepening hostility to Napoleon undoubtedly influenced her view of Germany – and *subjugated* Germany at that – as in some way an exemplary land, whose civilized peoples had been humiliated and traumatized by the brutality of their philistine conquerors. The official reaction to *De l'Allemagne* in France was quick and predictable. In his letter to Madame de Staël of 3 October 1810, Savary not only confirmed the ban on the book's sale but toughened the terms of her exile. 'It has seemed to me that the air of this country does not agree with you,' he wrote, 'and we are not yet reduced to searching for models among the peoples you admire. Your latest work is not French at all.'[42] In her *Dix années d'exil*, written between 1810 and 1813 but not published until 1821, four years after her death, Madame de Staël was to rail against the Imperial regime still more vehemently. And in a polemical tract of 1813 she was to dismiss its institutional flummery – senate, legislative body, and all – as 'that concert of high-flown praises' and as 'the imperial conservatories of flattery'.[43] She ended with an eloquent appeal to the nations of Europe to rise up and join forces to overthrow Napoleon and establish peace.

Within two years, Madame de Staël's wish would be fulfilled. Her enmity towards Napoleon persisted after his fall, and she was then in a safer position to indulge some caustic reminiscences. In her *Considérations sur les principaux événements de la Révolution française*, published posthumously in 1818, she could write:

> I had the distressing feeling that no emotion of the heart could ever reach him. He regards a human being like a fact or a thing, never as an equal. He neither hates nor loves. . . . The force of his will resides in the imperturbable calculations of his egotism; he is a chess master whose opponent happens to be the rest of humanity. . . . Neither pity nor attraction, nor religion nor attachment would ever divert him from his ends. . . . I felt in his soul cold steel, I felt in his mind a deep irony against which nothing great or good, even his own destiny, was proof; for he despised the nation which he intended to govern, and no spark of enthusiasm was mingled with his desire to astound the human race.[44]

Napoleon's 'little war' was waged with other prominent writers of the period, and for much the same reason: their supposed disobedience and lack of patriotism. His own view on the matter was crude. Finding time to write to Cambacérès on 21 November 1806, the very day of the Berlin decree which officially proclaimed the Continental Blockade, he protested that 'whilst the army does all it can for the glory of the nation, it must be admitted that our writers are doing their best to dishonour it. . . . People complain that we have no literature: it is the fault of the Home Minister [minister of the interior]. It's ridiculous to order an eclogue from a poet as one orders a muslin frock from the dressmaker's.'[45] The contradiction here between the freedom of artistic expression and the heavy hand of the State as the self-appointed arbiter of taste had apparently escaped Napoleon. There was a serious point to his passing remark in 1817 that 'the French language is not a well-made language. I ought to have codified it.'[46]

The ambivalence of some writers towards the Napoleonic regime is well illustrated in the literary and political career of Benjamin Constant, who was for many years Madame de Staël's lover, and the author of the Romantic novels *Adolphe* and *Cécile*. Early in the Consulate he was appointed to the tribunate, where he quickly fell foul of the first consul for his liberal views, and was among those expelled from it in the 'purge' of 1802. A long period in the political wilderness followed, as he went into exile and devoted himself to his work and the great loves which inspired it. In 1813, while in Germany, he also published *De l'esprit de conquête et de l'usurpation*, a polemical tract in which his denunciation of Napoleon was unrestrained. Yet only two years later, when it was hardly safe to do so, he made a sudden *volte-face* and a curious return to public life as a councillor of state during the Hundred Days. His influence on the drafting of the 'Additional Act to the Constitutions of the Empire', by which reform Napoleon hoped to win over the support of the liberal bourgeoisie, and which some at the time referred to as ' *la benjamine*', is well established. This intervention was almost a costly blunder, and his motives are indeed rather difficult to fathom. After the Second Restoration he went first to Brussels and then to London, where he published *Adolphe* in 1816. Having at last made his peace with Louis XVIII, he returned to France in 1818, and renewed his earlier political credentials, both as a journalist and as a leader of the Liberal opposition in the chamber of deputies. In that sense, and under another regime, his own wheel had come full circle.

It was Madame de Staël who had first brought Benjamin Constant into association with another group of writers and philosophers commonly referred to as the 'Ideologues', and she indeed who turned her famous *salon* in the Rue du Bac into a seminary of political opposition and liberal opinions. As Napoleon himself recalled on St Helena in October 1816:

Her [Madame de Staël's] house had become quite an arsenal against me; people went there to be armed knights. She endeavoured to raise enemies against me and fought against me herself. She was at once Armida and Clorinda. . . . After all, it cannot be denied that

Madame de Staël is a very distinguished woman, endowed with great talents and possessing a considerable share of wit. She will go down to posterity. It was more than once hinted to me, in order to soften me in her favour, that she was an adversary to be feared, and might become a useful ally; and certainly if instead of reviling me as she did, she had spoken in my praise, it might no doubt have proved advantageous to me; for her position and her abilities gave her an absolute sway over the *salons*, and their influence in Paris is well known.[47]

Madame de Staël and Benjamin Constant were not 'Ideologues' in the stricter philosophical sense, however, and their association with those more properly so called was largely confined to shared political views, especially during the Consulate.

The 'Ideologues' themselves might be described as a group of philosophers and writers who, at the end of the eighteenth century and the beginning of the nineteenth, extended the theory of sensationalism primarily associated with Condillac, notably in his *Traité des sensations* (1754) and *Logique* (1780), both of which had been heavily influenced by John Locke's ideas. They sought to demonstrate their notion of the perfectibility of man through a science of psychology based on observable organic reactions. They thought that artistic expression, for instance through creative literary works, should be judged by the organic impression it produced on man's senses, whether of reason or sensibility. Their political orientation was republican and therefore, under Napoleon, liberal. Their leader, '*le chef des idéologues*', is commonly identified as Destutt de Tracy (1754–1836), formerly a member of the committee of public instruction (1799–1800) and a staunch defender of the Revolutionary *écoles centrales*, who published several volumes under the title *Élémens d'idéologie* over the years 1801–15.[48]

Napoleon himself coined the term 'Ideologues' in 1800, abusively, intending it to mean a bunch of pretentious metaphysicians with dangerous revolutionary notions. The latter, in fact, were a diverse group, not in any sense a coherent 'school' of thought, and should more properly be seen as intellectual materialists, several of whom were prepared to assume public appointments under Napoleon. Besides the philosophers, they included Cabanis, well known for his medical studies, Volney the orientalist, the playwright Marie-Joseph Chénier, and some of the most outspoken critics of Napoleon in the tribunate.

Among the émigrés who returned to France under Napoleon's

amnesty of 1800 was the vicomte de Chateaubriand (1768–1848), who is best remembered for his last great work, the monumental *Mémoires d'outre-tombe*. He had spent part of his exile in America (1791–2), an experience he later distilled in exotic Romantic novels like *Atala* (1801), *René* (1805), and *Les Natchez* (1826). He broke with Napoleon in 1804, after the murder of the duc d'Enghien, giving up his diplomatic post in Rome. During the next few years he travelled widely, in Greece, in the Near East, and in Spain. On his return to France he devoted himself to literature and journalism, contributing regularly to the *Mercure de France* and to the *Journal des débats*. In spite of Napoleon's displeasure, he was elected to the Académie in 1811.

It is for one of his earliest works, *Génie du christianisme*, published in 1802, that Chateaubriand merits particular attention in the present context. He shared Madame de Staël's aesthetic interest in religion and religiosity, but in this work at least he turned his focus squarely on France itself to produce a sustained essay in Christian apologetics. It appeared at a receptive time, the Concordat between Napoleon and Pius VII having just been celebrated. Chateaubriand was not alone in sensing this change of mood. At about the same time a number of other writers were also responding to the renewed interest in Christian sentimentality after its buffetings during the Revolution. Fiévée's *La Dot de Suzette* (1798), Ballanche's *Du sentiment considéré dans ses rapports avec la littérature et les arts* (1801), Madame de Genlis's *La Duchesse de Vallière* (1804), and Madame Cottin's *Mathilde* (1805) all catered for such taste. *Génie du christianisme* was nevertheless the major influence in restoring literary and even philosophical respectability to the traditional Christian faith. It was to influence the more theological writings of Louis de Bonald and Joseph de Maistre, who are often seen as the principal apologists of the Catholic revival after 1815.

The work has four parts: dogma and doctrine, poetics, the *beaux-arts* and literature, and cults. From all of these angles it aimed to revive Christianity as a moral force and to stress its beauty as the most poetic and human of all religions, and also as the most favourable to liberty. It could be seen as an anti-*philosophe* tract, a plea for the spiritual regeneration of France, an attempt to offer an intellectual alternative to rationalism, through an emphasis on historical witness and aesthetic refinement. And yet it is surely more notable for its qualities as a work of art, for its personal poetic vision, than for its force as a reasoned apologia. In it, two Romantic impulses were evocatively joined: subjective sensibility, a belief in the unique value of individual experience, of the mind and emotions as creators of their own real world rather than as organic receptacles for the objective world outside them; and historicism, with its ancestral lore, images of antiquity, folk spirits, and even the cult of the dead. In the latter respect at least it anticipated the brooding fatalism of *La Vie de Rancé* (1844) and parts of the *Mémoires d'outre-tombe*, in which the old Chateaubriand seemed obsessed with the external signs of penitence, including mortification of the flesh, and sacrifice. His was one of the most passionate reactions against modernity, against the pretensions of science, against revolutionary philistinism, and against what he saw as the failed secular philosophies of his time.

Now, it has to be said that Chateaubriand's influence worked at a refined literary level, where an intellectual and aesthetic interest in religion was not always matched by the conventional regularity of outward observance. It was Louis XVIII who once wryly observed that 'all these great servants of the altar scarcely approach it. I would dearly like to know the name of M. de Chateaubriand's confessor.'[49] The lasting impression of Chateaubriand's literary works as a whole is one of pervasive melancholy rather than of hope and joy. If his interest in nature was sincere and abiding, he found particular affinity with its more sombre moods, which by all accounts were powerfully evocative very near home, around his ancestral seat at Combourg, near his native Saint-Malo. Here, in its richest essence in France, was the Romantic *Weltschmerz* we associate more readily with the German *Sturm und Drang*.

Chateaubriand yearned after the infinite, or what he once called 'the melancholy pleasure of horizons' (*volupté mélancolique des horizons*). If I have placed him alongside Madame de Staël, Benjamin Constant and the 'Ideologues' at the same crossroads of the Enlightenment and Romanticism, it is because he was himself conscious of being there. As he once wrote, 'I found myself between two centuries, as at the confluence of two rivers; I plunged into their troubled waters, distancing myself with regret from the old bank where I was born, swimming in hope towards an unknown shore.'[50] The turbulence of his struggle produced an enduring feeling of *malaise*, frequently melodramatic and sometimes self-pitying. 'Like Job,' he lamented in his *Mémoires de ma vie* (1826), 'I cursed the day that I was born.'[51] One of his contemporaries, Stendhal, whose senses were altogether more finely tuned to the pleasures and pains of the voluptuous world, had a phrase for such exponents of the *Je* and *Moi*. In his own unfinished autobiographical *Vie de Henry Brulard*, written some years later, he described Chateaubriand as 'this king of the *egotists*'.[52]

Egotism: the word serves almost as an epigraph for the various representations of power discussed in this chapter. The Imperial manifestations of military glory and civil grandeur were the most dominant of all, and it was the evocative and usually distorted recollection of these which also gave the Napoleonic legend its most charismatic appeal after 1815. Napoleon and his official entourage turned the personalized heroic ethic into a full-blown system, one which could be shared with all subjects willing to embrace it. In its crudest form, State propaganda was the most common means of its dissemination, although one may doubt whether the attempt to personify French patriotism in such an exclusive way actually convinced the great mass of the people at the time. In its more refined forms, the heroic ethic undoubtedly influenced the response of the intellectual and artistic élites of the Empire, whatever their political sympathies or ideological beliefs may have been. The writers, thinkers, scientists, educationalists, painters, architects, sculptors, and artists in general – in short, *all* who were exposed to the Napoleonic imperium had to react in some way to its political and military realities. Whether they were for or against the emperor, whether because of his favours or in defiance of his despotic methods, their individual reactions contributed much to the artistic vitality of his Empire. As a cultural '*dirigiste*', Napoleon may ultimately have failed to achieve most of his grandiose aims; but as a cultural catalyst, he had an extraordinary power to extract a response from his admirers and enemies alike.

. . . .

NOTES AND REFERENCES

1. June K. Burton, 'Heraldry', in Owen Connelly, ed., *Historical Dictionary of Napoleonic France, 1799–1815*, Westport, Conn., 1985, pp. 238–40.
2. Ibid., p. 239.

3. Lynn A. Hunt, 'Symbolism and Style', in Connelly, ed., *Historical Dictionary*, p. 461.
4. Ibid.
5. Nietta Aprà, *Empire Style 1804–1815*, Eng. edn, London, 1972.
6. Ibid., p. 3.
7. June K. Burton, 'Art', in Connelly, ed., *Historical Dictionary*, p. 29.
8. É.-J. Delécluze, *Louis David, son école et son temps*, Macula edn, Paris, 1983.
9. Anita Brookner, *Jacques-Louis David*, London, 1980.
10. Ibid., p. 129.
11. Quoted in ibid., p. 156.
12. Marie-Louise Biver, *Pierre Fontaine premier architecte de l'Empereur*, Paris, 1964.
13. *Letters of Napoleon*, selected, trans., and ed. by J.M. Thompson, Oxford, 1934, pp. 145–6.
14. Marie-Louise Biver, *Le Paris de Napoléon*, Paris, 1963, pp. 58–130.
15. Quoted in ibid., p. 33.
16. Claude Bergeron, 'Architecture', in Connelly, ed., *Historical Dictionary*, p. 19.
17. Ibid., p. 20.
18. Bruno Foucart, 'L'Artiste dans la société de l'Empire: Sa participation aux honneurs et dignités', *Revue d'Histoire moderne et contemporaine*, vol. 17, 1970, pp. 711, 718.
19. Robert B. Holtman, *Napoleonic Propaganda*, Baton Rouge, 1950, pp. 44–5.
20. André Cabanis, *La presse sous le Consulat et l'Empire (1799–1814)*, Paris, 1975, pp. 36–41, 66–84.
21. Holtman, *Napoleonic Propaganda*, pp. 17–22.
22. Cabanis, *La presse*, pp. 313–14.
23. Holtman, *Napoleonic Propaganda*, pp. 145–7.
24. Quoted in ibid., p. v.
25. Harvey Chisick, *The Limits of Reform in the Enlightenment: Attitudes toward the Education of the Lower Classes in Eighteenth-Century France*, Princeton, 1981, esp. pp. 5–17 and 278–90.
26. H.C. Barnard, *Education and the French Revolution*, Cambridge, 1969, pp. 169–75, 185–98.
27. Jacques Godechot, *Les institutions de la France sous la Révolution et l'Empire*, 3rd revised and expanded edn, Paris, 1985, pp. 738–9.
28. Quoted in Pieter Geyl, *Napoleon: For and Against*, Harmondsworth, 1986 impression (Peregrine Books), p. 133.
29. Félix Ponteil, *Histoire de l'enseignement en France. Les grandes étapes 1789–1964*, Paris, 1966, pp. 143–50.
30. Martin S. Staum, 'The Class of Moral and Political Sciences, 1795–1803', *French Historical Studies*, vol. 11, Spring 1980, pp. 371–97.

31. Antoine Léon, 'Promesses et ambiguïtés de l'oeuvre d'enseignement technique en France de 1800 à 1815', *Revue d'Histoire moderne et contemporaine*, vol. 17, 1970, pp. 846–59.
32. Godechot, *Les institutions*, pp. 745–6.
33. Ponteil, *Histoire de l'enseignement en France*, p. 110.
34. *The Mind of Napoleon: A Selection from his Written and Spoken Words*, ed. and trans. by J. Christopher Herold, New York, 1955, p. 14.
35. Thompson, ed., *Letters of Napoleon*, pp. 194–5.
36. Herold, ed., *Mind of Napoleon*, p. 14.
37. Emmanuel de Las Cases, *Mémorial de Sainte-Hélène. Journal of the Private Life and Conversations of the Emperor Napoleon at Saint Helena*, Eng. edn, 4 vols, London, 1823, vol. 1, part ii, pp. 130–1.
38. Herold, *Mind of Napoleon*, p. 14.
39. Ibid., p. 158.
40. Las Cases, *Mémorial*, vol. 3, part vi, p. 352.
41. Quoted by Simone Balayé in her introduction to Germaine de Staël, *De l'Allemagne*, Garnier-Flammarion edn, 2 vols, Paris, 1968, vol. 1, p. 19.
42. Quoted by Madame de Staël in her preface to *De l'Allemagne*, Garnier-Flammarion edn, vol. 1, p. 39.
43. A.-L.-G. de Staël, *An Appeal to the Nations of Europe against the Continental System*, Stockholm and London, 1813, p. 9.
44. Quoted in translation in Brookner, *David*, p. 136.
45. Thompson, ed., *Letters of Napoleon*, p. 164.
46. Herold, ed., *Mind of Napoleon*, p. 155.
47. Las Cases, *Mémorial*, vol. 3, part vi, p. 352.
48. Emmet Kennedy, *A Philosophe in the Age of Revolution: Destutt de Tracy and the Origins of 'Ideology'*, Philadelphia, 1978.
49. Quoted in Victor-L. Tapié, *Chateaubriand*, Paris, 1965, p. 153.
50. Quoted in ibid., p. 1.
51. François-René de Chateaubriand, *Mémoires de ma vie*, Librairie Droz edn, Geneva, 1976, p. 42.
52. Stendhal (Henri Beyle), *Vie de Henry Brulard*, Gallimard folio edn, 1973, p. 30.

Chapter 7

THE HISTORIOGRAPHICAL
IMAGES OF POWER

The apparently endless capacity of the French Revolution to generate historiographical debate was demonstrated, yet again, during the prolific harvest of its Bicentenary in 1989. For most writers, the Revolution was – and still is – the central event in the modern history of France, whether for good or ill. One might then overlook the fact that, in its rich diversity as well as sheer scale, Napoleonic historiography over the past two hundred years closely matches it. Indeed, during the last thirty years or so, the two subjects have come to be seen more and more as integral parts of the same historical process, or 'experience', which gave France the central institutions and social characteristics familiar to us today.

The enormous range of writings on Napoleon and the history of his times was skilfully analysed by Pieter Geyl in a fascinating historiographical survey, *Napoleon: For and Against*, first published nearly fifty years ago.[1] His long-ranging critique of the polemical as well as scholarly literature from the earliest contemporary accounts to the interwar works of the present century remains an invaluable commentary, but it was of course quite deliberately confined to French writers. Beyond France, in what once constituted the widely extended area of the 'Grand Empire', the literary and historiographical reactions to the Napoleonic hegemony had a pedigree no less old and (in some cases) no less distinguished. Many German and Italian writers in particular left fascinating accounts, often in poetic or dramatic form, both during the period of the Empire itself and in the formative years of the Napoleonic legend which followed its hero's death on St Helena in 1821. Most of them had had at least some direct experience of Imperial rule, and several had actually met Napoleon in person. Sadly, their works have found their way into English textbooks on the subject all too rarely.

The evolution of Napoleonic historiography up to the Second World War had three main features. The first, most common among the earliest writers, was a tendency to see Napoleon as a sort of metaphysical force which transcended all ordinary mortal bounds. Whether adulatory or otherwise, they conjured up the image of a 'superman', a military commander and civil ruler who was somehow larger than life, the embodiment of an extraordinary energy, a unique phenomenon in the history of humankind. The second and more enduring feature was the attempt, or rather a whole sequence of attempts, by later writers to reconstruct the Napoleonic past in terms of a living, moving present. In other words, each successive generation after 1815 was to reinterpret the Imperial legacy in a way that would seem relevant to its own current political concerns and changing ideologies, often with strong tendentious overtones. The polemical motives inspiring such 'lessons for our time' were most obvious in French literature on Napoleon, not surprisingly, but they were by no means confined to it. The third feature, particularly evident during the two or three decades preceding the Great War, was the genre of the 'grand idea'. It included several of the most prolific and distinguished writers, all of whom tried to encapsulate their perception of Napoleon's ambition and achievements in a dominant image, whose details could then be embellished at length. However variable and contradictory their particular views may have been, the search for an overriding theme was the common factor among them.

It is not my purpose here to trench on more recent trends in Napoleonic historiography, where the emphasis is less on the man and his deeds than on the underlying structures of his regime in a much wider sense. Discussion of these seems more appropriate in the Bibliographical Essay at the end of this volume. The present chapter has two main aims. One is to identify the essential features of Napoleon's ambition and concept of power, as he *himself* defined them. The first subsection therefore offers a brief appraisal of his own recorded statements on those closely related subjects at different stages of his career. Such pronouncements were regarded by many contemporary and later writers as a unique expression of his authentic will, almost as 'tablets of stone', and have been quoted at face value in countless secondary works ever since, notwithstanding their obvious self-contradictions.

My other aim is to outline what might be called the 'classic' images of power in the writings on Napoleon which preceded the new 'revisionist' approach of the past forty years or so. Those earlier accounts are refreshingly free of the academic specialization more familiar to us today. Writers then had no detailed knowledge of many of the historical sources we now take for granted. The distinction between subjective expression (which encouraged individuals to create their own impressions) and historical objectivity (in the Rankean sense of rigorous and impartial examination of the original documents of state) was far from established. Quantitative methods had not yet been revolutionized by the technical innovations which have led to the modern computer. 'Great history' could still be conceived of as an extension of great literature, of wider cultural movements, of political discourse, and of ideological debate. Authors, including a number of prominent politicians themselves, were not afraid to take sides in the debate. Imagination, polemical intent, sheer prejudice – everything indeed which might now be considered a matter of individual 'style' – left an impression on the literary genres of that time. In the last three sub-sections of this chapter, which review the most recurrent themes in the first century or more of Napoleonic historiography, I have attempted to give the general reader a sample of those earlier debates. If French writers have the lion's share of the coverage, those in other countries also receive some detailed attention and add a wider perspective to the whole debate. To avoid overloading the endnotes and references of the chapter, I have preferred to cite the titles of the most important works in the text itself, often in shortened form, and have also been selective in doing so.

· · · · · · · · ·

NAPOLEON ON NAPOLEON

As we have seen in the preceding chapter, Napoleon was one of the first to write his own history, or at any rate to assist in that process, through his regular military bulletins and other mouthpieces of his State propaganda. Since their historical value is by definition suspect, they need not concern us here.

Rather more authentic insights into his views on the exercise of power, as well as on his own ambition and destiny, can be gained from other sources, although allowances often have to be made for his changing moods and the self-contradictions to which these gave rise. His official correspondence alone, which was later collected and published on the orders of Napoleon III (his nephew) during the Second Empire, ran to no less than thirty-two volumes.[2] Apart from this and other major collections which appeared later, many of Napoleon's public or private utterances were recorded by his contemporaries, whether in the form of journals, or memoirs, or other writings of that kind. Among these latter, the *Mémorial de Sainte-Hélène* published in 1823 by his faithful companion in exile, Count Emmanuel de Las Cases, in which the more reflective grandiloquence of the fallen emperor was recorded at great length, is especially important.

In short, for what such evidence is worth, we have an ample stock of primary sources from which to construct a broad profile of how Napoleon saw himself. It is clear at once that he intimately associated his political power with his military prowess, and that this in turn was a function of his imperious character. 'What I am, I owe to strength of will, character, application, and daring', he wrote to his brother Jerome on 2 June 1805.[3] Sometime around 1811, according to Bourrienne's memoirs, he frankly acknowledged that 'my power is dependent on my glory, and my glory on my victories. My power would fall if I did not base it on still more glory and still more victories. Conquest made me what I am; conquest alone can keep me there.'[4] His similar remark to Chaptal, in which he was plainly conscious that he lacked the legitimacy of a true dynastic monarch, dates from roughly the same time: 'at home as abroad, I reign only through the fear I inspire. If I renounced this system, I would be dethroned before long. This is my position, and these are the motives that guide me.'[5] On this point at least he seems to have been consistent, returning to it many times during his final exile. In a conversation with Las Cases on 7 November 1816, for instance, he again insisted that 'situated as I was, deprived of hereditary authority, and of the illusion called legitimacy, I was compelled to avoid entering the lists with my opponents; I was obliged to be bold, imperious, and decisive'.[6]

The theme of power, as Napoleon perceived it, was played

out in many other colourful variations at different stages of his career. 'Power is my mistress,' he told Roederer in 1804, and then went on: 'I have worked too hard at her conquest to allow anyone to take her away from me or even covet her. Although you say that power came to me of its own accord, I know what it has cost me – the sufferings, the sleepless nights, the scheming.'[7] That was the year in which Napoleon became emperor of France. In 1809, after a longer savouring of his exalted status, he remarked to Roederer again that 'I too love power – but I love it as an artist. I love it as a musician loves his violin. . . . I love it for the sake of drawing sounds, chords, and harmonies from it.'[8] In the following pronouncement to Benjamin Constant on 10 April 1815, during the Hundred Days, he apparently had little regard for his (first) abdication only a year earlier: 'I wanted to rule the world, and in order to do this I needed unlimited power. . . . The world begged me to govern it; sovereigns and nations vied with one another in throwing themselves under my scepter.'[9] Less than three months later a different assembly of sovereigns if not nations would be compelling him to abdicate again and sending him into a more distant exile, this time for good.

'The world begged me to govern it'! There seems little doubt that Napoleon genuinely believed this, and for one good reason: a powerful sense of his own destiny. In fact, three elements were at play in his mind here – Destiny, fate, and luck – and his instinctive, at times even superstitious and pagan, reaction to them had clearly been influenced by a voracious reading of his favourite classical texts during the earlier years. Of the three, the call of Destiny was much the most powerful and inspiring to him. In his view, it came only to those few who were preordained for it, those marked out for special greatness, and capable of changing the course of history. As such, it was a noble call which *had* to be carried out, in his case through conquest, power, and personal glory. Fate, a more severe and unpredictable mistress, at once the soldier's friend and foe, was something to be suffered in the event, like military defeat, or exile, or sudden death. Mere luck or chance held few perils for Napoleon; indeed, he believed that they lay within his power to control or let slip. During the Russian campaign, for example, when he learnt on 23 October 1812 that Kutuzov had cut off his retreat along the Maloyaroslavets road, he asked not whether luck had let him down, but whether *he* had failed his luck.[10] And only a few months later, in the course of a conversation with Baron Fain at the start of the campaign of 1813, his attitude was even more resigned: 'I have made all the calculations: fate will do the rest.'[11]

The intimate interplay between the themes of Destiny, fate, and power is revealed in some of Napoleon's most memorable remarks, and these can be traced back to the years before Brumaire. 'Men of genius are meteors destined to be consumed in lighting up their century,' he wrote in an early manuscript, the 'Discours sur le bonheur' of 1791, which some might even be inclined to interpret as an uncanny premonition of the comet reportedly seen at the time of his death on St Helena, a rare event which had also apparently marked the death of Caesar.[12] Or again, in a letter to Manfredini of 1 February 1797, he said that 'there are things written in the great book of destiny that must be accomplished whatever one does' – perhaps most immediately in Italy, where his first victorious campaign was then well under way.[13] Ten years later, in a letter of 27 March 1807, he was to tell Josephine that 'all my life I have sacrificed everything – comfort, self-interest, happiness – to my destiny'.[14] Such a statement, at a time when his fortunes were riding high, almost suggests a sense of duty to fulfil his Imperial mission, which may not seem too surprising. Yet, more tellingly, the same belief lingered on even once he had lost power. In a conversation on the *Bellerophon*, the British warship he had boarded after his second abdication, Las Cases recorded the following remark in his entry for 2 and 3 August 1815: 'a man ought to fulfil his destinies; this is my grand doctrine: let mine also be accomplished'.[15] On St Helena Napoleon could even view his lost grandeur with a certain perverse irony. As he told Las Cases on 2 November 1816, 'my fate may be said to be the very opposite of others. A fall, usually has the effect of lowering a man's character; but, on the contrary, my fall has elevated me prodigiously. Every succeeding day divests me of some portion of my *tyrant's skin*.'[16]

The remaining element of Napoleon's concept of power is the nature of his ambition, as he himself perceived it. This is also perhaps the most elusive and difficult of all to pin down, since his views on the matter were often self-contradictory. In general terms, one may say that Napoleon formulated his own ambition in relation to his sense of personal destiny, and then used his military power as a vehicle for advancing both at the same time. But just how early did that ambition form in his mind, and how consistent was his own definition and pursuit of it? In the following remarks to Roederer, for instance, which were made during a conversation of 1804, he seemed almost to suggest that the issue was a red herring:

> As far as I am concerned, I have no ambition – or, if I have any, it is so natural to me, so innate, so intimately linked with my exist-ence that it is like the blood that circulates in my veins, like the air I breathe. It causes me to act neither more precipitately, nor in any way differently, than do the natural motives that move me. I never am obliged to fight either for or against ambition. Ambition never is in a greater hurry than I; it merely keeps pace with circumstances and with my general way of thinking.[17]

Those were the words of a man in the year of his elevation to the Imperial title, appearing to imply that what had borne him aloft had happened naturally, by the force of circumstance if not indeed by chance, as an extension of his own organic being into the external world around him. He would return to the subject much later on St Helena and, depending on his mood, express himself in rather similar terms. Thus on 11 November 1816 he told Las Cases that

> I never was truly my own master; but was always controlled by circumstances. . . . I was not master of my actions, because I was not fool enough to attempt to twist events into conformity with my system. On the contrary, I moulded my system according to the unforeseen succession of events. This often appeared like unsteadi-ness and inconsistency, and of these faults I was sometimes unjustly accused.[18]

This somewhat curious mood apparently lasted several more days, for on the following 20 November he even declared that 'I should very frequently have found it most difficult to affirm confidently, what had been my whole and entire thoughts on any given subject'.[19]

On other occasions during his last captivity, however, Napo-leon's reflections on the question of his former ambition had a quite different emphasis. In retrospect, his first Italian cam-paign seemed to have had a particularly formative influence on his 'general way of thinking'. According to Las Cases's re-cord of the conversations of 1–6 September 1815 aboard HMS

Northumberland, then on its way to St Helena, Napoleon once remarked that 'it was not till after Lodi [battle of 10 May 1796] that I was struck with the possibility of my becoming a decided actor on the scene of political events. – It was then that the first spark of my ambition was kindled.'[20] Here, at least, he was correctly associating his emerging ambition with the only thing that had given it any real substance at the time: military might. And yet, once he was settled on St Helena and the same subject had been discussed at greater length, he was often inclined to reconstrue it in more fanciful, irenic terms. Las Cases recorded one such conversation of 1 May 1816:

> Shall I be blamed for my ambition? This passion I must doubtless be allowed to have possessed, and that in no small degree; but, at the same time, my ambition was of the highest and noblest kind that ever, perhaps, existed! ... That of establishing and of consecrating the Empire of reason, and the full exercise and complete enjoyment of all the human faculties! And here the historian will probably feel compelled to regret that such ambition should not have been fulfilled and gratified![21]

Had he not then owed all his earlier Imperial glory primarily to his achievements as a military conqueror, to his relentless war-mongering? Napoleon gave this particular answer to the same companion on 11 November 1816:

> At Amiens [Peace of 25 March 1802], I sincerely thought the fate of France and Europe, and my own destiny, were permanently fixed; I hoped that war was at an end. However, the English Cabinet again kindled the flame. England is alone responsible for all the miseries by which Europe has since been assailed. For my part, I intended to have devoted myself wholly to the internal interests of France; and I am confident I should have wrought miracles. I should have lost nothing in the scale of glory; and I should have gained much in the scale of happiness. I should then have achieved the moral conquest of Europe, which I was afterwards on the point of accomplishing by force of arms. Of how much glory was I thus deprived!
>
> My enemies always spoke of my love of war; but was I not constantly engaged in self-defence? After every victory I gained, did I not immediately make proposals for peace?[22]

This whimsical self-image of Napoleon as an unrequited man of peace may strike us as thoroughly unconvincing, and rightly so; but for his immediate admirers at least, that myth was already a reality. Its place in his legend was assured. 'My history is made up of facts, and words alone cannot destroy them', he remarked to Las Cases on 21 October 1816.[23] What now follows is an attempt to distinguish between those 'facts' and 'words'.

· · · · · · · · · · · ·

HOW OTHERS VIEWED NAPOLEON: THE EARLY WRITINGS

Clearly, the *Mémorial* of the count de Las Cases did much to establish the positive aspect of the 'superman' image of Napoleon. It had a powerful influence on other disseminators of his legend, who also concentrated on his heroic deeds and legacy. All presented him as a ruler of unrivalled intelligence and wisdom, as a force for good, for necessary change, who swept away the last corrupt vestiges of the old regime in France and her annexed territories, who tried to do the same in her subject states and indeed in all Europe, who was driven to fight particular wars in order to establish a general peace, but whose work of renovation and reconstruction was cut short by an unholy alliance of foreign princes, the unenlightened enemies of progress. In this sense, he was seen as the child prodigy and true heir of the French Revolution, who in the full manhood of Imperial grandeur fulfilled its best ideals and ended its worst excesses. Order in place of chaos, stability in place of upheaval, unity in place of factionalism, strength in place of weakness – the picture was to become almost a stereotype among Napoleonists of the later nineteenth century.

Baron Bignon, a former Imperial diplomat who had once served in the duchy of Warsaw, should also have been a seminal influence on this panegyric tradition. Napoleon had commissioned him on St Helena to write the history of his reign, and indeed had left a handsome sum in his will for the purpose. In the event, this first multi-volume history of the Napoleonic period was published in stages only after a gap of some years, at the end of the Restoration and then a decade later during the July Monarchy. Meanwhile, having served in an official capacity under both the Bourbons and Louis-Philippe, and no doubt sensing the need to justify such conduct, Bignon left a more qualified account of Napoleon than might have

197

been expected. The passage of time had distanced him somewhat from the full-blooded commitment of earlier years. And so, while his underlying admiration is clear enough, he recognized that his former master had used despotic methods. These he was now inclined to see as the regrettable but necessary means by which order had been restored in the civil government of France and honour rekindled in her armies. His general interpretation was to be reinforced by Armand Lefebvre, whose account appeared in 1845, four years after Bignon's death. Apart from their natural admiration for Napoleon as the restorer of strong government and the greatness of France, the two authors shared a strong sense of Anglophobia. Lefebvre took that sentiment further, however, and from it constructed what almost amounted to a thesis of historical fatalism. He thought that Napoleon's foreign policy had been determined above all by his need to confront British treachery, and that this also justified even his most unfortunate mistakes.

The hostile variant of the 'superman' image left no place for any such excuses. It presented a much more gruesome picture of Napoleon as a hugely destructive and even demoniac force. It, too, had its origins in the earliest contemporary writings, most notably in those of Madame de Staël and Chateaubriand written during the Empire or shortly after its fall, even before the legend of Napoleon had assumed its posthumous mystique. Both those writers, of course, had fallen foul of his regime in different ways. For Madame de Staël, an early liberal admirer who soon became his outspoken enemy, Napoleon had once been the triumphant general of the Revolution, of whom so much had been expected, but who then systematically distorted all its finest principles by the abuse of power. After her enforced exile from France in 1803, she was in an easier position to mount her vitriolic attacks on him. They made much of his unbridled vanity and ambition, his childish infatuation with personal fame, his despotic methods, his callous disregard of the suffering caused by incessant wars, his notorious atrocities at home and abroad, his censorship of the arts and intolerance of any opposition. In all, the image she projected was that of a ruthless egotist, an unscrupulous manipulator of everyone around him, a rootless outsider without a true sense of fatherland, a philistine set loose on civilized peoples, a malign freak of history.

Madame de Staël's intimate friend, Benjamin Constant, whose

public interventions during the early Consulate were cut short by the 'purge' of the tribunate in 1802, was another prominent figure among Napoleon's liberal critics. His subsequent opposition from self-chosen exile was ultimately more ambivalent, however, as events were to prove. During the Hundred Days he suddenly rallied to the man whom he had branded in print as a latter-day 'Attila' or 'Genghis Khan' only a few weeks earlier. He accepted an appointment to Napoleon's restored council of state and was influential in drafting the more liberal 'Additional Act to the Constitutions of the Empire'. This still-born and impolitic initiative was to cost him some three years in prudential exile, before his return to public life in France. In the circumstances, Louis XVIII's pardon of one who had also championed Bernadotte's claim to the French throne in 1814 was generous indeed.

As for Chateaubriand, a former royalist and émigré, who once served Napoleon briefly in a diplomatic posting to Rome, the rupture came with the murder of the duc d'Enghien in 1804. An idiosyncratic voice of the Catholic literati, he was also disgusted by the emperor's cynical manipulation of the Concordat with the Church, and outraged by the later imprisonment of Pius VII. Increasingly, he came to see Napoleon as an enemy of the true religion. He had his chance to publish a bitter denunciation of the fallen emperor, and at the same time to vindicate the legitimist principles of monarchy, soon after the first abdication of Napoleon in April 1814. Unlike Madame de Staël, who died in 1817, Chateaubriand survived into the heyday of the Napoleonic legend. He took up his pen to refute it on more than one occasion before his own death in 1848, not least in his monumental *Mémoires d'outre-tombe*. If his influence on French Romanticism is well known, that on later Catholic writers of the nineteenth century, for the most part also hostile to Napoleon's Church policy, seems even more important in the present context.

The earliest writings on Napoleon outside France reveal, if anything, a still greater contrast of views about the man and his work. Most deal, whether directly or obliquely, with important themes of patriotism – even nationalism – emanating from the educated élites in lands which had been exposed for varying periods to French rule in one form or another. German and Italian works seem the most notable here, not only in sheer volume, but more significantly because they testify to an early expression of national sentiment. As such, they certainly influenced the ideological debates which were to accompany the movements for political unification in both countries during the half-century following the Vienna Congress. The historical background was a crucial point of departure here. In the course of the Revolutionary and Napoleonic wars, the many different states of which Germany and to a lesser extent Italy had consisted under the old regime all at some time experienced military conquest and (if Prussia and Austria are excluded) political subjugation by France. In some cases this went as far as direct annexation, on the Belgian model of 1795; in others, much more numerous in fact, it took the form of satellite status within Napoleon's new political groupings east of the Rhine and south of the Alps.

Reactions to French rule varied widely in the two countries, both at the time and after its collapse in 1814, but in general it is fair to say that the German view of Napoleon was the more hostile. Whatever the political and mercantile élites in Germany may have thought of collaboration with the French, when their public careers or business interests were at stake, the writers were much more inclined to condemn the Imperial system. If one thinks of Fichte, of Arndt, of C.F. Rühs, or of the Austrian chancellor Friedrich von Gentz, not to mention a host of lesser writers, the image – what more recent German historians sometimes call the '*Napoleonbild*' – was decidedly negative.[24] The emphasis is on the destructive impact of French rule: on military sacrifice and despoliation, on economic exploitation, and (perhaps most commonly) on the perceived outrage Napoleon had inflicted on the national pride, cultural identity, and religious sensibilities of the conquered German peoples.

It is small wonder then that, for such writers, the prevailing view of the Napoleonic Empire was antagonistic. In his *Geist der Zeit*, for instance, Arndt once called it 'a despotic military state'.[25] Conversely, the 'wars of liberation' (*Befreiungskriege*) of 1813–14 were hailed as a powerful upsurge of the German spirit against foreign domination. We have here an interesting anticipation of the more sustained Francophobic accounts of the Napoleonic imperium by later writers such as Sybel and especially Treitschke, when nationalist sentiment in the recently unified German *Reich* could express itself on a firmer political and military base. This important link illustrates the continuity of what was certainly the predominant '*Napoleonbild*' in German literature at least until the 1880s, after which the growing Anglo-German naval and imperial rivalry spawned a rather more favourable perception of Napoleon as an exemplary arch-enemy of Britain.[26]

Now, in the works of all those German writers named, the polemical intent was perhaps too powerful to produce a balanced and scholarly appraisal of their subject. It might be thought appropriate to include Droysen among them as well, because his view of Napoleon was generally very unfriendly. On the other hand, he was fair enough to concede that Imperial rule in Germany had also had its more positive side. It had, he thought, accelerated necessary reforms there, particularly through the impact of its legal codes and more uniform administrative practices on the old and fragmentary feudal order. He also had a remarkably astute insight into the long-term social effects of the whole Revolutionary and Napoleonic mutation. Even before Marx had stamped his inflexible 'class' dialectic on the process of history, Droysen had argued more pragmatically that Napoleon's enduring achievement had been to consolidate the 'bourgeois' gains of the Revolution in France. Niebuhr, in an earlier account, had similarly qualified his otherwise negative verdict by an important chronological distinction. He thought that Napoleon's work as first consul had indeed been beneficial, in restoring order to France after the upheaval of the Revolution, but that his incessant war-mongering as emperor steadily undermined the earlier reforms. Either way, Niebuhr was more concerned with the man and his actions than with the underlying social transformations of his time.

It is, however, in Ranke's work that the fullest, most informed, and most scholarly appraisal of Napoleon is to be found among the early German accounts. His firm rejection of the principles and work of the French Revolution made his attempt at an impartial study of the man who had once humiliated his native Prussia in war and dismembered it at the ensuing peace all the more striking. He saw Napoleon as not only the heir of the Revolution but also the embodiment of its reforming zeal, as an extraordinary human force in which all its energies were concentrated. His interest in diplomatic history led him to the conclusion that Napoleon's foreign policy could be properly understood only in the context of Anglo-French relations. The 'English question' thus became a key factor, one which made it all the more necessary for Napoleon to harness the resources of the European mainland in the struggle against his most implacable and elusive enemy. Since Germany was thus a crucial element of Napoleon's continental power-base, the argument proceeded logically enough to the 'Carolingian' view of his real ambition, about which more will be said later in this chapter. True to his rigorous historical method, above all, Ranke would not pass moral judgement on Napoleon, which set him apart from most of his German contemporaries.

The latter, it has to be said, included a curiously disparate minority of admirers and apologists. Of those who were most influenced by the spell of the Napoleonic legend, perhaps more in a literary than an ideological sense, Heine and Grabbe are the most noteworthy. They were responsive to the idea of a mighty emperor, who had once ruled most of western and central Europe, finally humbled in defeat and reduced to pitiable exile and painful death on a faraway island. Destiny incarnate, power and glory, but finally nemesis – this was the stuff that true Romantic heroes were made of. Heine's ethnic origins may also help to explain why his perception of Napoleon's work on behalf of Jewish emancipation, which in fact was far from liberal and aimed primarily at organizational control through the consistories and Sanhedrin, was so favourable.

Indeed, the myth of Napoleon as a great 'liberalizing' force who fulfilled the original ideals of the Revolution in Germany had other unlikely adherents there. A number of liberal writers like Rotteck, Schlosser, Müller, Aretin, Vogt, and Hebel all considered the interlude of French rule as a necessary break from the traditional shackles of the past. They recognized of course that Napoleon's methods had been despotic and that his subjugation of Germany had been a humiliation for its old dynasties, but they also thought that something good had come out of the trauma. Its effect had been to break down the structures of the old feudal order, of aristocratic and ecclesiastical privilege, and of the historic Holy Roman Empire itself, thereby preparing the way for German political union. Moreover, as the liberal reaction against Metternich's conservative 'system' grew in the later 1820s, so in retrospect Napoleon's reforms seemed all the more defensible. The presumption that he had consolidated 'bourgeois' interests, that his codes had outlawed legal privilege, and that he had been in favour of enlarged home markets unfettered by internal customs barriers and tolls, however questionable in fact, all appealed to the free trade

notions of those German writers. Yet if the passage of time
had thus made some strange bedfellows, the current of liberal
thought in Germany ran dry after the failure of the 1848 revolutions. The way ahead then favoured nationalist ideologues whose
vision of German unification was more authoritarian, more
statist, more militarist, and more sympathetic to the Prussian
(or '*Kleindeutsch*') model. In such company, the victor of Jena–
Auerstädt could arouse only hostile memories, and even these
were to be avenged at the expense of his nephew in the Franco-
Prussian War of 1870–71.

There remains the towering figure of Goethe, one of Napoleon's contemporaries and in many ways the most enigmatic
German witness of all. As an observer with the Prussian army
at the battle of Valmy (20 September 1792), he had already
given his celebrated pronouncement on the victory of the
Revolutionary warriors: 'here and today a new era dawns in the
history of the world'. Much later, when a new kind of French
warrior was in the ascendancy, he met Napoleon on three
occasions in October 1808, first at Erfurt and then twice at the
castle of Weimar. According to a fascinating modern account
of these audiences, the two men immediately formed something resembling a mutual admiration society, an impression
supported by Napoleon's memorable compliment to the poet:
'*voilà un homme!*'[27] It was then that Napoleon reportedly invited
Goethe to come to Paris and install himself as a sort of 'playwright laureate' in the Imperial cause. The emperor, who
always had a keen if rather crude sense of how distinguished
writers and artists might serve his propaganda, considered the
theatre a particularly effective forum for manipulating public
opinion. But Goethe, whose loyalty as a courtier of Duke Carl
August of Weimar remained firm, politely declined the invitation. And indeed, it would be very difficult to imagine him as
a political sycophant at any foreign court!

All the same, Goethe was enormously flattered by Napoleon's overture, as several of his writings show. In an earlier
letter to Knebel of 3 January 1807, he had referred to the
emperor as 'the most extraordinary phenomenon history could
have produced' since Caesar and Alexander – a grand tribute,
incidentally, which the French writer Stendhal was later to echo
in almost identical words in his adulatory *Vie de Napoléon* of
1837. On other occasions around that time Goethe would speak
of 'my Emperor', as recorded by a correspondent on 7 January

1809. And in later years, when it was extremely unfashionable to do so in his native land, he repeatedly expressed his view of Napoleon in terms such as 'superior intelligence' (1815), 'this compendium of the world' (1826), 'half-god' (1828), and 'incommensurable' (1829).[28] His own account of the meetings of 1808, written some sixteen years after the event, made it clear that he regarded them as the most extraordinary experience of his life. His admiration for Napoleon had not lessened during the intervening years, and he always valued the Legion of Honour bestowed on him shortly after the Erfurt gathering. He never ceased to view the emperor as a figure of supernatural power, as the embodiment of a sort of Manichean force in history which, for good or ill, could not be judged by the standards of ordinary men. More than once he excused, or at least tried to minimize, Napoleon's worst atrocities as necessary acts of state.

In short, however far removed he may have been from the prevalent consensus of his compatriots, Goethe did much to keep the favourable and awesome variant of the 'superman' image alive in Germany. In this respect he went much further than Schopenhauer, who had also met Napoleon, and who once remarked that 'Bonaparte is the finest embodiment of human will power'.[29] Hegel, not otherwise a sympathetic judge, was another who testified to the unique sense of wonder the emperor's mere physical presence on a scene could command. As he wrote to Niethammer on the eve of the battle of Jena on 13 October 1806, after witnessing Napoleon's entry into the town on horseback, he believed that he had seen 'the spirit of the world'.[30] Such views were to be reconstructed for their own purposes by other prominent German writers much later in the century. Nietzsche, for instance, in elaborating his theory of 'vitalism' from a rather different historical and ideological perspective, also singled out Napoleon as a supreme specimen of the 'superman' phenomenon.

In Italy, the reactions of the writers to Napoleon began somewhat earlier, which is hardly surprising if we recall the sensational impact of his first Italian campaign. Their wider historical context, too, was significantly different from that in Germany in several ways. The former glory of imperial Rome had lived on in the high culture of the Italian peoples for well over a millennium, but it had lost all political form long since. It is true that the Roman Catholic Church had often been cast in a successor role, and that Italy – unlike Germany – had not been politically divided by the Protestant Reformation. Yet if the pope's spiritual authority thus extended much more widely over all the Italian peoples, his secular sovereignty was more limited. It had been confined to the Papal States, to what might be thought of as the 'midlands' of Italy: Rome and its immediate environs in the Patrimony, Umbria, the Marches, Romagna, and the Legations.

On the eve of the French conquest, Italy's political fragmentation was real enough, and local particularism (*campanilismo*) prevailed almost everywhere. Even so, this scarcely compared with the huge complexity of *Kleinstaaterei* in Germany, where more than three hundred small states, each with its own titular sovereign, whether lay or ecclesiastical, had survived into the Napoleonic age. The concept of dynastic loyalty, especially when it implied allegiance to foreign sovereigns, then meant much less to Italian patriots. The enlarged sovereign kingdom of Sardinia-Piedmont-Savoy, which dated from 1718, did not command universal loyalty among them. In the lands of Venice and Genoa, notionally independent republics, power resided in local oligarchies which did not share their vision of nationhood (*italianità*). As for the rest, since Lombardy and Tuscany were ruled by the Habsburgs, Naples and Sicily by a branch of the Bourbon family, the whole idea of national 'liberation' through the intervention of a friendly foreign power seemed attractive to many of these same patriots when the first shocks of the French invasion were felt. There was of course a tradition of enlightened absolutism in Italy, notably in Lombardy and Tuscany, but its native roots were less firmly established than had been the case in Germany.

The critical year was 1796. Then, as a modern historian has written, it may be said that 'the *Settecento* ended and the Revolution came to the peninsula; the modern history of Italy begins with the physical presence of the French army'.[31] This may also help to explain why so many Italian writers responded to the French conquest with more apparent enthusiasm than their German counterparts in the early years. Their hostility to the old ruling dynasties, their strong Anglophobia, and a sense of their own military impotence – all made it easier for them to welcome a triumphant French general of Corsican origins as the heroic instrument of their patriotic cause. Pindemonte, Fantoni, Monti, Cesarotti, and Giordani, for example, in spite of their misgivings and some mercurial changes of allegiance, all at some time hailed Bonaparte as a great liberator and were hopeful that his initial work of reconstruction in Italy would mark the dawn of their brave new world. Their reaction, which in some cases persisted well into the years of the Empire, was also shared by a number of lesser writers. It was often so adulatory that they have sometimes been portrayed as self-interested time-servers. And indeed, one has to remember the presence of the censors and the pressure of official indoctrination gathering force behind them, especially after the French victory at Marengo in June 1800. Their desire to curry favour with the new regime probably owed a good deal to their natural instincts of careerism.

For other reasons, too, we need to be wary of such literary reactions to the invasion. They were certainly not typical of Italian public opinion more widely, especially in the face of the republican sentiments and anticlerical excesses of the French conquerors. The latter, as Stuart Woolf has rightly reminded us, had to confront the antipathy of the popular masses, who associated them and their Italian sympathizers with godless 'Jacobinism'. Urged on by nobles and clerics, the peasants in many regions raised violent revolt on a number of occasions during the early years of the new satellite republics, not least in 1799, when (with Napoleon away in Egypt) the Austro-Russian army forced the French to retreat from the peninsula.[32] In fact, as Woolf again observes, 'popular risings marked the whole period of Napoleonic domination in Italy'.[33]

It is equally clear that some of the more prominent writers themselves were openly hostile to the French, while the reaction of others was at best ambivalent. In the former group, Alfieri must surely have pride of place. Before his death in 1803 he had lost no opportunity to express his contempt – his '*misogallismo*' – for the Revolution, then for Napoleon, and indeed for everything he associated with the new order in France. In his eyes, the French invaders were barbarians and the enemies of true freedom. Foscolo, too, took years to get over the outrage he felt at Napoleon's betrayal of Venice by the Treaty of Campo Formio in October 1797. Although he later assumed a more placatory attitude towards the emperor, accepting that something good for Italians might come out of his rule after all, the natural honesty of Foscolo's underlying dislike of the man often expressed itself when others were much more servile in their adulation. Gioia's reaction, at first, followed a reverse sequence. In 1796 he had apparently believed that Napoleon was 'the guardian angel of Italy', and his optimism lasted beyond Marengo into the early phase of the Italian Republic. But in 1802 his tone changed, as disillusionment with the political methods imported from France set in. If his outward collaboration with them continued nevertheless, his formal tributes to Napoleon thereafter were motivated less by genuine admiration than by his Anglophobia and by his patriotic vision of an Italy eventually rid of all foreign interference.

Others again, like the southerners Cuoco and Lomonaco, had always been inclined to adopt a more consistently moderate and pragmatic position. For them, French rule was a necessary step towards eventual freedom within a unified peninsula, and for Lomonaco in particular this also meant freedom from the incubus of the Catholic Church. They therefore took the view that what was necessary could not be evil. They believed that Italians first had to learn the methods of efficient government from their conquerors before they could realize their patriotic ideal of self-rule. In other words, they saw Napoleon as a means to an end; the end itself lay in the future. Small wonder, then, that these contemporary observers are now seen as important early prophets of the Risorgimento.

We, too, would do well to take a longer view of all those changing literary currents in Italy during the years of Napoleonic rule. The subject has been treated in all its various phases by Eileen Millar in an illuminating monograph which covers the period from 1796 to 1821.[34] She shows that the writers in Italy reacted in some way to every stage of the French presence there: from the time of Napoleon's first Italian campaign of 1796–97, to the interlude of the satellite republics which followed in broken sequence until 1805, to the heyday of the Imperial annexations and dependent kingdoms of Italy and of Naples within the 'Grand Empire', and to the eventual disintegration of the Napoleonic imperium in the peninsula during the years 1813–15. Taken as a whole, such reactions left an enduring legacy which was to have an important influence on the ideological currents inspiring the later movements for Italian unification. Having revitalized the concept of '*italianità*', they could be seen as the nursery stage of the Risorgimento, from which the likes of Balbo, d'Azeglio, Mazzini, Cavour, and others could all draw lessons in their turn.

And so, while Italian literature did not lack its voices hostile to French rule during any part of the Napoleonic period, its positive response remained the more typical. Its heroic themes became still more pronounced after 1815, and especially after 1821, when they were infused by Romantic embellishments of the Napoleonic legend. The return of the Austrians and the Neapolitan Bourbons, indeed the restoration of so much of the old fragmentary political structures in Italy at the Vienna Congress, made many writers all the more inclined to lament the lost years of Imperial rule. The full melancholy of remembered grandeur ultimately reduced to pitiful exile on St Helena is nowhere better captured than in Manzoni's epic poem, 'Il Cinque Maggio', written in immediate response to the news of Napoleon's death in 1821. Its awesome and tragic image of the now departed 'man of destiny', who stood above ordinary mortals, was a lasting monument to his legend. Three years later Carlo Botta published the four volumes of his *Storia d'Italia dal 1789 al 1814*, from which Italian historiography on Napoleon, more strictly defined, made its first real departure. This work, written during the author's exile in Paris, achieved an impartiality remarkable for its time. Botta, who formerly had collaborated in government with the French in his native Piedmont, receiving the Legion of Honour for his services, was in no doubt about the unhappy consequences of Napoleon's tyrannical methods in Italy. Yet, like so many others, he also stood in awe of 'the fatal Napoleon', recognized his unique genius, and (as he wrote in his concluding pages) shared the sense of 'mingled wonder, terror, pity, grief, and pleasure' which memories of the emperor still evoked.

In Britain, by contrast, the predominantly hostile reactions to Napoleon among contemporary writers more closely matched the German than the Italian, albeit for very different reasons. From an 'official' point of view, this was only to be expected, given the need to strengthen public morale as well as mobilize material resources for the prolonged French wars of 1793–1815. Yet the subject itself, which seems potentially so full of interest and importance, has been strangely neglected since the pioneering work of F.J. Maccunn was published over eighty years ago.[35] His evidence suggests that characteristic views of Napoleon can be found in the writings of prominent politicians, diplomats, journalists, and literary figures alike, quite often from an early stage of the wars. Indeed, such reactions can be traced back to the time of Napoleon's Egyptian campaign of 1798–99, when the British interest in his military designs first became widely evident, and then continued throughout the years of the Consulate and Empire, and on into his period of exile on St Helena. A number of British visitors to France during the interludes of peace also left valuable accounts of the state of that country under his rule in 1802–3 and then after his abdications in 1814 and 1815.

The published speeches of men like Pitt, Fox, Sheridan, and Windham, for instance, offer insights into the parliamentary consensus which gathered, irrespective of party, against the threat which Napoleon posed to Britain and (it seemed for a time) to her interests in the Levant. Similarly, the correspondence and diaries of diplomats like Castlereagh, Malmesbury, Sir Arthur Paget, and Cornwallis, who at different times conducted peace negotiations with the French, reflect the nuances of public opinion among the British political class. Wellington's views have a particular interest, too, although they were mostly recorded in retrospect. A wider readership was assured by a number of prominent journals. The *Courier*, which was to all intents and purposes a mouthpiece of official wartime propaganda, usually presented Napoleon as an enemy without redeeming features; the *Times* was, if anything, even more extreme and consistent in its angry denunciations of him as a cowardly imposter; and the *Quarterly*, for its part, also added to this chorus of tory demonology. Alongside these, there were the more scurrilous fulminations of occasional publications like the *Anti-Jacobin* (1798) and the *Anti-Gallican* (1803), in which Napoleon was seen as an uncouth military adventurer hell-bent on plundering his conquered victims. His reported atrocities were magnified to produce the greatest possible revulsion among British readers. James Gillray, the celebrated caricaturist, depicted 'Little Boney' as a puny creature cowering before the beefy figure of John Bull, while lesser cartoonists also drew him in the coarsest light. The more moderate whig view was represented by the *Edinburgh Review*, whose military assessments in particular were commendably well informed and at times unusually fair.

Whatever their medium of expression, the tories were agreed that Napoleon was a vulgar upstart, devoid of any gentlemanly breeding, and a dangerous war-monger whose egotistical and despotic ambition had to be resisted. They saw him as the heir

209

of the militarism and lawlessness of the Jacobins, and condemned all their works without distinction. Those of them who
held office during the ministries of Pitt and Addington were
outraged by Napoleon's military interventions in Italy, Switzerland, and Egypt, as well as by his apparent designs on Malta
and Turkey. They considered him solely responsible for the
rupture of the short-lived Peace of Amiens in 1803. Having
weathered the crisis of Hoche's failed landing in Ireland in
1797, they were genuinely alarmed by Napoleon's more elaborate Boulogne flotilla project of 1803–5 for a direct invasion
of southern England. Their propaganda against him reached
a particularly high pitch in those years, while, more practically,
they also worked overtime to strengthen the defences of the
Channel coast.[36]

This particular scare eased after the battle of Trafalgar in
October 1805, only to be replaced by the new, more indirect
threat of Napoleon's Continental Blockade, officially declared
in November 1806. After Britain had become directly involved
in the Peninsular War in 1808, and when Napoleon's annexation of Holland in 1810 revived fears of a possible French
invasion of England, the whole area of conflict had widened
alarmingly. The tory propaganda-machine was then stretched
to the limit to rally public morale, especially after the collapse
of the Portland ministry which followed the fiasco of its
Walcheren expedition of 1809. When crisis overtook the domestic economy and social unrest also worsened around that
time, the public mood was generally sullen. So it largely remained until news of the disaster suffered by the Grand Army
in Russia in 1812 brought a welcome respite and strengthened
the British resolve to drive the French out of the Peninsula and
to subsidize the Allied Coalitions which would eventually bring
Napoleon down.[37] But during the anxious years preceding that
final conflict, no words were too harsh, no cartoons too crude,
to vilify his image, even though he was then at the height of his
continental hegemony.

The whig politicians and publicists, who were largely out of
office during this period, attacked Napoleon for rather different reasons. A good many of them, so far from denouncing the
French Revolution without discrimination, had responded
enthusiastically to its initial phases. Some indeed had prompted
Burke's celebrated *Reflections* of 1790 by comparing it favourably
with the English Revolution of 1688–89. In their view, Napoleon

210

was its complete antithesis, a military tyrant who had usurped its finest principles of peaceful reform. That, for instance, was the unyielding line of William Burdon's broadside, *The Conduct and Character of Napoleon Bonaparte*, published in 1804, the year in which the Imperial title was inaugurated. But, at the same time, the political consensus among whigs and radicals was much less solid than that of their tory opponents. Some, like Fox and Sheridan, were disposed at first to take an expedient view of Brumaire, especially when Napoleon in due course seemed more responsive to peace negotiations with Britain. They had an older and much stronger dislike for the exiled Bourbons, whose restoration they opposed in principle. Their position was compromised by the resumption of hostilities in 1803, then further weakened by the death of Fox in 1806 and by the failure of the coalition ministry of 1806–7 in which he had served to agree terms of peace with France. Even the 'Friends of Peace', the Nonconformist and largely extra-parliamentary radicals who had opposed Pitt's attempts to destroy the French Revolution by war, had no liking for Napoleon. Some were prominent in the patriotic resistance movements against him, and if the pacifism of most persisted during the wars of the Empire, it was because they believed that peace with him would be expedient for Britain.[38]

In any event, the whigs never orchestrated a wholly coherent front against Napoleon. A few, Earl Grey and Lord Holland most notably, shared a faintly disguised sympathy with his reforms in France, albeit with a public discretion appropriate to their rank. Radicals like William Cobbett, Francis Burdett, Samuel Whitbread, and J.C. Hobhouse are also often regarded as his apologists, although this impression may have been a reverse function of their still stronger bias against the tories. The case of the literary critic William Hazlitt, at least, needs no such qualification, even if his views certainly pose some curious moral equations. While his radicalism and animus against the British establishment were rooted in a Nonconformist and partly Irish background, he was also positively attracted to what he saw as Napoleon's brave fight against the effete autocracies of Europe. His adulation never waned, and in his *Life of Napoleon*, published much later in 1830, he extolled the virtues of his hero as one who had done more than any other to challenge the iniquitous principle of the divine right of kings.

Those were the exceptional voices, however; reactions among

the British literary fraternity were otherwise much more consistently hostile. The dark image of Napoleon as a liberticide recurred time and again in their writings, notwithstanding their own differences of political affiliation. Coleridge, whose early tergiversations later hardened into an inveterate antagonism towards Napoleon, vented his spleen almost entirely in prose. Others chose the medium of poetry. Of these latter, Wordsworth and Southey (who was to become poet laureate in 1813) were most outstanding among the whig writers who had become bitterly disillusioned by the later course of the Revolution in France, and especially by what followed it after Brumaire. Wordsworth had branded Napoleon as a 'Robespierre on horseback' from an early stage of his campaigns, an image which the poet invested with all the accoutrements of systematic banditry as the wars of conquest were relentlessly extended, and which may have been the original source of Carlyle's later remark that Napoleon 'belonged to the brigand species'.[39] Wordsworth also came to believe that the heroic spirit of nationality, which at different times he rather indiscriminately attributed to the Prussians, the Spaniards, the Austrians, the Tyrolese, the Russians, and of course the English *par excellence*, would eventually overcome Napoleon.

Walter Scott, again, who also made much of the 'bandit' image, added another, more idiosyncratic note to the chorus of abuse. His unremitting hatred of Napoleon stemmed mostly from the almost 'feudal' reverence which he, as a high tory, always felt for the proper hierarchy of social status. In this respect, his sympathies were diametrically opposed to those of Hazlitt. Characteristically, he depicted Napoleon as a low-born and ill-mannered brute, driven by reckless greed to acts of unconscionable barbarism. The emperor's eclectic literary tastes, which ranged from a self-professed love of Ossian, of Rousseau, and of Goethe's *Werther*, to a whole assortment of classical texts, seemed a vulgar sham to one infatuated with the neo-chivalric niceties of the Gothic revival. Scott's social prejudices against Napoleon were implicit in attenuated form in such poems as 'The Vision of Don Roderick' (1811) and 'The Field of Waterloo' (1815). Yet nothing here could match the sustained animosity he later poured into the nine volumes of his *Life of Napoleon* (1827), a poorly researched work of virtually no historical value, and which has not on the whole found much favour with literary critics either. For Byron, on the other hand, the passage of time at least brought a change of tone. If he despised the emperor-in-power, just as he despised all autocrats as enemies of Liberty, he was markedly less hostile to the emperor-in-captivity. This shift of emphasis is explained in part by his abhorrence of the Holy Alliance formed in 1815, but mostly perhaps by his artistic response to the pathos of Napoleon's ultimate fate on St Helena, which prompted the classical analogy of Prometheus chained to his rock.

Whatever their political affiliations may have been, British contemporaries who expressed their views on Napoleon had one thing in common. Unlike their German and Italian counterparts, they never experienced the shock of conquest in their homeland, and of course they were never exposed to direct subjugation by the French. They did not have to engage in the pragmatic art of collaboration with the enemy. Their country was not exploited in a material sense. After Trafalgar, Britain was more than ever master of the high seas, already set on a course of major imperial expansion across the world. Both the hostility which the vast majority of British writers felt towards Napoleon, and the relative warmth of his few admirers, were expressed in a context in which he or his army had no physical presence. Their response was inspired more by the principles, or perhaps rather the lack of principles, he was perceived to represent, and by the spell his very person cast over the literary and artistic circles of that time.

Among most of the British political élite, even the unreformed parliamentary system had bred a comfortable sense of a free people governed through tried and enlightened institutions. By comparison, the Napoleonic Empire seemed like an extended network of military despoliation. The Continental Blockade of 1806–13, which in fact posed a grave threat to many of Britain's traditional economic outlets abroad, could be construed as an impracticable policy born of desperation. To overcome it, Britain could count on the ascendancy of her navy, on her ability to blockade the enemy coastline almost at will, and on the native ingenuity of her commercial and industrial classes. Outside of the Iberian peninsula as from 1808, she did not have to mount sustained military campaigns on the European mainland; subsidies to her continental allies would achieve the purpose by less painful means. In short, whatever the curiosity Napoleon always aroused, and the sneaking regard which some at least had for his military genius, British contemporaries could form their impressions of him in a mood of patriotic and insular superiority. It was this spirit, perhaps, which most enabled British society to face the recurrent crises and sustain the heavy burdens of the French wars, until victory finally came.

. . . .

THE PAST RELATED TO THE PRESENT

It should, then, be abundantly clear that both the adulatory and the black legend of Napoleon had their roots in the earliest contemporary accounts, and that these were by no means confined to French writers. On the other hand, reinterpretation of the Napoleonic legacy in terms that would seem immediate and exemplary to contemporaries of later generations was a feature of French historiography, above all others, during the century or more up to the Second World War. Indeed, from this angle we have to view Napoleon as part of a process of change running right across the period of the French Revolution and the Empire. The watershed is not then 1799, nor 1804, nor any other particular year in the process of empire-building, but the longer experience of 1789–1815, when the organic life of the French nation was seen as having been irreversibly transformed. The Bourbons might well return, but their inheritance was the new order in France, not the old regime. What happened after 1815 was that the ideological conflicts of that earlier period were relived, as constitutional regimes succeeded each other, from the Bourbon Restoration to the July Monarchy, from the Second Republic to the Second Empire, and finally to the Third Republic. The Great Revolution and First Empire thus became a fertile source for writers of all ideological persuasions to relate to the political issues of their own times. Whether they were for or against Napoleon, whether he was seen as the grand consolidator of the work of the Revolution, or rather as a despot who rode roughshod over its principles, was often a reflection of their attitude to the immediate regimes under which they were writing.

For those whose first loyalties were to the Catholic faith, the Revolution continued to be seen as an evil force, destructive of the traditional ties of 'King and Church'. Its secular dynamic, in their view, had generated a plague of godless apostles motivated by impiety and greed, who had desecrated so many churches and other holy places. And Napoleon's role, most notably in his

214

later abuse of the Concordat with Pius VII, had been to accentuate the humiliation of the Church, by browbeating its clergy into submission, by imprisoning its supreme pontiff, and by giving enduring legal sanction to the confiscation and sale of its lands. This theme is evident early on in the writings of Joseph de Maistre and Chateaubriand, and it was to recur again and again in comte d'Haussonville's five-volume work, *L'Église romaine et le premier Empire*, published in 1868–69. The standpoint of the last-named writer was of course significantly different. As a liberal Catholic, d'Haussonville drew his inspiration much more from Lamennais, and (like his mentor) had uneasy relations with Rome. He was also an admirer of Madame de Staël, who had herself been raised in a Swiss Protestant family, to which he was distantly related by marriage.

For radicals and republicans, by contrast, it was natural enough to celebrate the guiding principles of the Great Revolution, and by extension to see Napoleon as the usurper of that bold, humanitarian, and universalist vision of reform. Never mind the departures from those principles which had already undermined their practical attainment as early as 1789 itself. Never mind the brutal excesses of the Jacobin Terror. Never mind the self-interested élite which had entrenched itself in outwardly republican forms, and through a highly exclusive franchise, under the regime of the Directory. Never mind the despoliation of occupied and annexed lands during the Revolutionary wars of conquest. The early ideal of 'Liberty, Equality, Fraternity' had survived all that. It would have been logical enough for these writers to conclude that Napoleon had distorted and finally abandoned the great vision by his despotic methods and incessant wars.

Some, like François Mignet, Auguste Barbier, and Jules Michelet (especially in his last works), certainly argued largely in that sense. For Michelet in particular, the true hero of the Revolution had been the common people, and he could hardly approve of their mute subservience under Napoleon's pitiless regime. It is, however, an intriguing fact that other republican writers of the mid- to later nineteenth century were much more ambivalent in their reconstruction of the Napoleonic past. All had difficulty in coming to terms with the militarism implicit in the nostalgia for '*la gloire*' and '*la grandeur*' associated with the Bonapartist cults. At the same time, the Concordat remained as an instrument of state to safeguard the old 'Gallican Liberties' and prevent legitimists and ultramontane diehards from engrossing power, as they had once done under Charles X (1824–30). Napoleon had, after all, tried to put the priests in their place and made an effort to incorporate the religious life of Protestants and Jews within his authoritarian system. His perceived anticlericalism thus provided one crucial link with which later republicans and radicals could find affinity. His Civil Code, too, was an established monument to the social order which had emerged from the Revolutionary land sales, a sacred charter for those of the bourgeoisie and better-off peasantry who had bought property confiscated from the Church and the émigrés back in the 1790s. His prefectures, though in other respects an undesirable instrument of State centralism, could have useful executive functions in the republican cause, not least in curtailing the activities of its internal enemies.

Among those who might be thought of as classic liberals rather than committed republicans, Adolphe Thiers was the outstanding figure. A minister under the Orleanist monarchy and later a founding father of the Third Republic, he could reconcile his liberalism with the most adulatory account of Napoleon written by a major politician during the nineteenth century. Deeply influenced by the Napoleonic legend, his monumental *Histoire du Consulat et de l'Empire*, which appeared in twenty volumes between 1845 and 1862, had a huge public appeal. Like other admirers of Napoleon, Thiers was moved by a deeply ingrained Anglophobia, and this in turn led him to see the 'English menace' as a justification for many of Napoleon's most serious miscalculations. Before him, Victor Hugo had similarly reconciled his own liberal principles with an instinctive admiration for Napoleon. *His* reaction almost certainly had much more to do with literary inspiration, since Napoleon brilliantly embodied all the greatness and dynamic energy Hugo looked for in a true Romantic hero.

The out-and-out Napoleonists were of course the most nostalgic of all writers, and their role in disseminating the legend was vital to its popular appeal. They could see no major blemish in their hero's achievements. Everything he had done had been necessary and for the best. It had been undertaken to serve the interests of France and of Europe. What had frustrated him was the cynical alliances of foreign tyrants and spoilers, Britain foremost among them, forcing war on Europe when he had sought peace, and ultimately contriving to bring him down just as his grand design of European integration was coming to fruition. For the adherents of the Napoleonic legend after 1821, the terrible human cost of the wars of the Consulate and Empire raised no great moral discomfort. The abuses of conscription, the financial burdens of incessant campaigns, and the systematic exploitation of conquered territories did not trouble them either. They saw all this as the inevitable price Napoleon's subjects had had to pay for his heroic fight against malevolent enemies. The brutality of his exemplary punishments meted out to recalcitrant individuals or villages were either ignored or else condoned as necessary acts of state. The same construction could also be put on his relentless censorship, his manipulation of official propaganda, and his ruthless treatment of opposition groups more generally. It was as if ordinary human judgement stood suspended before a genius called by Destiny to act above it.

The Napoleonists, of course, were much less interested in making excuses for than in orchestrating homages to their hero. They pointed to his appeal, however selective and circumstantial it may have been in fact, across classes and professions. They liked to think that he had inspired all conditions of men with a common purpose, that he had opened his army and his civil state to the patriotism in the hearts of all subjects. He had given ordinary soldiers a sense of pride in serving him, a willingness to march whenever and wherever he called on them to do so, whatever the privations, and to accept the greatest risks with courage in the cause of the Eagle standards. Higher up the ranks, his officer corps had attracted men of talent from all social backgrounds. In inaugurating his Imperial nobility, he had not so much brought back the social and legal distinctions formally abolished by the Revolution, but rather given all his most faithful servants a chance to aspire to and share in the just rewards of honour. He had, as Las Cases boldly declared, 'created titles, the qualifications for which gave the last blow to the old feudal system'.[40]

In short, when celebrated in such terms, Napoleon had been an emperor for all the people, and the wide appeal of his legend seemed later to vindicate that belief. Its evocation of the glorious Imperial past was physically present for all Parisians to see in some of the city's most imposing public monuments: the Arc de Triomphe de l'Étoile (finally completed under the July Monarchy), the Arc du Carrousel, and the statue

217

of Napoleon on top of the Vendôme column (to which Hugo dedicated a rousing Ode in 1830, and whose history during the nineteenth century was one of literal ups and downs) – among others. The legend was kept alive not only among the *grognards* of the Old Guard and their descendants; it had passed into French folklore in a much more pervasive way. For how else could Napoleon's later admirers account for the public awe which followed the return of his mortal remains to Paris in 1840? How else could representations of the legend in the popular works of Stendhal, or Hugo, or even Balzac be explained? How else could the legend have recurred in more marginal writings, such as de Musset's autobiographical *Confession d'un enfant du siècle* (1836), or in the verses of the *chansonniers* P.-J. Béranger and Émile Debraux? How else could it have inspired even foreign adherents like Mickiewicz, the Polish exile, whose ritualistic homages at the Napoleonic shrines assumed an almost religious fervour? How else could the bronze statue by the sculptor François Rude at Fixin in Burgundy, which represented Napoleon as a Christ-like figure in the process of resurrection, have attracted so many pilgrims after its inauguration in 1847?

Indeed, how else would the subsequent career of Louis Napoleon, the son of the great emperor's brother Louis and Hortense de Beauharnais, have been conceivable at all? It may be helpful here to distinguish between the Napoleonic legend, as revealed through its various artistic expressions or through other fanciful manifestations of the Napoleonic cults after 1815, and Bonapartism in its more practical political and institutional forms. The scholarly account of Frédéric Bluche goes some way towards explaining the symbiotic relationship between the two, although it covers only the first half of the nineteenth century.[41] The subject has also been analysed more recently by Robert Gildea in an excellent essay which offers a much longer perspective.[42] He identifies Bonapartism as a major theme in modern French history right up to the present day, and shows that the claim to political 'legitimacy' was one of its most recurrent features from the start. In default of any widely acknowledged dynastic right among the political élites after 1815, or at any rate after 1870, the claim came to be based essentially on the presumption of a popular mandate. The earliest source of that mandate lay less in Napoleon's own plebiscites of 1800, 1802, 1804, and 1815, which had been State-managed affairs, whose apparently massive majorities had actually disguised a high

218

rate of abstention among the electorate.[43] It lay much more in the spontaneous rally of the so-called 'federations' to his restored regime during the Hundred Days. These had been most prominent among the administrative personnel of some provincial towns like Rennes and Dijon and among the artisans of certain Paris sections.[44]

Such memories of 'popular Bonapartism' lived on in the legend after 1815, even as French society became more industrialized and more urbanized. Bernard Ménager has shown how the myth of Napoleon as an emperor of the people in due course strengthened the electoral appeal of Louis Napoleon.[45] It would be difficult otherwise, given the pathetic failure of the latter's attempted *coups d'état* at Strasbourg (October 1836) and at Boulogne (August 1840), to explain how his formulation of Bonapartist doctrine in *Des Idées napoléoniennes* of 1839 could have had the impact it later did. Clearly, if the author of this curiously hybrid work had not yet learnt how to get his military act together, he had a much better sense of where to strike his readers. He argued with specious clarity that the Imperial laws had established 'civil equality, in accordance with the democratic principle; hierarchy, in accordance with the principles of order and stability'; that 'the base [of the Imperial system] is democratic, because all power comes from the people, while the organization is hierarchical.'[46] Such simplisms, especially the claim that Bonapartism stood for popular rights and welfare, as well as for social order and strong government, eventually had their effect in the presidential elections under the Second Republic in December 1848, conducted on the new basis of universal manhood suffrage. At first, Louis Napoleon had to accommodate his populism within the existing republican forms, which in due course he found increasingly frustrating. After his *coup d'état* of 2 December 1851, he was in a stronger position to turn the Imperial myth which had helped to bear him aloft into a new political reality.

Exactly a year later the Second Empire of Napoleon III was proclaimed. His title itself deferred to the intervening dynastic rights of the uncrowned Napoleon II, son of the first emperor, the former King of Rome and Duke of Reichstadt, 'the Eaglet' of the legend, who had died at the palace of Schönbrunn in 1832. Practical exposure to the reconstituted Imperial system provoked the first sustained reaction against the Napoleonic legend, and at the same time against Thiers's enthusiastic celebration of it. Tocqueville's vindication of the moral principles of Liberty in his well-known text of 1856 was explicitly clear. His criticism of the new emperor's despotic methods masquerading as plebiscitary democracy was perhaps necessarily more oblique, but also unmistakable. He saw these as the latest variant of a long process of governmental centralization going back to the old regime. Victor Hugo, whose literary attraction to '*Napoléon le Grand*' has already been noted, soon became altogether less infatuated with the current incumbent, '*Napoléon le Petit*', as he contemptuously entitled a work published on that subject in 1852. Having espoused the republican cause as an elected deputy in 1848, he withdrew his early support for Louis Napoleon in the following year. Exiling himself from France after the latter's *coup d'état*, he chose to spend the long interlude of the Second Empire on Jersey and then on Guernsey.

It may perhaps seem ironic that two at least of the more notable historical reactions against Thiers and the legend were published in the 1860s, when, as some modern writers have argued, Napoleon III was set upon a major adjustment of policy that would eventually lead to his so-called 'Liberal Empire'. Edgar Quinet, a friend and former academic colleague of Michelet at the Collège de France, felt obliged by the events of 1851 to seek refuge in Switzerland. As a liberal polemicist with an aversion to all dogmatic systems, he had a number of axes to grind. He had already earned a reputation as an enemy of Catholicism through his earlier invectives against the Jesuits. Later, in an interpretation of the Revolution published in 1865, he had a more obviously secular target. His attack here was directed against centralized government in general and against its former Jacobin exponents in particular, who (incidentally) had certainly not been friendly to Jesuits. Stressing the dictatorial nature of that regime, he saw Napoleon as its true military heir, but he did not develop his case beyond the Imperial coronation of December 1804.

By comparison, the first volumes of Pierre Lanfrey's new *Histoire de Napoléon*, published in 1867, appeared to be more scholarly. They were certainly much more substantial, since this author set out to demolish Thiers and the Napoleonic legend in systematic detail. In pursuing his resolve, however, he was actually a good deal less impartial than his advertised intentions seemed to suggest, and also more fortunate than

220

Thiers in one important respect. He had access to most of the recently published volumes of Napoleon's official correspondence, and these he was able to quarry with consummate skill, trained journalist that he was. The partisan selections he made from them provided just the sort of 'ammunition' he felt would give his counter-blast an authentic ring. The picture of Napoleon which emerged was consistently hostile, both as to his base character and his cruel methods, and devoid of any mark of greatness. In constructing it, Lanfrey of course had another, more tendentious purpose. He wanted, by association, to denigrate the character and regime of Napoleon III as well.

In the event, that same result was soon to be achieved much more by the impact of military conflict than by the influence of any writer. After the humiliating French defeat by the Prussians in 1870, apologists of the Napoleonic legend for some time resembled voices crying in the wilderness. Gaps formed among the witnesses of the blood, so to speak, with the death of the former emperor in 1873 and with that of his son, the Prince Imperial, in the Zulu War of 1879. In due course, a renewed attack on everything Napoleon and his legend had stood for was launched by another prominent writer, Hippolyte Taine. Once a liberal enthusiast of the 1848 revolution, he had been thoroughly disillusioned by the experience of the Paris Commune of 1871. The first three volumes of his major work, *Les origines de la France contemporaine*, which appeared in 1876, were a scathing denunciation of the Great Revolution. In dwelling at length on the excesses of its 'spontaneous anarchy' and 'mob' rule, he not only castigated its destructive vulgarity; he also provided embittered conservatives with a still more vitriolic vocabulary for that exercise. In two further volumes covering the Napoleonic regime, but which were not published until 1890–93, Taine showed himself an equally unrestrained critic. Everything the old emperor had done, all the institutions he had founded, were contemptuously portrayed as an odious extension of his brutal Corsican mentality, as functions of his unbridled egotism, and as proof of his insatiable desire to dominate all about him. This was indeed the very quintessence of the black legend; and it, too, was exaggerated beyond all reasonable proportion.

Ironically, Taine had also missed his ideal moment. He had joined the polemical debate on Napoleon too late to remain its dominant voice for long. It is true that much of the early running against him was made by a lesser intellect, the ageing Prince Napoleon, the second son of Jerome Bonaparte by Catherine of Württemberg, until his own death in 1891. His credo, often formulated in near-republican terms which combined anticlericalism with a strong plebiscitary appeal, is usually seen as the most politically radical version of Bonapartism yet enunciated. As such, it seemed suspect to the political élites of the Third Republic. In any event, the prince's quarrel with Taine was not the major reason for another revival of the Napoleonic legend during the later 1880s and 1890s. Much more significant here was the public perception of weakness and corruption in high republican circles themselves.

The Boulanger affair, which peaked in 1888–89, and which has sometimes (but rather inappropriately) been likened to a failed Bonapartist coup, was one expression of that public mood. The Wilson, Panama, and Dreyfus scandals, coinciding as they also did with the effects of the Great Depression in France, all accentuated the sense of alienation felt by many on the disillusioned Right and Left alike. The xenophobia common among these fragmented political groups had at least two dimensions. One, most obvious among the *revanchistes*, was aimed at recovering the 'lost provinces' of Alsace and Lorraine, following their 'rape' by Germany in 1871. The other, whose roots went back much further, was a resurgence of Anglophobia. Intensified by the imperial disputes of the late nineteenth century, it very nearly led to war over Fashoda in 1898. Britain was seen as the prime example of effete parliamentary liberalism, and the revolving ministers of the 'Opportunist' Republic as a supine breed who lacked the courage to challenge the imperial pretensions of 'perfidious Albion'.

By that comparison, the historical apologists of the Napoleonic legend could at least claim to be reviving collective memories of a true national hero. Three in particular were prominent around that time. Henry Houssaye, whose work appeared in four volumes between 1888 and 1905, returned to the idea that the interests and ultimately tragic destiny of the great emperor had been identical with those of France. His argument was unfortunately vitiated by a narrow concentration on the years 1814–15, and so by his failure even to consider why Napoleon had got himself into such a desperate position in the first place. Arthur-Lévy, again, whose two accounts were published in 1892 and 1902, had at least the merit of covering

Napoleon's career as a whole. His attempt in the first to offer an intimate insight into his subject's generous spirit certainly had its appeal. At the same time, he spoilt his case by too many mawkish excesses and by concentrating so much of his hostile fire on Taine. In his second work, which was more concerned with foreign policy, he drew lavishly on the St Helena record of Las Cases to peddle yet again its original myth that Napoleon had been a man of peace, whose wars were thrust upon him against his will, and who had paid the price of being much too tolerant towards implacable enemies in his ascendant years.

Count Albert Vandal, finally, who also shared the current Anglophobia and anti-parliamentary sentiments of other contemporary writers, held no reverence whatever for the work of the Great Revolution or for the view that Napoleon had fulfilled its finest ideals. On the contrary, his *L'Avènement de Bonaparte* (1903) was an eloquent restatement of an older thesis that Brumaire had been a great watershed, separating the orderliness and grandeur of the Napoleonic years from the chaos, squalid factionalism, and national degradation of the Revolutionary upheaval. That was very much the message that Napoleonic propaganda had repeatedly disseminated at the time, and indeed in most other respects Vandal was inclined to interpret his subject in Napoleon's own terms. In an earlier three-volume work of 1891–96, he had similarly extolled his hero's greatness in foreign policy by a highly partial account of the emperor's relations with Tsar Alexander I from 1807 to 1812. Here, Vandal concluded that Napoleon's overriding aim had always been the general peace of the world, a notion which his Russian foe exposed to the massive French invasion of 1812 would no doubt have considered a rum construction of events.

· · · · · · · · · · · · ·

IN SEARCH OF A GRAND THEME

Among the thousands of writings on Napoleon published before the Second World War, some might almost be likened to elaborate symphonies in which a central theme was played out through all the constituent movements. The authors in question, who tried to explain Napoleon's achievements in terms of a grand idea, or a dominant image that would encapsulate all others, had one thing in common: they were all looking for the vital key to unlock his real ambition. This interpretative device had been implicit in some of the earlier accounts, of course, and its first extended exposition can probably be found in the monumental work of Thiers cited earlier. Using a largely narrative framework, he concluded that Napoleon's overriding ambition had been nothing less than the construction of a 'universal empire'. For this author, then, the Imperial vision was never confined to France, or even to continental Europe more widely, but took on truly global proportions. He appeared to think that Napoleon ultimately hoped to conquer the world. Just how he might have done so without a dominant navy, at a time when Britain's mastery of the seas was so abundantly clear, was a difficulty Thiers never really confronted.

Clearly, the whole scale had to be reduced, and it *was* reduced in the major works of two prolific writers which began to appear some thirty to forty years later. One was Albert Sorel, whose admiration for Napoleon was qualified by his own detached, as it were 'Olympian', view that even great men were bound to act within the constraints of historical necessity. His *L'Europe et la Révolution française* was published in eight volumes between 1885 and 1904, of which the last four dealt with Napoleon's foreign and military policy. If they have a binding theme, it surely lies in their emphasis on the essentially *continental* dimension of the subject. Sorel particularly stressed the importance of the 'natural frontiers' of France (the Pyrenees, the Alps, and the Rhine) as the determining factor in Napoleon's ambition. These frontiers, the argument went, he had to some extent inherited from the Revolutionary wars at the time of Brumaire. It was his compulsion to bring them entirely under French rule once and for all, if necessary by the creation of buffer states, that chiefly motivated his subsequent campaigns and political embellishments further afield, and also precluded any prospect of lasting peace with enemy Powers.

From this assumption Sorel developed his compelling thesis of historical fatalism, in which Napoleon appeared less as the master of his own destiny than as an involuntary agent driven by circumstances to secure the sacred 'natural frontiers' at all costs. In this respect, he was only the most spectacular custodian of an older mission, which itself marked an underlying continuity in French foreign policy since the Revolution, and whose origins can be traced back to the reign of Louis XIV. Yet the ineluctable force of history and logic of geography, as Sorel applied them to Napoleonic imperialism, was not without its irony. One may well ask what vital interests of France, or even of extended France, really *had* to be defended in Moscow. And, by ignoring many obvious foreign sources, Sorel's centrifugal view of Napoleon's military dynamic did not adequately explain the understandable anxiety or even the negotiating position of the Allied Coalitions at different times during the wars. In view of this, critics like Raymond Guyot and Pierre Muret not unreasonably considered Sorel's work too systematic and inflexible.

Frédéric Masson, by contrast, whose ardent admiration for Napoleon was altogether less impersonal, saw his achievements as the working out of a much more voluntary plan, and attributed its ultimate collapse in large part to human fallibility. The thirteen volumes of *Napoléon et sa famille*, which appeared over the years 1897–1919, were a sustained attempt to explain Napoleon's ambition in the light of a Corsican 'clan spirit', itself typical of local custom. Viewed in such terms, he was moved by a native sense that his personal success could also elevate his family to positions of power and honour, and that they would eventually form the pillars of his own glorious European dynasty. This scheme had its origins in Napoleon's modest advancement of his brothers and sisters after he had won fame as a general during the Revolutionary wars. Later, once he was master of France, he expanded it into a much more grandiose plan to 'house the family' (*caser 'la famiglia'*) on the satellite thrones of his 'Grand Empire'. The aim was laudable, Masson thought, and it had been conceived in the fullness of Napoleon's generous spirit. But the family, alas, were to let him down. Their disobedience, ingratitude, and on occasion even treachery were a cruel reward for the trust he had placed in them. Without him, they could never have risen so far; with his fall, their own was inevitable. In all, Masson's work was a poignant reconstruction of a human story which moved from insular obscurity to Imperial grandeur, before ending in tragedy. By taking it back to its first roots, and by elaborating the theme of an enduring Corsican instinct in Napoleon's evolving ambition, his treatment of the subject was unusually perceptive and original.

Other writers, however, revived the notion that Napoleon had a much wider imperial vision beyond the heartland of continental Europe. Émile Bourgeois, for instance, constructed an intriguing thesis based on 'the oriental mirage' in Napoleon's foreign policy. The idea that Napoleon's secret ambition was the creation of a great emporium to the east, one which would give France command of the Mediterranean and the rich Levantine trade routes, was elaborated in the second of the author's four-volume work, *Manuel historique de politique étrangère*, published in stages over the years 1892–1926. Although the evidence for this underlying plan was scattered and presumptive, for what it was worth, Bourgeois milked it dry. He pointed to Napoleon's early interest in the Adriatic during the late 1790s, to his recurrent hopes of acquiring the Ionian Islands, to his Egyptian campaign of 1798–99 (which ended of course in the French military evacuation of 1801), to his conflicting designs on Constantinople and search for a closer alliance with Turkey, and to his annexation of the 'Illyrian Provinces' in 1809, which seemed a strategic springboard into a vaster Balkan hinterland. If such a bold plan ever persisted in Napoleon's mind, we could probably agree with Bourgeois's conclusion that its constant deceptions undermined the integrity of his European diplomacy and were harmful to French interests nearer home. It would, however, be safer to say that the plan itself was at best an occasional chimera. If Napoleon's early fascination for the Levant is indisputable, the harsh reality of French naval eclipse, especially after Trafalgar, made such youthful fancies all the more remote.

More convincing was the thesis of Édouard Driault, presented at length in the five volumes of his *Napoléon et l'Europe* (1917–27), that Napoleon's ambition was chiefly motivated by 'the Roman ideal'. It was not of course an original idea. More than fifty years earlier, Edgar Quinet's cited work had already anticipated something similar, in arguing that Napoleon's ultimate aim was a sort of universal Roman monarchy, a caesaro-papist establishment reminiscent of a Constantine or a Theodosius, and that his Concordat with Pius VII was a necessary (if sadly miscalculated) preparatory step to its attainment. Yet Driault developed the analogy much more fully. He thought that it implied not just the conquest and assimilation of the whole of Italy to French rule, which up to a point was actually achieved, but the creation of a wider French empire in the Mediterranean basin as well. He reinforced his case through all the outward embellishments of Napoleon's neo-classical pretensions: political nomenclature, art, medals, coins, palaces, columns, triumphal arches, and so on. It was as if the emperor wanted each of his subjects to be able to say: '*civis napoleonicus sum*'.

Where, however, would the dynamic of that grand design come from? Driault, in an accompanying theme, gave a clear answer: from the energy of the French Revolution, at once destructive *and* constructive, which Napoleon embodied in his own person. As the strong man of the Revolution, he became the most effective disseminator of its principles beyond France, sweeping away all the political and social institutions of the old regime before him. The 'Roman ideal', as an end, would thus be served by the means of revolutionary change, and in Driault's view the two became organically linked in Napoleon's mind and policies. Taken as a whole, this interpretation had something to commend it, not least the evidence of many of Napoleon's recorded utterances; but it was also too trusting of appearances, of Imperial display and flummery, and of the emperor's own grandiloquence. Driault looked at his subject from France – outwards. He did not adequately explain the diversity of native reactions to Napoleonic rule in Italy, including the violent uprisings in many parts. Too often, he took Napoleon's stated will for the deed. And, once again, there is the fundamental problem of the French navy. At the height of the Empire, it could not even secure safe access to Sicily, within sight of the Italian mainland, let alone mount a serious challenge to the more distant islands or shores of the Mediterranean.

Driault's work also made much of another motif, the Carolingian analogy, which he was inclined to see as a transitional stage in Napoleon's ambition, before the grander Roman imperial idea overtook it. For a number of other writers, however, the Carolingian analogy seemed much more convincing *in its own right*. It was for instance implicit in Charles Schmidt's *Le grand-duché de Berg (1806–1813)* of 1905 and then again in Marcel Dunan's *Napoléon et l'Allemagne* of 1942, both works of exemplary scholarship, where the German aspect of the question is understandably uppermost. Hellmuth Rössler's much more explicit treatment of it some years later certainly owed something to those and to other earlier works, Driault's included.[47] Briefly put, the thesis stresses the essentially Latin and Teutonic foundations of Napoleon's 'Grand Empire', as can be seen in the broad similarity between its 'map' and that of Charlemagne's empire. It explains Napoleon's true Imperial design logically enough in primarily *continental* rather than global or maritime terms. It highlights the practical options open to him across the Rhine and beyond the Alps, and it more closely reflects the evidence of the policies he actually pursued there. In its most refined form, it could be considered an empirical thesis.

This is not to say that the Carolingian analogy had no place in the historiography of the nineteenth century, or that it lacked the more fanciful flourishes of some of the other grand images discussed above. On the contrary, it was germane to the Napoleonic legend from the earliest days, and for one very good reason: Napoleon himself was its original source. At his Imperial coronation in Notre-Dame, he self-consciously flaunted the regalia (replicas in fact) of his celebrated Frankish progenitor as symbols of his just inheritance. At his coronation as King of Italy in Milan in May 1805, he likewise assumed the Iron Crown of Lombardy, which he again placed on his own head. At his meeting with Tsar Alexander I at Erfurt in 1808, he had another chance to demonstrate his 'Carolingian' status as the sovereign of a new western empire to the thirty-four vassal or allied princes of Germany then assembled before him. On many other occasions, too, he made a point of projecting himself as a 'new Charlemagne' as well as a 'new Caesar' – indeed, as an emperor who had surpassed all earlier ones in history.

And so, through whichever variation we follow it, the genre of the 'grand idea' leads us back to the primary source which always inspired it: Napoleon himself. The first century or more of Napoleonic historiography thus ended where it had begun, with a presumptive elaboration of his Imperial vision and of the heroic deeds which gave it outward form. In this and the preceding chapters I have tried to set the polemical rhetoric of that historiographical debate against the more factual historical record, to distinguish the reality of Napoleonic power, as it was implemented and experienced at the time, from the myths with which it was later embroidered. In the same way, since both the heroic and black legends of Napoleon have coloured so many earlier perceptions of his enduring legacy, we might well ask just how much of his Imperial design and which of his celebrated achievements *actually* survived his fall. The short conclusion which follows is an attempt to answer the question empirically.

. . . .

NOTES AND REFERENCES

1. Pieter Geyl, *Napoleon: For and Against*, Harmondsworth, 1986 impression (Peregrine Books).

2. Napoleon I, *Correspondance de Napoléon Ier publiée par ordre de l'empereur Napoléon III*, 32 vols, Paris, 1858–69.
3. Ibid., vol. 10, p. 474; quoted in *The Mind of Napoleon: A Selection from his Written and Spoken Words*, ed. and trans by J. Christopher Herold, New York, 1955, p. 43.
4. Quoted in Herold, *Mind of Napoleon*, p. 242.
5. Quoted in ibid.
6. Emmanuel de Las Cases, *Mémorial de Sainte-Hélène. Journal of the Private Life and Conversations of the Emperor Napoleon at Saint Helena*, Eng. edn, 4 vols, London, 1823, vol. 4, part vii, p. 110.
7. Quoted in Herold, *Mind of Napoleon*, p. 257.
8. Quoted in ibid., p. 260.
9. Quoted in ibid., p. 276.
10. Comte Philippe-Paul de Ségur, *Un Aide de camp de Napoléon: Mémoires du comte de Ségur*, ed. by Louis de Ségur, 3 vols, Paris, 1894–95, vol. 2, pp. 219–20.
11. Quoted in Herold, *Mind of Napoleon*, p. 45.
12. Quoted in ibid., p. 40.
13. Napoleon I, *Correspondance*, vol. 2, p. 294; quoted in Herold, *Mind of Napoleon*, p. 40.
14. Napoleon I, *Correspondance*, vol. 14, p. 553; quoted in Herold, *Mind of Napoleon*, p. 40.
15. Las Cases, *Mémorial*, vol. 1, part i, pp. 57–8.
16. Ibid., vol. 4, part vii, p. 53.
17. Quoted in Herold, *Mind of Napoleon*, p. 47.
18. Las Cases, *Mémorial*, vol. 4, part vii, pp. 133–4.
19. Ibid., p. 256.
20. Ibid., vol. 1, part i, pp. 150–1.
21. Ibid., vol. 2, part iii, pp. 197–8.
22. Ibid., vol. 4, part vii, pp. 132–3.
23. Ibid., vol. 3, part vi, p. 353.
24. Hans Schmidt, 'Napoleon in der deutschen Geschichtsschreibung', *Francia*, vol. 14, 1986, pp. 530–60.
25. Quoted in ibid., p. 532 n.
26. Besides ibid., see also: Heinz-Otto Sieburg, *Deutschland und Frankreich in der Geschichtsschreibung des 19. Jahrhunderts*, 2 vols, Wiesbaden, 1954, 1958; and Michael Freund, *Napoleon und die Deutschen. Despot oder Held der Freiheit?*, Munich, 1969.
27. Gonthier-Louis Fink, 'Goethe et Napoléon. Littérature et politique', *Francia*, vol. 10, 1982, p. 365.
28. All quoted in ibid., pp. 374–5.
29. Quoted in Geyl, *For and Against*, p. 349.
30. Quoted in Fink, 'Goethe et Napoléon', p. 375.
31. J.M. Roberts, 'Italy, 1793–1830', in C.W. Crawley, ed., *The New Cambridge Modern History*, vol. 9, Cambridge, 1965, p. 412.

32. Stuart Woolf, *A History of Italy 1700–1860: The Social Constraints of Political Change*, London, 1979, pp. 181–3.
33. Ibid., p. 218.
34. Eileen Anne Millar, *Napoleon in Italian Literature 1796–1821*, Rome, 1977, to which I am much indebted for the material used in these paragraphs on the Italian writers.
35. F.J. Maccunn, *The Contemporary English View of Napoleon*, London, 1914.
36. Richard Glover, *Britain at Bay: Defence against Bonaparte, 1803–14*, London, 1973, pp. 77–124; and Clive Emsley, *British Society and the French Wars 1793–1815*, London and Basingstoke, 1979, pp. 99–123.
37. John M. Sherwig, *Guineas and Gunpowder: British Foreign Aid in the Wars with France 1793–1815*, Cambridge, Mass., 1969, pp. 284–344.
38. J.E. Cookson, *The Friends of Peace: Anti-War Liberalism in England, 1793–1815*, Cambridge, 1982.
39. Quoted in Maccunn, *Contemporary English View*, pp. 232, 233 n.
40. Las Cases, *Mémorial*, vol. 1, part ii, p. 270.
41. Frédéric Bluche, *Le Bonapartisme. Aux origines de la Droite autoritaire, 1800–1850*, Paris, 1980.
42. Robert Gildea, 'Bonapartism', in *The Past in French History*, New Haven and London, 1994, pp. 62–111; the essay on 'Grandeur' in the same vol., pp. 112–65, also has some illuminating discussion of another major Napoleonic theme.
43. E.g. Frédéric Bluche, *Le plébiscite des Cent-Jours, avril–mai 1815*, Geneva, 1974.
44. R.S. Alexander, *Bonapartism and Revolutionary Tradition in France: The Fédérés of 1815*, Cambridge, 1991.
45. Bernard Ménager, *Les Napoléons du peuple*, Paris, 1988.
46. Louis-Napoleon Bonaparte, *Des Idées napoléoniennes*, London, 1839, pp. 100, 113–14.
47. Hellmuth Rössler, *Napoleons Griff nach der Karlskrone. Das Ende des alten Reiches 1806*, Munich, 1957.

Chapter 8

CONCLUSION:
THE REAL LEGACY

The period known as the Hundred Days (from 20 March to 22 June 1815) after the celebrated 'Flight of the Eagle' from exile on the island of Elba must surely rank among the most extraordinary episodes in the history of empires. The hectic trail of Napoleon's triumphant return to Paris, and the hurried departure of the Bourbons less than a year after the First Restoration of Louis XVIII, were their own testimony to the emperor's personal charisma among his '*ralliés*' and to the fear he struck in those who had deserted him. To the witnesses of such astonishing events, it seemed as if this last supreme assertion of his will-power could reverse the tide of history and master even his most inevitable fate.

And yet, from another more practical angle, there is also something curiously artificial about the whole episode. Napoleon's partial restoration of the Imperial institutions and personnel, now in a significantly modified form calculated to win over his former liberal critics, was a deceptive ruse. The 'Additional Act to the Constitutions of the Empire' promulgated on 22 April would in all probability have remained no more than a political fig-leaf, with or without the circumstantial assistance of Benjamin Constant. If it was indeed ratified by a referendum, the very high level of abstentions among all official and civilian groups eligible to vote suggests a pervasive public indifference to the initiative, and certainly also the outright hostility of many among them.[1] The former tribunate had of course been abolished once and for all in August 1807. The legislative body, last summoned for the two sessions of 1813, had been formally adjourned in January 1814, as Napoleon marched to the front to meet the Allied invaders, although a rump of

231

legislators had been reassembled to add their own confirmation of sorts to his first deposition early in the following April. That assembly was not revived in its old form during the Hundred Days; under the terms of the 'Additional Act', it was to be replaced by a new and greatly enlarged chamber of representatives, chosen directly by the reconstituted electoral colleges. The former Imperial senate, which only a year before (1–3 April 1814) had performed what had now turned out to be the premature last rites by announcing a provisional government and Napoleon's deposition, was similarly superseded by a new chamber of peers, a scrabbled and unconvincing variant of Louis XVIII's upper house of the same name, but shorn of the old hereditary aristocracy.[2]

Napoleon's new pretensions as a civil ruler with a reforming mission, who among other gestures had again proclaimed equality before the law and now also the freedom of the press, were of course never really put to the test. His more characteristic determination to raise another army and reopen the war seemed in itself a contradictory move. The outcome at Waterloo on 18 June 1815 provoked no widespread outcry on his behalf in France, but rather a mood of weary resignation, as the mass of the people again awaited the return of the Bourbons, this time assuredly 'in the baggage-train of the Allies'. The 'federations' raised for the defence of the Empire in a few French towns during the Hundred Days, including parts of Paris, were not typical of popular opinion as a whole. But their very formation lived on in the Napoleonic legend, at once perpetuating his heroic cult and the myth of 'popular Bonapartism'. Among their adherents later in the century, distance only made the heart grow fonder.

Judged in terms of its *actual* results, however, the Hundred Days amounted to a non-event in the civil state. None of Napoleon's constitutional and political innovations during those months survived his fall. All the social accretions of grandeur which had accumulated during the earlier years – the senatoriates, the titles of the Imperial nobility, and the land-gifts attached to many of them – had in effect disappeared at or even before his first abdication on 4 and 6 April 1814, although Louis XVIII was often magnanimous in bestowing his own honours on some at least of their former beneficiaries. With the exception of Davout, for instance, the surviving Napoleonic marshals received the Grand Cross of the Order of Saint-Louis, while Victor, Oudinot,

Marmont (the 'traitor' who had surrendered Paris to the Allies in 1814), Macdonald, and Gouvion Saint-Cyr, all of whom had refused to rally to Napoleon during the Hundred Days, were to enjoy special favours from the Bourbons.

Napoleon's military initiative during the Hundred Days and its diplomatic consequences ended of course in composite disaster. At an earlier stage, by the first Treaty of Paris (30 May 1814), the Allies had been willing to allow France her frontiers of 1792, which included the former papal enclaves of Avignon and the Comtat Venaissin, parts of Belgium and of the Rhenish left bank, and Savoy. As such, the Bourbons had been granted a truncated but still significant version of the vaunted 'natural frontiers'. Moreover, by that same treaty, France had recovered all her captured overseas colonies from Britain, with the exception of St Lucia, Tobago, and Mauritius. In Europe, then, Louis XVIII had inherited appreciably less territory in 1814 than Napoleon had done in November 1799; but abroad, the king had regained very much more than the emperor had ever been in a position to command or bequeath.

The second Peace of Paris (20 November 1815), which followed the complex Vienna Settlement finally agreed on 9 June that year, was altogether a much more punitive document. France was reduced to her frontiers of 1789, although she was again allowed to keep Avignon and the Comtat Venaissin, as well as Mulhouse in upper Alsace ('reunited' with the French Republic in 1798) and in the event nearly all of Alsace-Lorraine. The larger part of the annexations of the Revolutionary Republic was thus removed, and none of Napoleon's own annexations after Brumaire survived the treaty. Viewed purely in terms of its territorial extent, the shape of France immediately after the Vienna Congress represented the total obliteration of everything Napoleon had ever achieved by conquest. All that physically remained of his famous exploits on the battle-field were the monumental buildings, the heroic sculptures, the triumphalist paintings, and the other public emblems of his former glory. But was it really for this that over 900,000 Frenchmen, victims of the land wars of the Empire, had ultimately fought and died? On top of its harsh territorial provisions, the second Peace of Paris imposed a war indemnity of 700 million francs on France, to be settled within five years, and pending its payment an Allied army of occupation of 150,000 men was to be maintained on her northern and eastern frontiers. By the end of 1815, the reality of '*la gloire*' cast a very dim light in France, which makes its brilliant incandescence in the later Napoleonic legend seem all the more remarkable.

It was not, then, as a military commander or imperial conqueror that Napoleon bequeathed his real legacy to France. What survived his fall was still of lasting importance, but it lay almost entirely in the sphere of his *civil* rule. Indeed, it may even seem a little ironic that so much of this institutional legacy had its origins not in the heyday of the Empire but in the earlier years, and more especially those of the Consulate. The following bare chronological record alone confirms the point: the Bank of France (6 January 1800), the prefectures (17 February 1800), the Concordat with the Catholic Church (signed on 16 July 1801, and officially published on 8 April 1802), the State secondary schools or *lycées* (1 May 1802), the Legion of Honour (19 May 1802), the bimetallic standard or '*franc de germinal*' (28 March 1803), and, perhaps most monumentally of all, the Civil Code (21 March 1804). All those innovations preceded the proclamation of the hereditary Empire on 18 May 1804, and were in due course to become defining institutions of Imperial rule itself. All were to survive Napoleon's fall in one form or another, even if some, the Concordat most notably, had a troubled and erratic history during the later nineteenth century. Several of Napoleon's later measures, such as the Code of Civil Procedure (1806), the Commercial Code (1807), the Criminal Code and Code of Criminal Procedure (1808), and the Penal Code (1810), as well as the arbitration boards (*Conseils de prud'hommes*) established in most of the major towns as from March 1806 to settle industrial disputes, were also to play their part in French institutional life long after his second abdication on 22 June 1815, albeit in modified form.

In all those respects, Napoleon had clearly set out to *civilize* his legacy, and to a large extent he succeeded. While so much of the subsequent historiographical debate focused on his posturings as a new Caesar or Charlemagne, it was perhaps rather more as a new Justinian that his institutional reforms affected the mass of the French people after 1815. Of course, his achievements as a lawgiver lay quite as much in a grand consolidation of the earlier Revolutionary reforms as in his own innovations. Most important of all, he gave full and definitive legal sanction to the Revolutionary land sales, obliging both the Church and (with some notable exceptions) the émigrés to accept the loss of their property alienated during the 1790s. In that sense, he could be seen as the emperor of the bourgeoisie, whose material gains from the Revolution he was anxious to protect, but at the same time we should remember that many hundreds of thousands of well-to-do peasants had also bought national lands and were similarly secured in their new possessions under his Civil Code. As a result, a new concept of 'notability' gained official status under the Consulate and Empire. Identified with landownership above all, but on a very much wider social base than under the old regime, the Napoleonic *notables* formed the bulk of an essentially *post*-Revolutionary élite. As such, they defended their material gains with tenacity, not least during the aristocratic and clerical revival under the Bourbon Restoration. They and their heirs were to remain a large and prominent group in French society and politics during the rest of the nineteenth century.

Napoleon's legacy also has a bearing on another and wider question already raised in an earlier chapter of this volume. How far may he be regarded as a prophet of the modern State? If the nature of his government stood for anything substantial and enduring in French history, it was the elaborate system of State centralism. Its guiding principles of authoritarian rule from the centre and from the top, radiating out to the provinces and towns through a uniform hierarchy of officials, have been a defining feature of French politics ever since. Something at least of their institutional framework survived all subsequent changes of constitutional regime, and elements of it persist even in the parliamentary democracy of the Fifth Republic today. Alexis de Tocqueville, writing in the 1850s, thought that the whole process of political and administrative centralization in France had its roots well back in the old regime, and that it had been continuous right up to his own day.[3] Such a view is mistaken in many of its details and also detracts from Napoleon's major contribution to the same process. 'Modern', 'open to talents', and 'meritocratic' his government may not always have been; but what he bequeathed to subsequent generations, whether they liked it or not, was a stronger and more efficient structure of State centralism than anything which had gone before. Even the Bourbon monarchs, whose vitriolic rhetoric against him might have suggested otherwise, retained his basic prefectoral system. For one thing, it seemed to provide them with an effective executive arm to counter-balance the new legislative chambers Louis XVIII had conceded in his Charter of 4 June 1814.

If, however, we turn to the long-term effects of Napoleon's civil rule *beyond* French frontiers, the record seems very much patchier. His administrative 'model' had its most enduring influence in the lands which lay closest to France and which (even before Brumaire in some cases) were annexed relatively early, such as Belgium and Luxemburg (1795), the departments of the Rhenish left bank (formed early in 1798 and fully incorporated in 1802), and Piedmont-Liguria (1802–5). There, too, the process of secularization had run a fuller course by the end of the Empire. But elsewhere, in those parts of Italy, Illyria, Holland, and Germany annexed later, and in the various satellite states carved out of the spoils of conquest in the years 1805–8, local resistance to the Napoleonic reforms was a major obstacle. In countries where seigneurial privilege and serfdom were still prevalent, Napoleon's advertised policy of 'rationalizing', 'modernizing', and 'defeudalizing' the traditional agrarian structures was often frustrated, and the French legal and social reforms barely took root.[4] Indeed, his own 'spoils system' itself undermined the official aims of his reforms in many parts of Italy, Germany, and Poland. Feudalism persisted there, as it did in Spain, and the traditional authority of the landed aristocracy long outlived the intrusion of the Imperial reformers. The social effects were conservative rather than radical, and Napoleon's legacy lacked lasting foundations. Ironically, this actually made it easier for the statesmen at the Vienna Congress to uphold the principle of dynastic legitimacy and to restore so much of the old social order in those countries.

If to such unintended results one adds the relentless exactions of the Grand Army in the subject states and the one-sidedness of Napoleon's Continental Blockade, founded on his declared priority of 'France first', then his ultimate legacy to Europe beyond French frontiers simply did not match the irenic purpose and constructive effects so often claimed for it. For most of the peoples of the 'Grand Empire', his rule amounted to a system of deliberate exploitation in the interests of his own grandeur. Even so, with the bicentenary of Brumaire now only a little more than three years away, it seems to me a fair bet that some politicians and media pundits in France, for their own tendentious reasons, will want to hail Napoleon as one of the great early architects of European integration, as the

champion of a Europe without frontiers. They will find specious evidence in his legend to support them, as so many generations of commentators have done since 1815, but it will
have very little to do with his *real* legacy.

. . . .

NOTES AND REFERENCES

1. Frédéric Bluche, *Le plébiscite des Cent-Jours, avril–mai 1815*, Geneva,
   1974.
2. Irene Collins, *Napoleon and his Parliaments 1800–1815*, London,
   1979, pp. 145–8, 161–2, 167–8.
3. Alexis de Tocqueville, *L'Ancien régime et la Révolution*, Paris, 1856.
4. The varying efficacy of the French administrative 'model' in all the
   lands of the 'Grand Empire' is discussed in detail in Stuart Woolf,
   Napoleon's Integration of Europe, London, 1991.

BIBLIOGRAPHICAL ESSAY

Very few subjects in French and European history have attracted more attention from writers of all persuasions than Napoleon. The massive literature which has accumulated over the years on the man, his times, his regime, his achievements, and indeed his shortcomings, is unusually rich. While it is a prolific field for any historian to work in, it is also a daunting one. It poses constant problems of selection, and I too have *had* to be highly selective in my approach to this bibliographical essay.

The 'classic' themes in Napoleonic historiography up to the Second World War, as seen from the angle of French writers, were admirably set out in Pieter Geyl's pioneering survey of 1949, *Napoleon: For and Against*, which has since been republished several times in a standard paperback edition (Peregrine Books, Harmondsworth, 1986 impression). My own detailed review of that historiographical tradition, to which the penultimate chapter of the present volume is devoted, now enables me to concentrate very largely on secondary studies published since the war. In making my selection of these, I have tried to cater mainly for the needs of my most likely readership, and so have paid special attention to works (including translations) available in English. A number of important texts in French have not been translated, however, and since my topical and regional coverage would be unbalanced without them, I thought it best to include them here as well. But first, readers may wish to have some brief guidance on the principal primary sources, dictionaries, reference works, and bibliographies available for this vast subject.

. . . .

PRIMARY SOURCES

Full translations of the official *Correspondance de Napoléon Ier publiée par ordre de l'empereur Napoléon III* (32 vols, Paris, 1858–69) are not available. English readers may, however, turn to the volume of *Letters of Napoleon,* selected, translated, and edited by J.M. Thompson (Oxford, 1934; London, 1954), which remains a useful source. More important still is the fascinating collection gathered in *The Mind of Napoleon: A Selection from his Written and Spoken Words,* edited and translated by J. Christopher Herold (New York, 1955; 3rd pbk edn, 1969), which offers telling insights into his mercurial moods and changing opinions on a great variety of topics at different periods of his life. It includes a fair sample of the many memoirs and/or journals written by Napoleon's contemporaries and published at various times during the nineteenth century. Of these, pride of place must go to the *Mémorial de Sainte-Hélène* (8 vols, Paris, 1823), published by Count Emmanuel de Las Cases, his companion in exile. It had a crucial role in disseminating Napoleon's legend after his death, and it remains an indispensable source for many of his most celebrated pronouncements. The English translation which soon appeared under the same main title (4 vols, London, 1823) is now unfortunately not widely available, and a modern English edition of the *Mémorial* is certainly long overdue.

Contemporary documents of the Napoleonic period have appeared in a number of works over the past two centuries, although mostly in scattered and rather inaccessible form. The recent collection, *A Documentary Survey of Napoleonic France,* edited and translated by Eric A. Arnold, Jr (Lanham, Md, 1994), will therefore be all the more valuable to English readers. Its contents are set out in chronological order and include many of Napoleon's major laws, decrees, proclamations, instructions, treaties, and the like, as well as the full texts of his Concordat with Pope Pius VII and of the Constitutions of the Year VIII (December 1799), the Year X (August 1802), the Year XII (May 1804), and of April 1815 (Additional Act). Professor Arnold has more recently published a supplement to this work (Lanham, Md, 1996).

. . . .

DICTIONARIES, REFERENCE WORKS, AND BIBLIOGRAPHIES

Of the recent dictionaries now widely available, two are outstanding. The *Dictionnaire Napoléon* (Paris, 1987; new edn, 1989), published under the direction of Jean Tulard, assembles the expertise of various specialists and has already established itself as a major work of reference. English readers are fortunate to have a similar and no less authoritative text in Owen Connelly, ed., *Historical Dictionary of Napoleonic France, 1799–1815* (Westport, Conn., 1985). For more specialized military coverage, they may refer to the extensive, reliable, and well-illustrated work of David G. Chandler, *Dictionary of the Napoleonic Wars* (London and Melbourne, 1979). Much useful material (including military chronologies, chronologies for the domestic and international affairs of all the major European states, information on their rulers and governments, potted biographies of the leading figures of the Napoleonic Empire, and maps) is also available in a recent manual by Clive Emsley, *The Longman Companion to Napoleonic Europe* (London and New York, 1993).

The huge complexity of institutional changes in the French state from the end of the old regime to the end of the Napoleonic Empire is comprehensively analysed in Jacques Godechot, *Les institutions de la France sous la Révolution et l'Empire* (3rd revised and expanded edn, Paris, 1985). First published in 1951, this remains much the most authoritative source on the subject, with accompanying bibliographies, and it ranges extensively over the constitutional, political, administrative, military, judicial, financial, economic, social, and religious developments in French public life during the Revolution, Consulate, and Empire. Very regrettably, it has never been translated into English. Many of the general or more specialized studies referred to below also have good bibliographies on the Napoleonic (and indeed Revolutionary) period, but the most detailed guide to the mass of modern literature available is Jack A. Meyer, *An Annotated Bibliography of the Napoleonic Era. Recent Publications, 1945–1985* (New York, 1987).

· · · · · · · · · · · ·

STANDARD GENERAL TEXTS

Of the many earlier general histories still widely available, most have not weathered the more recent trends in Napoleonic studies particularly well. Two notable exceptions among these standard introductions to the subject are Felix Markham, *Napoleon* (London, 1963), also published in an American/Canadian paperback edition (New York and Scarborough, Ont., 1963), and Owen Connelly, *French Revolution/Napoleonic Era* (New York, 1979), whose second edition has appeared quite recently in a handsome paperback volume (Fort Worth, Tex., 1991). Both are erudite works, which treat their subject with clear and scholarly detachment, yet add enough narrative and episodic colour to hold the reader's interest. As general introductions to Napoleon's career and to the nature of his regime, they have scarcely been bettered. Another long-serving work of comparable merit is J. Christopher Herold, *The Age of Napoleon* (London, 1964; Penguin pbk edn, Harmondsworth, 1969). It is enriched by the author's impressive command of the primary sources (letters, memoirs, and journals) for his subject. The result is an animated portrait which is at once eminently readable, critical, yet sympathetic.

Two other general histories also deserve particular notice here. Georges Lefebvre's monumental *Napoleon* (Eng. edn, 2 vols, London, 1969; pbk edn, 1974) had originally appeared in French in the '*Peuples et Civilisations*' series (1st edn, Paris, 1936; 5th revised and expanded edn, Paris, 1965). Although some of its material has since been superseded, not least its treatment of the Grand Army, the sheer scale and erudition of the work has ensured its place among the 'classics' of Napoleonic historiography. Indeed, Pieter Geyl (in the work cited above, p. 376) was prompted to describe it as 'a textbook for the history of the world during the period 1799–1815'. A master of the French style sometimes called '*terne*' (meaning literally 'dull' or 'colourless', but in this case perhaps more properly 'factual' or 'impartial'), Lefebvre did not allow his Marxist sympathies to distort his rigorous empirical method. He was often critical of Napoleon's policies and did not minimize his mistakes; but he recognized the unique personal power, the 'spiritual fire' and genius of the man, and he refrained from passing easy moral judgement on him.

241

The Fontana paperback by D.M.G. Sutherland, *France 1789–1815: Revolution and Counterrevolution* (London, 1985), finally, has several virtues. Although most of its chapters cover the Revolutionary decade, it offers a broad view across the whole period up to 1815. It is particularly good in reminding us that counter-revolutionary movements (in the plural indeed) were a significant feature of French political, social, economic, and not least religious history during much of that time. Napoleon was the first to neutralize them effectively, but at the expense of the libertarian and egalitarian ideals of the Revolution. The author's own earlier research on the west country of France, more especially on the *Chouanneries* in the Breton departments, gives his account an interesting provincial angle. This testifies to the tenacity of popular customs in the rural areas, which even the great machine of Napoleon's centralized state could never break down. The book offers a salutary warning against any simple equation of Paris with France, and makes a good case for the diversity of social life in the provinces throughout the Napoleonic years.

. . . .

MORE SPECIALIZED TOPICAL AND REGIONAL STUDIES

French historians have long recognized that Napoleon's Corsican background had a lasting influence on the formation of his personality and on the evolution of his military, political, and dynastic ambitions. Without that background, we cannot properly understand his strong sense of clan and his life-long belief in a heroic personal destiny. Fortunately, more published works in English are now available on this elusive subject than was once the case. The essential introduction to it is provided by Dorothy Carrington in two fascinating studies: *Granite Island: A Portrait of Corsica* (Harmondsworth, 1984 impression), which ranges widely over the history of the island, its people and their customs; and *Napoleon and his Parents: On the Threshold of History* (London, 1988), which publishes important new archival research on Napoleon's youth and education up to 1786. The whole subject has also had more collective discussion at conferences in the United States in fairly recent years, most notably by Thadd E. Hall, Dorothy Carrington, Jean Defranceschi, John M.P. McErlean, and Harold T. Parker, 'Corsica and Corsicans during the Revolutionary Era (1755–1815)', in

The Consortium on Revolutionary Europe: Proceedings 1986 (Athens, Ga, 1987). Among these latter scholars, Parker is certainly the best known for his pioneering research into the early influences on Napoleon's character. His article, 'The Formation of Napoleon's Personality: An Exploratory Essay', *French Historical Studies*, vol. 7 (Spring 1971), is an outstanding contribution to this debate, on which he has also published several other interesting 'probes' over the years.

If we turn next to the period of Napoleonic rule itself, most of the more specialized accounts of the central institutions of government (the council of state, the senate, the legislative body, and the tribunate) have been published in French. Readers who have the language will find much of this often very technical matter digested into clearer form in Jacques Godechot, *Les institutions de la France sous la Révolution et l'Empire* (3rd revised and expanded edn, Paris, 1985). For those who do not, the best introduction in English is Irene Collins, *Napoleon and his Parliaments 1800–1815* (London, 1979), a work which fully justifies what may at first seem its unlikely title, and which is enlivened throughout by apposite quotation from a wide variety of primary sources. Thomas Beck, *French Legislators, 1800–1834* (Berkeley, 1974), although more confined in its institutional range, offers a longer diachronic perspective and is also an authoritative prosopographic study. These works can be supplemented by the relevant part (chiefly chapter 8) of Clive H. Church, *Revolution and Red Tape: The French Ministerial Bureaucracy 1770–1850* (Oxford, 1981), which also has much more detailed coverage of the Directorial bureaucracy during the years immediately preceding Brumaire. At the level of departmental government, English readers will benefit from the account by Edward A. Whitcomb, 'Napoleon's Prefects', *American Historical Review*, vol. 79 (1974), which does not discuss the official functions of the prefectures within the Napoleonic state, as such, but offers valuable new evidence on the social and professional composition of the prefectoral corps itself.

Relations between Church and State form a major subject throughout the period 1789–1815. Indeed, the importance of Napoleon's Concordat with Pope Pius VII cannot be fully grasped unless the scale of the schism in the French Church during the Revolution is recognized. Much the best introduction to this crucial background is John McManners, *The French Revolution and the Church* (London, 1969; Westport, Conn., 1982).

Details of the Concordat itself are fully discussed in the now rather old text by H.H. Walsh, *The Concordat of 1801: A Study of the Problem of Nationalism in the Relations of Church and State* (New York, 1933); and also in somewhat less detail in H. Jedin and J. Dolan, eds, *History of the Church*, vol. 7, *The Church between Revolution and Restoration* (New York, 1981). The structural problems implicit in that agreement from the start are analysed in the short essay by Jean Godel, 'L'Église selon Napoléon', *Revue d'Histoire moderne et contemporaine*, vol. 17 (1970), which is an excellent digest of his own more detailed research on the concordatory church in the diocese of Grenoble, *La reconstruction concordataire dans le diocèse de Grenoble après la Révolution (1802–1809)* (Grenoble, 1968). Probably the most accessible, and certainly the most readable, account of the rupture in relations between the emperor and the pope is E.E.Y. Hales, *Napoleon and the Pope: The Story of Napoleon and Pius VII* (Garden City, NY, 1961; London, 1962).

The wider question of Catholic ordinations, the status of the different clerical orders, and popular religiosity in France during the early decades of the nineteenth century is treated best in Claude Langlois's detailed study of a Breton diocese, *Le diocèse de Vannes au XIXe siècle, 1800–1830. Un diocèse breton au début du XIXe siècle* (Paris, 1974). English readers will find something of the same ground more briefly covered in Ralph Gibson, *A Social History of French Catholicism 1789–1914* (London, 1989). The shortest cut to the religious revival which immediately preceded the Concordat is Olwen Hufton's illuminating essay, 'The Reconstruction of a Church 1796–1801', in Gwynne Lewis and Colin Lucas, eds, *Beyond the Terror: Essays in French Regional and Social History, 1794–1815* (Cambridge, 1983). On the Protestant communities in France, there is nothing in English to compare with Daniel Robert, *Les Églises Réformées en France, 1800–1830* (Paris, 1961); but on the Jews, readers may usefully consult Frances Malino, *The Sephardic Jews of Bordeaux: Assimilation and Emancipation in Revolutionary and Napoleonic France* (University of Alabama, 1978), and Simon Schwarzfuchs, *Napoleon, the Jews and the Sanhedrin* (London, 1979).

Other branches of Napoleon's civil rule are not so well served by English works. There is some discussion of his educational policy in Robert B. Holtman, *The Napoleonic Revolution* (Baton Rouge, 1967), and rather fuller treatment of censorship and State propaganda in an earlier book by the same author, *Napoleonic*

244

Propaganda (Baton Rouge, 1950). The important subject of legal codification remains sadly neglected, although readers may still profitably consult the collection of essays in B. Schwartz, ed., *The Code Napoleon and the Common-Law World* (New York, 1956), which deals with various aspects of the Code across a wide chronological and international perspective. A good modern synthesis of Napoleon's attempts to manipulate the visual arts and official symbols of the Empire in the interests of his own grandeur is very much needed. Meanwhile, there are short but authoritative statements by June K. Burton on 'Art' and 'Heraldry', by Claude Bergeron on 'Architecture', by Jean Henry on 'Sculpture', and by Lynn A. Hunt on 'Symbolism and Style', in Owen Connelly, ed., *Historical Dictionary of Napoleonic France, 1799–1815* (Westport, Conn., 1985), where further bibliographical references (mostly in French) are also given under the respective entries.

The social history of the Napoleonic period, more especially the formation and endowment of an Imperial élite, is one of the subjects on which major research has been conducted in France, Germany, Italy, and to a lesser extent in the English-speaking countries during recent decades. Since much of this is an essential part of the new 'revisionist' approach in Napoleonic historiography, the main titles are noted and discussed in the next sub-section of this essay. A good general survey of the topic appears in chapter 6 ('The Social Classes') of Louis Bergeron, *France under Napoleon* (Eng. edn, Princeton, 1981). Much the same may be said of the burgeoning research into Napoleon's treatment of the annexed departments and subject states of the Empire, which is also more properly discussed in the next sub-section. For more general coverage here, English readers can refer to Owen Connelly, *Napoleon's Satellite Kingdoms* (New York, 1965; pbk edn, 1969), as well as the comprehensive study of Stuart Woolf, *Napoleon's Integration of Europe* (London, 1991).

Napoleon's economic policy and its effects are discussed in many of the older texts, some of which are rather specialized and technical. English readers will find an authoritative digest of much of this matter in chapter 7 ('Economic Life: Take-off or Stagnation?') of Louis Bergeron, *France under Napoleon* (Eng. edn, Princeton, 1981). There is no real substitute for Bergeron's major doctoral study, *Banquiers, négociants et manufacturiers parisiens du Directoire à l'Empire* (Paris, 1978), but English readers

245

may wish to consult my own doctoral thesis, *Napoleon's Continental Blockade: The Case of Alsace* (Oxford, 1981), and chapter 6 ('The Imperial Economy') of my earlier textbook, *The Napoleonic Empire* (Macmillan Studies in European History, Basingstoke and London, 1991), where some of the same ground is covered. The seminal article by François Crouzet, 'Wars, Blockade, and Economic Change in Europe, 1792–1815', *Journal of Economic History*, vol. 24 (1964), remains the best short general account of commercial and industrial dislocation and regional reorientation under the impact of the maritime wars.

Studies of Napoleon's army and military campaigns are, of course, legion. Of the great many works available, four are likely to be most accessible and useful to English readers. David G. Chandler, *The Campaigns of Napoleon* (London, 1966, 1993), has long been a standard text, which on the whole puts a favourable gloss on Napoleon's genius as a commander. It is supplemented by a stimulating volume of articles, essays, and lectures by the same author, *On the Napoleonic Wars: Collected Essays* (London and Mechanicsburg, Pa, 1994), which span his distinguished career as a military historian. A rather more demystifying account is provided by Owen Connelly, *Blundering to Glory: Napoleon's Military Campaigns* (Wilmington, Del., 1988), whose central argument that Napoleon's genius as a commander lay less in systematic planning than in brilliant improvisation in the field is nicely subsumed in its provocative title. The most recent textbook by Charles J. Esdaile, *The Wars of Napoleon* (London and New York, 1995), is very much more than a history of the campaigns. While it discusses the latter, and also deals with the structure of Napoleon's armies, its most original contribution lies in a detailed analysis of the wider political, social, and economic repercussions of the wars across Continental Europe during the years 1803–15, and of their whole impact on international relations.

Fortunately, we now know much more about the *unheroic* side of the Grand Army's rank and file; and here, too, some of the most notable recent research on conscription and on the twin problems of desertion and draft evasion has been published in English. Alan Forrest's penetrating study, *Conscripts and Deserters: The Army and French Society during the Revolution and Empire* (New York and Oxford, 1989), brings a wide chronological and regional perspective to those endemic problems, and can be highly recommended to readers. Isser Woloch's earlier

246

work, 'Napoleonic Conscription: State Power and Civil Society', *Past & Present*, no. 111 (May 1986), another major contribution to this important debate, has been extended more recently to include the Revolutionary origins of conscription, along with all its accompanying social tensions, in the last main chapter of his valuable study, *The New Regime: Transformations of the French Civic Order, 1789–1820s* (New York, 1994; pbk edn, 1995).

Some of the better general histories cited above (more particularly those by Felix Markham, J. Christopher Herold, and Jean Tulard) have chapters on Napoleon's final exile and on the legend which spread in Europe after his death in 1821. The *Mémorial de Sainte-Hélène* (1823) by Las Cases is again the essential starting-point here, but the subject has also been treated in some detail by modern writers. There is an elementary introduction to it by Duncan MacIntyre, *Napoleon: The Legend and the Reality* (London, 1976), which manages to pack quite a lot into its fifty-eight pages, and a rather fuller account by Richard B. Jones, *Napoleon: Man and Myth* (London, 1977). One especially evocative detail in the heroic annals of the Grand Army was the remembered glory of Napoleon's Imperial Guard. Henry Lachouque, *The Anatomy of Glory* (Eng. edn, London and Melbourne, 1978), adapted from the French by Anne S.K. Brown, with a new introduction by David Chandler, gives a lively and often moving account of the celebrated Guard.

Much of the Napoleonic legend after 1815 was kept alive by nostalgic and fanciful rituals, which had their own peculiar power and attraction for its adherents. The history of 'Bonapartism' during the nineteenth century, insofar as it was a distinct ideological force, often had much more practical and serious military, political, and institutional manifestations. The origins of 'popular Bonapartism' during the Hundred Days are fully discussed in R.S. Alexander, *Bonapartism and Revolutionary Tradition in France: The Fédérés of 1815* (Cambridge, 1991). Frédéric Bluche, *Le Bonapartisme. Aux origines de la Droite autoritaire, 1800–1850* (Paris, 1980), and Bernard Ménager, *Les Napoléons du peuple* (Paris, 1988), trace the same phenomenon over a much wider period, and assess its importance to the later ascent of Louis Napoleon. For an even longer trajectory across time, readers would do well to consult Robert Gildea's splendid essay, 'Bonapartism', in *The Past in French History* (New Haven and London, 1994), which treats its subject as an important recurring theme in French history up to the present day.

. . . .

RECENT TRENDS IN NAPOLEONIC HISTORIOGRAPHY

The earliest signs of a new 'revisionist' approach in Napoleonic studies appeared around 1960, but had their first major collective airing at the various international conferences which marked the bicentenary of Napoleon's birth in 1969. Of these latter, two in particular have had a seminal influence on later research in France and Germany. The more important was the conference organized by the Société d'Histoire moderne and held at the Sorbonne on 25 and 26 October 1969, whose papers were published shortly afterwards in a special number entitled 'La France à l'époque napoléonienne' of the *Revue d'Histoire moderne et contemporaine*, vol. 17 (1970), as well as in the *Annales historiques de la Révolution française*, vol. 42 (1970). The other was the Bremen conference of 27–30 September 1969, whose proceedings appeared some four years later in *Francia*, vol. 1 (1973), the journal of the German Historical Institute in Paris, which had sponsored the event. Until these new departures, the traditional view of the Napoleonic imperium had been formed mainly in the context of military and political history, in which biography was often the favoured literary form. Most earlier writers had focused chiefly on the career of Napoleon himself or on his more immediate entourage, whether in his army, or in his civil state, or in his closer family and dynastic relationships.

The current genre of research has tended to shift the emphasis more towards the underlying structures of the Napoleonic regime. From such an approach, a broader and less episodic perspective has emerged. Indeed, it is now fashionable to view the Revolutionary and Napoleonic 'experience' not so much as a succession of ruptures which ended in military dictatorship, but more as an evolving process with important themes of continuity across the *whole* period. The social, professional, economic, and (in the widest sense) cultural aspects of that process have had much more attention than had been the case hitherto. The regional focus, too, has widened considerably. More and more, the annexed departments and the subject (or 'satellite') states of France have been brought into the reckoning. This is perhaps most evident in the major research into the long-term effects of Napoleonic rule in Germany and Italy, which has been carried out by scholars in both those countries during the past thirty years or so.

Much of this new research, regrettably, has never been translated into English, and since so much of it has appeared in the form of specialized monographs, it is not widely available to English readers even in the original languages. I made an attempt to communicate some of its most important findings in my earlier textbook, *The Napoleonic Empire* (Macmillan Studies in European History, Basingstoke and London, 1991), within the limitations of space then available to me. Two major studies by French historians, which deal with similar 'structural' questions in much more detail, are also available to English readers in translation. One is Louis Bergeron, *France under Napoleon* (Eng. edn, Princeton, 1981), which has sometimes been seen as an exemplary model of the *Annales* method applied to Napoleonic history. The other is Jean Tulard, *Napoleon: The Myth of the Saviour* (Eng. edn, London, 1984), a longer book which includes more narrative. Unfortunately, the English edition is sometimes marred by poor translation.

Both Tulard and Bergeron have also made major contributions to the process of identifying and classifying the Napoleonic *notables*, from official lists published during the Consulate and Empire, and this remains an active area of current research. The important findings of Tulard's earlier articles were incorporated in the detailed commentary of his later volume, *Napoléon et la noblesse d'Empire* (Paris, 1979), which also publishes a complete list (by rank of title) of the Imperial nobility (1808–15). As such, it has superseded the older manuals and armorials, and is now widely regarded as the definitive text on the subject. Some of Bergeron's earlier work on the *notables* was undertaken in collaboration with other historians and, for almost the first time, made systematic use of modern computerized techniques at the École des Hautes Études en Sciences Sociales to broaden their social catchment area as far as possible. The most comprehensive results are published in Louis Bergeron and Guy Chaussinand-Nogaret, *Les «masses de granit». Cent mille notables du Premier Empire* (Paris, 1979). These same two scholars have directed the major series of *Grands notables du Premier Empire* (Centre National de la Recherche Scientifique, Paris, 1978–), which still continues. The various volumes of the series which have appeared to date give biographical notices on the 'most distinguished' citizens of each department during the later years of the Empire.

The general conclusion which emerges from all the studies

noted above is that most of the Napoleonic *notables* had played a public role of some kind during the Revolutionary period, whether in central, departmental, or local administration, or in the judicial services. They, and a good many landowners and *rentiers* besides, had similarly enhanced their 'notability' through the purchase of national lands before Brumaire. Such threads of social and professional continuity across the whole period are clear.

As for the annexed departments and subject states of the Empire, the ambitious study of Stuart Woolf, *Napoleon's Integration of Europe* (London, 1991), is now the most comprehensive account in English of the varying impact of Napoleonic rule in the many lands which together constituted the 'Grand Empire'. Woolf examines its various regional angles in terms of a central theme – that Napoleonic government beyond French frontiers was based on an administrative 'model' of 'uniformity' and 'modernity' – and assesses how far it was effectively (or indeed *not* effectively) implemented there. Some at least of his material is also available in shorter article form: most notably 'French Civilization and Ethnicity in the Napoleonic Empire', *Past & Present*, no. 124 (Aug. 1989); and 'The Construction of a European World-View in the Revolutionary-Napoleonic Years', *Past & Present*, no. 137 (Nov. 1992). In these last works, more particularly the first, Woolf relates the administrative 'model' to the wider question of what he believes was a deliberate French policy of 'cultural imperialism' at that time. His main arguments here are not without their critics, but they remain an interesting and challenging lead in current Napoleonic studies, on which more research needs to be done.

Two other recent books in English, which similarly offer valuable information on and interesting insights into the current 'structuralist' approach to Napoleonic history, also merit special attention here. One is a study by Martyn Lyons, *Napoleon Bonaparte and the Legacy of the French Revolution* (Basingstoke and London, 1994), whose debt to Woolf's work is acknowledged in several places. It stresses the socio-economic continuities in French history of that time and, with some refreshing effect, plays up Napoleon's role as the heir and executor of the Revolution rather than his role in liquidating its ideals. If the chapters on his foreign policy and military expansion sometimes draw on old and now somewhat dated texts, those on the domestic ramifications of his rule (especially on the composition and functions of the political, social, and cultural élites of the Empire) are commendably up to date.

The other account, by Isser Woloch, *The New Regime: Transformations of the French Civic Order, 1789–1820s* (New York, 1994; pbk edn, 1995), takes a much wider view, in which the 'Napoleonic episode' (as some French historians call it) is discussed as a part of a longer process of change in French history. Its title is nicely chosen to mark a departure from our more familiar associations with 'the old regime', while also stressing important themes of continuity in French civic life. It combines much important new archival research with penetrating commentary to explain the senses in which the relationship between the State and French society at large were transformed over those thirty to forty years. Its wide perspective helps us to situate Napoleon's achievements, or the lack of them, in major areas of public policy which had not always been well served in earlier accounts. These cover the evolving (but also often stalling) process of political participation; changes in the laws and indeed in the whole institutional structure of French justice; the main advances and then official retreats in primary education; the rise and fall of Revolutionary charity (*bienfaisance*), as well as the ups and downs of public philanthropy and social welfare; the ways in which conscription impinged on French society at different times over the period; and several other aspects of the State's intrusion into village life (for instance through its budgets, policing and roads). In all, Woloch unearths many interesting local details of French civic life which had simply been passed over in earlier accounts.

CHRONOLOGY

1768   France acquires Corsica from the Republic of Genoa

1769   Birth of Napoleon in Ajaccio, 15 August

1779   Napoleon enters the military school of Brienne, April

1784   Passes from Brienne to the Royal Military School in Paris, October

1785   Graduates as a sub-lieutenant from the Royal Military School, September; begins service in La Fère Regiment at Valence, November; commissioned as a lieutenant there

1788   Enters the artillery school in Auxonne, June

1789   Meeting of the States General in Versailles, 5 May; Napoleon leaves Auxonne, September; takes eighteen months of Corsican leave

1791   Resumes duty at Auxonne, February; promoted to first lieutenant, April; Louis XVI accepts new monarchical Constitution, 14 September; French annexation of Avignon and the Comtat Venaissin, 14 September; first meeting of the Legislative Assembly, 1 October; Napoleon joins the volunteer Corsican National Guard, October

1792   Elected lieutenant-colonel in the Corsican National Guard, 1 April; Ajaccio riot, 8–12 April; France declares war on Austria (and Prussia), 20 April; Napoleon promoted to captain, 28 May; First Coalition (Austria and Prussia) against France, 26 June; deposition of Louis XVI, 10 August; first public meeting of the National Convention formally proclaims the abolition of the monarchy and inauguration of the French Republic, 21 September; French annexation of Savoy, 27 November

252

1793   French annexation of Nice, 31 January; France declares war on Britain and Holland, 1 February, and then on Spain, 7 March; revolt of Corsican patriots against France, March; Bonaparte family takes refuge on French mainland, June; French recapture of Toulon from the British and royalists, immediately followed by Napoleon's promotion to brigadier-general, December

1794   Napoleon posted as artillery commander to the French Army of Italy, February; coup of 9–10 Thermidor Year II/27–8 July eliminates Jacobin government

1795   Napoleon refuses to take up a posting to the Army of the West, May; struck off the officer list, 15 September; proclamation of the republican Constitution of the Year III, 23 September; French annexation of Belgium and Luxemburg, 30 September; Napoleon suppresses a royalist revolt in Paris ('whiff of grapeshot'), 13 Vendémiaire Year IV/5 October; promoted to divisional general in the Army of the Interior, 16 October, and then to its *général en chef*, 26 October; inauguration of the executive Directory, 1–3 November

1796   Napoleon appointed commander of the French Army of Italy, 2 March; marries Josephine de Beauharnais, 9 March; start of his first Italian campaign, April

1797   Mantua falls to the French, 2 February; Treaty of Tolentino with the Papacy, 19 February; preliminary Peace of Leoben ends first Italian campaign, 18 April; royalists eliminated in *coup d'état* of 18 Fructidor Year V/4 September; Treaty of Campo Formio with Austria, 17 October

1798   French departments formed on German left bank of the Rhine, January; French annexation of Geneva, 26 April; start of Napoleon's Egyptian campaign, May; Second Coalition (Britain, Austria, Russia, Naples, and Turkey) formed against France, as from May (but not completed until June 1799); Jourdan–Delbrel Law establishes regular conscription in French armies, 5 September

1799   Napoleon leaves Egypt, August; returns to Paris, October; *coup d'état* of 18–19 Brumaire Year VIII/9–10 November – end of the Directory, and appointment of Bonaparte, Sieyès, and Ducos as provisional consuls; Constitution of the Year VIII/13 December appoints Bonaparte as first, Cambacérès as second, and Lebrun as third consuls; appointment of the council of state, 22 December; installation of the senate, 27 December

1800 Installation of the legislative body and tribunate, 1 January; Bank of France founded, 6 January; plebiscite approves Constitution of the Year VIII, 7 February; fundamental law reforming the government of France (prefectures, sub-prefectures, cantons, communes), 17 February; amnesty to émigrés, 2 March; start of Napoleon's second Italian campaign, May; battle of Marengo ends campaign, 14 June; further amnesty to émigrés, 20 October; bomb plot (*'machine infernale'*) against Napoleon, 24 December

1801 Treaty of Lunéville with Austria, 9 February; Concordat with Pius VII signed, 16 July (ratified in Rome on 15 August and in Paris on 10 September); surrender of French army in Egypt to the British, August

1802 Napoleon president of the Republic of Italy, 26 January; 'purge' of the legislative chambers, January–March; Treaty of Amiens with Britain, 25 March; official publication of the Concordat (with the Organic Articles), 8 April; further (almost general) amnesty to émigrés, 26 April; education law establishes the *lycées*, 1 May; foundation of the Legion of Honour, 19 May; Constitution of the Year X/4 August proclaims Napoleon consul for life; French annexation of Piedmont, 11 September

1803 Creation of the senatoriates, January; Napoleon 'Mediator' of the Swiss Confederation, 19 February; Boulogne camp established for the invasion of England, 11 March; reform of the currency (*'franc de germinal'*), 28 March; rupture of the Peace of Amiens and renewal of war with Britain, May; introduction of an industrial work record-book (*livret*), 1 December

1804 Suppression of the Cadoudal conspiracy against Napoleon, February–March; execution of the duc d'Enghien, 20 March; proclamation of the Civil Code, 21 March; Constitution of the Year XII/18 May proclaims Napoleon hereditary emperor; first eighteen marshals of the Empire named, 19 May; Imperial coronation in Notre-Dame, 2 December

1805 Creation of the Kingdom of Italy, March; Napoleon crowned King of Italy in Milan, 26 May; Eugène de

Beauharnais appointed viceroy of Italy, 7 June; French annexation of the Ligurian Republic (Genoa), 30 June; Third Coalition (Britain, Austria, and Russia) formed against France, August; surrender of Ulm, 20 October; battle of Trafalgar, 21 October; battle of Austerlitz, 2 December; Treaty of Pressburg with Austria, 26 December

1806 Joseph Bonaparte appointed king of Naples and Joachim Murat grand duke of Berg, March; creation of the twenty-two 'ducal grand-fiefs of the Empire', March; Imperial Catechism published, April; law on the 'University of France', 10 May; Louis Bonaparte appointed king of Holland, June; creation of the Confederation of the Rhine, 12 July; Fourth Coalition (Britain, Prussia, Russia, and some smaller states) formed against France, July; dissolution of the Holy Roman Empire, 6 August; Prussian mobilization, August; battles of Jena (Napoleon) and Auerstädt (Davout), 14 October; Berlin decree declares Continental Blockade against Britain, 21 November

1807 Battle of Eylau, 7 February; battle of Friedland, 14 June; Treaties of Tilsit with Russia, 7 July, and with Prussia, 9 July; creation of the kingdom of Westphalia (Jerome Bonaparte) and of the duchy of Warsaw (Frederick Augustus of Saxony), July; abolition of the tribunate, 19 August; Junot's occupation of Lisbon starts Peninsular War, November; Milan decrees extend terms of the Continental Blockade to neutrals, 23 November and 17 December

1808 Occupation of the Papal States, February; Murat appointed Napoleon's lieutenant-general in Spain, February; inauguration of new titles of the Imperial nobility, 1 March; decree of the Imperial University, 17 March; Spanish National Assembly in Bayonne, May–July; Joseph Bonaparte crowned king of Spain, while Murat and Caroline Bonaparte transfer to the kingdom of Naples, July; Napoleon and Tsar Alexander I meet at Erfurt, October; Napoleon assumes personal command of the French Army of Spain, November

1809 Napoleon leaves Spain after battle of Corunna, 16 January; Fifth Coalition (Britain, Austria, and Spanish insurgents) formed against France and start of the Wagram campaign, April; French annexation of the Papal States,

17 May; battle of Aspern–Essling, 21–2 May; Napoleon excommunicated by Pius VII, 11 June; battle of Wagram, 5–6 July; start of Pius VII's captivity in Savona, July; Treaty of Schönbrunn with Austria, 14 October, and formation of the 'Illyrian Provinces of the Empire'; senate pronounces Napoleon's divorce from Josephine, 16 December

1810 *Officialité* in Paris confirms the divorce, 14 January; establishment of Napoleon's *Domaine extraordinaire*, January; Rome annexed to Empire, 17 February; Napoleon marries Marie-Louise of Austria, 2 April; annexation of Holland to Empire following abdication of Louis Bonaparte, July; Trianon tariff modifies Continental Blockade, 5 August; Fontainebleau decree toughens customs surveillance, 18 October; annexation of part of Hanover, the Hanse towns, and the grand duchy of Oldenburg to Empire, December

1811 Birth of an heir (the 'King of Rome'), 20 March; Napoleon summons a national council of French and Italian bishops in Paris, June

1812 Nucleus of Sixth Coalition (Russo-Swedish alliance, with British support) formed against France, March; Pius VII removed from Savona to Fontainebleau, June; start of Russian campaign, June; battle of Borodino, 7 September; Napoleon enters Moscow, 14 September; start of the retreat from Moscow, October; Napoleon returns to Paris, 19 December

1813 The 'Concordat of Fontainebleau' signed and then repudiated by Pius VII, January; Treaty of Kalisch (Russia and Prussia), 26 February; Prussian declaration of war on France, 16 March; battles of Lützen, 2 May, and of Bautzen, 21 May; secret Treaty of Reichenbach (Austria and Allies), 27 June; Austria joins the final Grand Alliance and declares war on France, 12 August; 'Battle of the Nations' (Leipzig), 16–19 October; Wellington's advance from Spain through south-west France, October–December

1814 Allied crossing of the Rhine starts the campaign of France, January; Pius VII removed from Fontainebleau back to Savona, January; Allied Treaty of Chaumont, 1 March; Marmont surrenders Paris to the Allies, 31 March; Pius VII taken into Italy and gains his freedom,

March–April; Napoleon deposed by the senate, 2 April; his first abdication, 6 April; First Restoration of Louis XVIII and his return to Paris, 1–3 May; start of Napoleon's exile on Elba, 4 May; first Treaty of Paris, 30 May; Congress of Vienna assembles, September (lasts until June 1815)

1815 'Flight of the Eagle' from Elba, February; Napoleon returns to Paris, 20 March, and start of the Hundred Days (20 March–22 June); Additional Act to the Constitutions of the Empire, 22 April; battle of Waterloo, 18 June; Napoleon's second abdication, 22 June; his journey to St Helena aboard HMS *Northumberland*, August–October; second Peace of Paris, 20 November

1821 Death of Napoleon on St Helena, 5 May

1823 Publication of the *Mémorial de Sainte-Hélène* by Las Cases

1840 Return of Napoleon's remains to Paris

. . . .

MAPS

1. Batavian Republic
2. Belgium
3. Left bank of the Rhine
4. Savoy
5. Helvetic Republic
6. Nice
7. Piedmont
8. Cisalpine Republic
9. Ligurian Republic
10. Parma
11. Modena
12. Lucca
13. Tuscany
14. Roman Republic
15. Parthenopean Republic
16. Piombino
17. Montenegro
18. Ionian Islands (to France)
19. Ragusa
20. Trentino

1.   Europe, January 1799

1. Kingdom of Holland
2. Minor German territories excluded
   from Confederation of the Rhine
3. Bayreuth
4. Neuchâtel
5. Helvetic Confederation
6. Republic of the Valais
7. Kingdom of Italy
8. Parma
9. Ligurian Republic
10. Lucca
11. Piombino
12. Kingdom of Etruria
13. Papal States
14. Istria/Dalmatia
15. Ragusa
16. Montenegro
17. Tyrol/Vorarlberg (to Bavaria 1805)
18. Venetia (to Kingdom of Italy 1805)
19. Hanover (to Prussia 1806)
20. Hamburg
21. Salzburg (to Austria 1805)

2. Europe, September 1806

French Empire
(frontiers of 1804)

French Empire
(annexations 1804–6)

French occupation/
administration

French satellites/allies

Fourth Coalition

SWEDEN

RUSSIA

PRUSSIA

SAXONY

AUSTRIAN
EMPIRE

HINE

OTTOMAN
EMPIRE

KINGDOM OF
NAPLES

SICILY

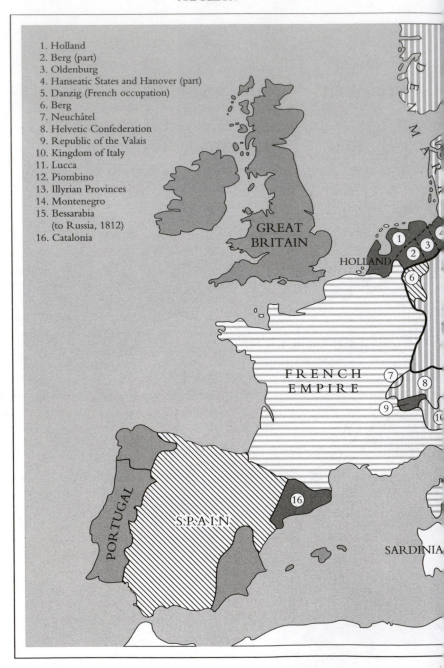

1. Holland
2. Berg (part)
3. Oldenburg
4. Hanseatic States and Hanover (part)
5. Danzig (French occupation)
6. Berg
7. Neuchâtel
8. Helvetic Confederation
9. Republic of the Valais
10. Kingdom of Italy
11. Lucca
12. Piombino
13. Illyrian Provinces
14. Montenegro
15. Bessarabia
    (to Russia, 1812)
16. Catalonia

3.   Europe, May 1812

SWEDEN

RUSSIA

French Empire (frontiers
of December 1809)

French Empire
(annexations 1810–12)

French occupation/
administration

French satellites/allies

Great Britain and
dependencies

Frontier of Confederation
of the Rhine

⑤

PRUSSIA

DUCHY
OF WARSAW

OF THE RHINE

AUSTRIAN
EMPIRE

⑮

⑬

⑩

⑪

OTTOMAN
EMPIRE

⑭

②

KINGDOM OF
NAPLES

SICILY

4. Departments of the French Empire at its height in 1812

Key to map

------ Frontier of the French Empire

—— Boundaries of departments

• ROUEN *Chef-lieu* of department

Key to names of departments

1	Bouches-de-l'Elbe	34	Manche	67	Cher	100	Pyrénées-Orientales
2	Ems-Oriental	35	Calvados	68	Nièvre	101	Hérault
3	Bouches-du-Weser	36	Orne	69	Côte-d'Or	102	Haute-Loire
4	Frise	37	Eure	70	Haute-Saône	103	Ardèche
5	Ems-Occidental	38	Seine-et-Oise	71	Doubs	104	Lozère
6	Ems-Supérieur	39	Seine	72	Charente-Inférieure	105	Gard
7	Bouches-de-la-Meuse	40	Seine-et-Marne	73	Charente	106	Isère
8	Zuiderzee	41	Marne	74	Haute-Vienne	107	Drôme
9	Yssel-Supérieur	42	Meuse	75	Creuse	108	Vaucluse
10	Bouches-de-l'Yssel	43	Moselle	76	Allier	109	Bouches-du-Rhône
11	Lippe	44	Meurthe	77	Sâone-et-Loire	110	Mont-Blanc
12	Bouches-de-l'Escaut	45	Bas-Rhin	78	Jura	111	Hautes-Alpes
13	Deux-Nèthes	46	Finistère	79	Gironde	112	Basses-Alpes
14	Bouches-du-Rhin	47	Côtes-du-Nord	80	Dordogne	113	Alpes-Maritimes
15	Lys	48	Morbihan	81	Corrèze	114	Var
16	Escaut	49	Ille-et-Vilaine	82	Cantal	115	Corse
17	Dyle	50	Loire-Inférieure	83	Puy-de-Dôme	116	Simplon
18	Meuse-Inférieure	51	Mayenne	84	Loire	117	Doire
19	Roer	52	Maine-et-Loire	85	Rhône	118	Sesia
20	Pas-de-Calais	53	Sarthe	86	Ain	119	Pô
21	Nord	54	Indre-et-Loire	87	Léman	120	Stura
22	Jemmapes	55	Eure-et-Loir	88	Landes	121	Montenotte
23	Sambre-et-Meuse	56	Loir-et-Cher	89	Basses-Pyrénées	122	Marengo
24	Ourthe	57	Loiret	90	Lot-et-Garonne	123	Gênes
25	Seine-Inférieure	58	Yonne	91	Gers	124	Taro
26	Somme	59	Aube	92	Hautes-Pyrénées	125	Apennins
27	Oise	60	Haute-Marne	93	Lot	126	Méditerranée
28	Aisne	61	Vosges	94	Tarn-et-Garonne	127	Arno
29	Ardennes	62	Haut-Rhin	95	Haute-Garonne	128	Ombrone
30	Forêts	63	Vendée	96	Ariège	129	Trasimène
31	Sarre	64	Deux-Sèvres	97	Aveyron	130	Tibre
32	Rhin-et-Moselle	65	Vienne	98	Tarn		
33	Mont-Tonnerre	66	Indre	99	Aude		

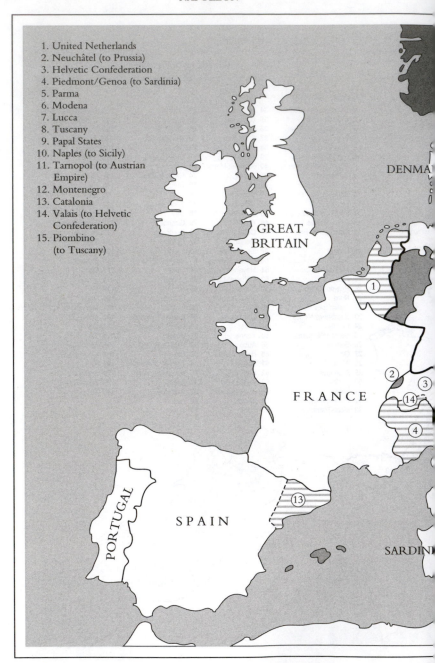

1. United Netherlands
2. Neuchâtel (to Prussia)
3. Helvetic Confederation
4. Piedmont/Genoa (to Sardinia)
5. Parma
6. Modena
7. Lucca
8. Tuscany
9. Papal States
10. Naples (to Sicily)
11. Tarnopol (to Austrian
    Empire)
12. Montenegro
13. Catalonia
14. Valais (to Helvetic
    Confederation)
15. Piombino
    (to Tuscany)

5. Europe after the Congress of Vienna

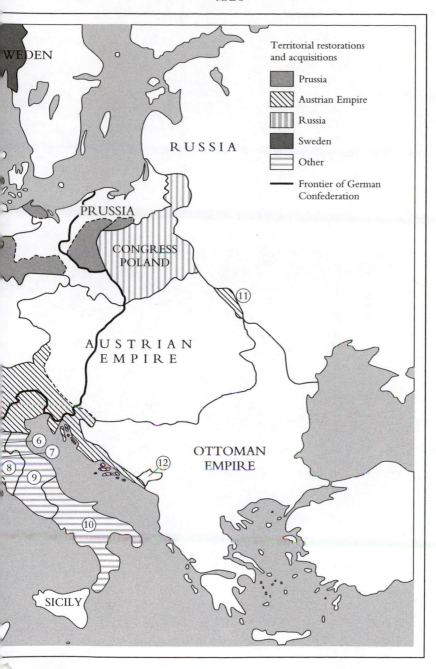

SWEDEN

RUSSIA

Territorial restorations
and acquisitions

Prussia

Austrian Empire

Russia

Sweden

Other

Frontier of German
Confederation

PRUSSIA

CONGRESS
POLAND

11

AUSTRIAN
EMPIRE

OTTOMAN
EMPIRE

6

7

8

9

12

10

SICILY

INDEX

Note: the topical sub-divisions of the main entries which follow are set out in alphabetical order, except in particular cases (most notably that of Napoleon himself) where readers may find the broadly chronological sequence more helpful.